Still, I Cannot Save You

Still, I Cannot Save You

A Memoir of *Sisterhood, Love*, and *Letting Go*

Kelly S. Thompson

McCLELLAND & STEWART

This edition published 2023

McClelland & Stewart and colophon are registered trademarks of
Penguin Random House Canada Limited.

Library and Archives Canada Cataloguing in Publication data
is available upon request.

ISBN: 978-0-7710-5184-5
ebook ISBN: 978-0-7710-5185-2

Book design by Kate Sinclair
Cover photograph: Daniel T. Neff
Typeset in Janson MT Pro by M&S, Toronto

Printed in Canada

The excerpt on p. vii is from "To Countess Lili Kanitz-Menar (July 16, 1908)"
from *The Dark Interval: Letters on Loss, Grief, and Transformation* by Rainer Maria Rilke,
translated by Ulrich Baer, copyright © 2018 by Ulrich Baer. Used by permission of
Modern Library, an imprint of Random House, a division of Penguin Random
House LLC. All rights reserved.

The photograph on page 277 is reprinted courtesy of
Jessica Dozois (Girls on Film Photography).

Names and identifying details of some individuals have been altered for the sake
of privacy. Portions of this book have appeared in publications that include *Room*,
the *Humber Literary Review*, and *M(o)thering: An Anthology* (Inanna Publications,
2022). Thank you to those publishers for seeing the value in these stories.

McClelland & Stewart,
a division of Penguin Random House Canada Limited,
a Penguin Random House Company
www.penguinrandomhouse.ca

1   2   3   4   5   27   26   25   24   23

Penguin
Random House
McCLELLAND & STEWART

To Dad and Mom

We loved her fiercely, and what a gift that has been.

"No constellation is as steadfast, no accomplishment as
irrevocable as a connection between human beings which,
at the very moment it becomes visible, works more forcefully
in those invisible depths where our existence is as lasting as
gold lodged in stone, more constant than a star."

—Rainer Maria Rilke, *The Dark Interval*

prologue, 2007

I waited for Meghan on a bench at Georgian Mall in Barrie, anxiously tapping my foot as acid gurgled up my throat. Everything smelled like damp down and the greasy food court, a combination that made me nauseated. At twenty-three years old, I was sure I had an ulcer—another thing to blame my sister for, along with the dark rings around my eyes, the literal pain in my neck, the deepening divide between me and our parents.

I nudged a loose chunk of ice with my boot, edging it towards the escalator while chewing on my Orange Julius straw. *It's important to make an effort to connect*, said the Al-Anon leader, *but only when the addict in your life can accept your boundaries.* Choosing our meeting place and time had felt like some kind of boundary, even as the emotional ones slipped away from me like Jell-O.

A tinny version of "White Christmas" blared through the overhead speakers, and it felt stupid, suddenly, my gift idea for Mom and Dad: a photo of their grown kids with Santa to replace the only other version they have, taken in 1984. In that picture,

Meghan's bald, three-year-old head is stark against the colourful backdrop of St. Nick's workshop, her plaid skirt wrinkled, her face marred with tears. Of course, she's small for her age, freckled and thin, with the feeding tube just removed. Her gaze focuses somewhere beyond the camera, likely on Mom and Dad, who would have been hovering nearby with plastic bags— checked twice for holes—in case chemo side effects had Meghan filling that Zehrs bag with hot bile. Cradled in Santa's arm beside my sister, I am just five months old, somehow managing a look that straddles angry and jaded. In the centre of the picture, Santa's head is tilted towards Meghan in a gesture of sympathy. The picture has remained an emblem of suffering and sadness, stored with the family Christmas decorations but never displayed. I wanted our parents to have a new snapshot, with both daughters smiling this time.

The clock above the Gap indicated noon. Meghan was thirty minutes late. But then, for the last five years of birthdays, celebrations, anniversaries, she'd been late or hadn't shown up at all, so I had learned to not expect her, while Mom and Dad maintained loose hope, laying her place setting and then saying nothing when clearing it all away, unused. Still, Meghan had promised she'd be at the mall for eleven thirty. Said *yes* all three times I called to remind her. Arranging this visit was the first time we'd spoken in six months. Seven?

It was my second Christmas as an officer in the Canadian Armed Forces, and while my posting to Kingston, Ontario, was decent in terms of location, I kept making the three-hour drive to Barrie on weekends when the comradeship I had imagined I'd find in the military failed to materialize. *Call your sister*, Mom would say each time I dropped my bags in the foyer. *She misses you.*

Except it wasn't my sister who missed me; it was Mom missing whatever it was sisters were meant to share but which no longer existed between Meghan and me. Plus, tracking Meghan was a Herculean effort thanks to a trail of numbers no longer in service, addresses no longer valid. Sometimes I humoured Mom and dialled while she hovered near the kitchen landline and feigned that she wasn't listening. *She's not here*, a stranger often groggily relayed once the line connected. Or, *Meghan who?*

I slurped the dregs of my drink and stood to toss it in the garbage just as Meghan approached, although it took me a moment to register that it was, in fact, her. Her curvy shape, once so like my own, had melted into the straight edges of a young boy. Hanging from her body were a pair of baggy jeans and a zip-up, one of those sporty polyester numbers from the seventies, although she'd never been one to exercise. She hesitated when she saw me, then picked at the point of her upper lip, which was raw and bleeding—a nervous tic she'd had since childhood. Face to face, we leaned into an awkward hug. She didn't smell of the Herbal Essences and Calgon body sprays I remembered, instead reeking of chemicals and something smoky that made my eyes water.

As we pulled apart, Meghan's plasticky purse slipped off her shoulder and onto the floor, scattering condoms, change, and clumps of lint. Also, an Altoids tin mottled with burn marks. I stood there like a statue and imagined the contents of the tin as she scrambled to collect her things. She'd missed my first legal drink, my first apartment, my graduation from York University followed by my first military move to Kingston. And what had I missed? I could barely stand the thought.

"Hi," I said to break the spell. She stood, purse righted, and barely met my chin. Even though I was three years younger, almost to the day, I was six inches taller. For some reason, the difference never failed to surprise me.

"Hey."

"Thanks for meeting me."

"No problem."

She gathered her sheet of long brown hair into a ponytail, wisps of grey sneaking through the box dye, as they had since she was a teenager. Taking full stock of her was a stab to the gut: her cheeks were sunken; skin colourless; hip bones jutting; teeth that looked like they hadn't been brushed in weeks. A stranger, really.

"You're crazy-thin." I reached out to tug at the loose waistband of her jeans.

"I'm fine," she barked, swatting me away, spittle gathering at the corner of her mouth. And then she adjusted her zipped sweater and gave her shoulders a shimmy so that the veil of anger lifted like Mr. Hyde reverting to Dr. Jekyll form. I'd almost forgotten how exhausting it was, the constant emotional merry-go-round.

"We better line up," she muttered, moving towards the throng of children in line for Santa. Keen to get the photo over with.

"Want to walk through the Bay first?" I had a weird desire to keep her in sight after what had been years of avoidance because now she was within arm's reach, and I didn't want her to disappear again. "There's this perfume. Thought we could get it for Mom for Christmas. Split the price." We both knew we wouldn't split the price, but I would still add Meghan's name to the gift tag and hate her while I did it. She shrugged but followed silently until we hit the department store's wall of floral scent.

The hum of activity allowed Meghan to move through the shoppers unnoticed, and she wandered to the edge of the accessories area, fiddling with gaudy earrings, her fingers blackened like they'd been dipped in ink. With one eye trained on my sister, I approached the Chanel counter, where a salesperson tapped a polished nail on the glass case. My attention ricocheted between Meghan and the salesperson as plumes of perfumed air choked my other senses and a headache bloomed, making me squeeze the bridge of my nose.

"Can I help you?" The salesperson smiled, cracking her painted foundation.

"Yeah, hi. Uh, I'm just looking for something for my mom. This one here." I called out to Meghan to distract her, holding the Chanel in the air. "Meg! This one. What do you think?"

She didn't turn to face me. Instead, she slipped the rhinestone earrings into her purse, patting the bag when they reached the bottom. Next, she lingered over a brown belt, letting the leather slide between her middle and pointer fingers. My stomach churned and I turned to the clerk, whose focus was trained on the debit machine where she hoped to make a sale. When I turned back, the belt had disappeared into Meghan's bag too, no one the wiser except for me. It is such a special sort of pain, to love someone you don't like very much.

I quickly paid for the perfume, half ignoring the salesperson who asked three times if I wanted gift wrap, if I needed a gift receipt. Meghan busied herself near the cosmetics until I snatched the offered bag tufted with tissue paper and grabbed my sister by the elbow, stalking away at a pace she could barely match. Once outside the store, both of us breathing heavily, I froze. Her zip-up had bunched around her forearm, revealing a line of bruises under my white-knuckled grip. Drugs or men? With Meghan, the damage could have been caused by either. I stumbled backwards and raised my chin to the ceiling, concentrating on the pot lights while drawing in big, calming breaths, like my anxiety workbook had told me to. *You can only control what is within your control.*

"We should get the photo done. I have other stuff to do today," I said, my voice strained.

"Fine." Her face was set in a challenge. *Say it. I dare you. I double-dog dare you.*

We joined the line that curled around Santa's workshop, which was made of painted wood and cardboard that looked somehow polished when topped with cotton snow. A small gingerbread house was perched near wooden elves that mechanically nodded their heads back and forth while Rudolph's nose shined tomato-tinged light on the scene.

The queue inched forward, and the eighty-year-old Santa remained cheerful for each shot, his motorized scooter a reminder of real life, parked inconspicuously behind the giant present display. Although he lacked the belly paunch, it was clear that his greyish-white beard was as real as his enthusiasm. He waved at everyone who walked by. Even teenagers couldn't resist a half-hearted flop of their hands in return.

Meghan cooed and waggled her fingers at twin boys ahead of us in a stroller, their matching blond curls twirling around their ears. "They're beautiful," she said to the mother, who regarded my sister—the sunken cheeks, the stained teeth, those black fingers—like she was wielding a knife. Meghan stepped back, just straight enough to feel the burn, while I swallowed my own silent shame.

As we waited, she alternated between picking her lip and scratching at invisible, non-existent bumps on her arm while I checked my BlackBerry for messages, as though each required an urgent response.

"Busy with work?"

"Super busy." I clicked a few more words before dropping the phone into my purse.

Meghan had no idea what my job as a logistics officer entailed, really, but then she'd never inquired about it or military life in general. If she had asked, I'd have told her that my boss was awful, that the sexual harassment was so pervasive that not even an ugly uniform staunched the jeers at my breasts, and that my leg—which I'd broken during basic training—hadn't healed, which put my career in jeopardy, with the likelihood of a medical release. I wanted to tell my sister everything, but I no longer knew the point.

"What about you? Work going well?" I asked.

"It's okay. Fine, I guess."

The previous week, I'd visited the tanning salon where Meghan claimed to be a receptionist, only to find out she'd been fired. We'd spent the last few years like this: Meghan lied about having a job, about where she got money, about how she spent her day, about who she spent her day with. But she couldn't lie to me—at least, not well and not for long—and our parents remained none the wiser. We were the veritable CIA of sisterhood, knowing our confidential information could implode our family roles: me, the reliable but judgmental fixer, and Meghan, the sweet, affectionate cancer survivor. So, we embraced the irony of knowing one another better than anyone else and yet not knowing each other at all.

Meghan started to vibrate, and a sheen of sweat glistened on her forehead.

"You alright? You don't look so great."

"Geez, thanks." She licked her bleeding lip, tongue darting out like a snake's.

"I mean sick. You look like you're going to be sick." I kept my arms at my sides, resisted pressing a cool hand to her forehead as she used to do to me when we were little, when I played the role of ill child and she the caring mother. In our play world, I was the sick one subjected to a lifetime of checkups, needles, and prodding, whereas in real life, Meghan was the patient, with her annual remission appointments. But in our shared pink bedroom, she'd press the Fisher-Price stethoscope to my chest, stick the plastic thermometer in my mouth, and pull the covers to my chin. *I'll take care of you,* whispered with such care that nothing had ever felt truer. So because my sister had nearly died and we had tried to make a game of it, I felt born into my phobia of illness, of vomit, of anything associated with cancer. Part of me resented how easily she moved in the world without that fear.

"I'm fine, Kell. Fuck. I'm not going to throw up on you, if that's what you're freaked about. Jesus, aren't you over that stupid phobia yet? You're not five anymore. It's not cute."

I gawped, aware of how easily she made me feel like that ashamed and anxious five-year-old. It was a constant effort to keep the vulnerable version of myself tucked away and out of sight when Meghan so easily used it as a weapon.

"Ho, ho, ho!" Santa called, distracting us by grabbing his belly and shaking what little was there. The camera-snapping elves waved us over.

"Hi, Santa." Meghan's tone was childlike and wheedling.

"What brings you ladies to see ol' Santa?" He didn't ask what we wanted for Christmas, perhaps sensing that what we wanted and needed would not be remedied by a present under the tree.

Meghan and I each hovered over one of his knees, aware of his frailty, our thigh muscles quaking with the effort.

"We're redoing our Christmas photo for our parents," I said through clenched teeth, sounding more irritated than I expected. It was hot under the lights and my purse felt so heavy on my shoulder. And it was late. I still had the drive back to Kingston ahead of me and a meal plan to create for the week and so much adult stuff to do.

"And what was wrong with the last one?"

Meghan's bottom lip quivered and she tucked her chin to her chest.

"Whoa, hey now, it's okay." Santa rubbed her arm in the comforting way of grandpas, but looked to the elves, his wranglers, and then at me—as if any of us could manage the situation. I gave Santa a look that assured him I, too, was powerless. *Don't fall for it.* Meghan was always crying, expertly manipulating our guilt. This all made me feel so overwhelmingly tired that I wanted to curl up on the red carpet that was spread at our feet and wake up at Christmastime next year.

"We look pretty miserable in our last photo." I had to clear my throat to keep my own surprise tears at bay. "She had cancer and I was a colicky newborn. It's not a very happy picture for our parents."

"Well then, let's create a new memory," Santa replied, as though we were in a Hallmark movie and he was relieved to have an easy solution to our anguish.

Meghan sniffled in response. Thompson Crying Face takes mere moments to develop but hours to dissipate—skin blotchy and swollen, nose dripping. This photo didn't stand a chance in hell. I passed Meghan a tissue from my purse, and she honked and blew. The parents waiting in line seemed divided between compassion and irritation, some tapping their toes in annoyance while others cocked their heads in sympathy.

"Ready, girls?" Santa asked, a bony arm wrapped around each of us. The costumed camera operator waved a stuffed reindeer, finger hovering over the shutter button. I heard the jingling of bells somewhere distant, or close by, I couldn't be sure, and on cue, Meghan plastered on a smile that was frightening in its suggestion of happiness. The shutter went off, a flash sparked, and we stood in unison, finally making eye contact with one another. It was only then that I noticed her glassy, dilated pupils, wide and black like the prized marble we used to fight over as kids.

As we walked away, photo in hand, Meghan asked why I was crying. I explained that it was just allergies, plus my eyes were watering from the flash. I lied. Meghan knew it. Another secret kept.

one, 2011

Mom drummed the steering wheel with her slender fingers as we puttered up Highway 400 from the Toronto airport. She was driving her usual twenty kilometres under the speed limit, which led to a stream of drivers shooting past to give us the finger or shake their fists from rolled down windows.

"It's good to have you back, Moo."

Despite the October chill, I leaned into the vent to blast AC on my armpits as I fought off a hot flash—another parting gift from my dying thyroid in the wake of the radiation I'd just had.

"There's something depressing about being a twenty-seven-year-old woman who can't feed or look after herself." The words sounded self-pitying even as they left my mouth. Back in Vancouver, I had a two-foot stack of dishes in my sink, five half-eaten jars of peanut butter abandoned on countertops, and a pile of laundry so high that I'd stopped wearing underwear. Between the Graves' disease and the treatment for it, I could barely scrape myself off the floor to brush my teeth.

"Medically, it's well documented that stress can bring Graves' disease on." Mom, a nurse for thirty years, adopted a particular tone when donning her clinical hat as opposed to her mothering one. It was authoritative and clipped, like Dad giving orders to his army troops during his lifelong military career. "Leaving the military wasn't exactly a smooth ride for you."

"I didn't *leave* the military. I was medically released." The distinction felt necessary, and my throat thickened with phlegm. In the wake of my recent health crisis, it was ironic to have been ousted from the Forces after eight years of service for a broken leg that wouldn't heal and not because of the disease that had recently landed me in hospital.

For the previous four months, I had worked at charting a new path, dancing so close to my West Coast writing life dream. I was dating my friend Joe from basic training, had landed a job in book publishing, and was renting a nice apartment that overlooked the mountains, but within weeks of arriving in the city, it was clear I couldn't ignore my symptoms. Extreme weight loss and hunger. A tremor that prevented me from eating soup. A constant, racing pulse. The endocrinologist claimed I had the worst case of Graves' disease he'd ever seen and arranged radiation, leaving me reliant on medication. My short stint as a civilian was proving to be total bullshit.

"Well, there's no one in Vancouver to help you, so coming home was the only real option, no?" Mom said, ever the realist. "Besides, your father and I don't mind looking after you for a while."

Don't mind.

For a while.

My jaw ached from clenching. I picked at the tinted film on the window of Mom and Dad's new Mercedes, which they'd purchased after I'd moved. There was something heartbreaking about watching my world continue to function, happily even, despite my removal from it.

"It's a good thing you waited until your sister moved in with Bernard, though. It would have been tight in the house with the two of you." It felt pointless to mention that their home had two guest rooms, each with its own bathroom, alongside more than two thousand square feet of furnished suburbia. But it wasn't square footage she was talking about, and it felt pointless to mention that, too. "Your sister has been doing so well," Mom continued. "A year sober."

I didn't want to talk about Meghan. Didn't want to think about her either. I wanted a tepid bath and then to pull the comforter over my head and disappear into time.

"Bernard." I tested the word out loud. "Stupid name." It wasn't stupid, particularly, but I felt better for having made the slight. My sister and her boyfriend had been dating only a few months, but he had a reliable job as an electrician and Mom said he seemed nice. But then, she thought everyone was nice.

"Don't be rude. It's French."

"Does he speak French?"

"I don't think so." Mom flicked the signal light to ease off the highway to Barrie, causing the truck driver behind us to bleat his horn.

"Aren't people in addiction recovery meant to stay single until they're, like, comfortable with themselves?" Was I the only one who worried that if this relationship went down the drain, Meghan's tenuous hold on sobriety might snap like a guitar string? And was that even my concern to fret about when we were veritable strangers? We'd spoken sporadically during the year that she'd lived with Mom and Dad, whenever she picked up one of my calls to my parents, her tone routinely blithe. We'd chat about the benign stuff you'd discuss with an acquaintance, like plans for the weekend or if we'd seen any good movies lately, but those calls had ended when she moved in with Bernard. I didn't even know her new phone number. While I had hoped that we'd return to one another once she was sober, adulthood had made me a realist, and not every story of sisterhood has a tidy ending. Not having a relationship with my sister was familiar and stable, and after life in the Forces, I craved stability.

"You can't help when you meet your person, and your sister has met her person." Mom rapped her knuckles on the dash in a way that indicated I was not to take this further. "Why don't we stop in to see her at work before we go home?"

"Not right now, Mom. I'm exhausted from the flight." I had set off radiation alarms at the airport, and had sheepishly passed the nuclear medicine form to the security agent while a string of guards waited in the wings and red lights swirled their warnings.

"You said Graves' means you're always hungry, so you can grab a bite, too. We'll just pop in real quick."

Mom steered into the Mucho Burrito parking lot before I could resist further and stood outside the entrance to wait out my resistance. She motioned for me to follow and I gave in, pushing the car door open with a grumble of displeasure.

Inside the restaurant, Spanish music blared too loud for conversation, echoing off the rows of metal tables and benches that lined the walls. The smell of hot food tickled my nostrils, making me want everything on the menu, which I stared at dumbly until a familiar voice chirped, "Welcome to Mucho Burrito. What can I get you today?"

My sister beamed, clearly expecting our arrival. Her dark hair was captured in a hairnet, a themed visor clapped on top, and she was barely able to see over the sneeze-guard that protected the flour tortillas and pots of shredded cheese. She was exactly the same but entirely different.

And I had absolutely no idea how to respond.

"Ta-dah! What do you think?" She spun, modelling the all-black uniform that was meant to conceal splatters of the inky beans that simmered in the warmer, and then paraded back and forth between her busy co-workers. Feet away, a customer at the register barked that no, she did not want the ninety-nine-cent guacamole, thank you very much, and when the hell did avocadoes become so damn expensive? She would add her own at home, where she didn't have to take out a mortgage for the spread. The teenager serving her gave a curt nod, like he'd heard this all before, and with the speed of a well-trained superhero, whipped her burrito into a smooth aluminum bullet. I was inexplicably transfixed.

"Kell?" Meghan was waiting for me, shaking jazz hands this way and that. I stared, mouth open, and could not stem the tide of anger.

For the fifteen years of choosing cocaine and opioids over her family.

For stealing money from the sock drawer of the Alzheimer's patient she was hired to care for. The daughter threatened charges and Mom and Dad paid for her silence.

For the car crash during a drug run without insurance or a licence or valid plates. Another addition to the unpaid tab she owed to our parents.

For all the times she stole from our wallets.

For the promised sister get-togethers where I would wait one hour, then two, drinking piss-warm teas alone.

And, worst of all, for the fact that in that moment, I was the only one considering this list of grievances when faced with evidence of how far she'd come.

"Great. It's great." I couldn't manage another word. This was an olive branch she was wobblily extending, but the risk of reaching for it made the branch feel more like a barb. As kids, we'd played WrestleMania on Mom and Dad's bed, re-enacting all the body slams and arm clotheslines, our scrawny limbs poor substitutes for the muscled specimens we admired on television. Miraculously, neither of us was ever hurt, always careful of where we fell so that we landed in heaps of frilly dresses and Rainbow Brite dolls. And then we would lie there, clutching our stomachs while we laughed. I knew she wouldn't hurt me on purpose, and she knew the same about me. But standing in the fast-food restaurant, I didn't know anything at all.

Mom was grinning so wide it looked like she might cleave open, and she reached across the partition to pat Meghan's arm, a gesture I found off-putting. For years, Meghan had placed herself on the fringes of our family, but it was clear that it was me who no longer fit. The lights felt overwhelmingly bright, and I kept squinting and blinking into the starkness, feeling adrift.

Meghan dashed about, corralling co-workers like a sheepdog. "This is my sister! Come meet my sister!" Staff rushed to shake my hand like they knew all about me, some of them taking a moment to scrub their fingernails under the tap. They gave Meghan congratulatory squeezes, knowing looks of kindness. She was clearly well-liked, working hard, but then, she'd always been easy to like.

"I'll have to hug you later," she said to me, pointing to a camera that was trained on the stainless-steel counters. She said this like us hugging was a regular thing, like it hadn't been something that only happened at Christmas. "Our boss watches everything." She rolled her eyes and winked. I had never seen my sister wink.

"Right." I could think of nothing else to say because all the things I wanted to discuss were impossible to dig into at the counter of Mucho Burrito.

"So, what can I get you? I'll make it special."

"Oh, yeah. Uh, I'll have a Mucho-size beef burrito, please."

She made a face of wide surprise. "Whoa, Kell, it's really, really big. Like, I've never seen anyone manage it, and I've been here a year. Jenny, you ever seen someone finish a Mucho?"

The woman operating the quesadilla press held up her pointer finger. "Just once. Think he was a bodybuilder or something."

"I can manage. Beef, please."

Mom didn't order anything, which seemed to disappoint Meghan. She went down the line of fillings and, at my command, sprinkled in beans, rice, scoops of overcooked meat that looked the same as the other tubs of protein. She slapped a dollop of guacamole onto the centre of the tortilla and spread it loosely around. "This is usually extra." Another wink. She shakily passed the burrito, an obscene thing approximately the size of a newborn, over the Plexiglas barrier. "Do you think it'll be good?" Her eyebrows steepled and she pressed her lips together. Hopeful. Nervous.

"It'll be great, thanks." I waggled the burrito about and nearly got a wrist cramp.

"We'll see you later, okay, Meggie?" Mom said as Meghan dropped a packet of nacho chips into a to-go bag.

"Hey, Kell," she called out when we were nearly at the door. Meghan was the only person who ever called me Kell. I hated it. "Now that you're home, we can hang out a bit. Maybe. If you want."

Still, a dumbstruck look on my face. Was she thinking back to the trial, as I was? It was only two years ago that she'd been caught stealing from the grocery store where she worked and snorting drugs in the storeroom. Afterwards, she had called me, so high she could barely speak, desperate for me to vouch for her in court. *Well, this is all very interesting news, Ms. Thompson,* the judge had said when I told him about the stealing, the lying, the litany of debts paid for and covered up by our parents. I told myself that by being honest, I was saving her somehow, but also, some part of me wanted Meghan to hurt an iota as much as her self-destruction hurt me.

The judge ordered a fine and no jail time, but said that Meghan should enter a drug program—a gift of a sentence that I couldn't help but think was attributable to the white, middle-class parents who sat behind the defence table. Now she stood before me in a visor and an apron, smelling of refried beans. And she was sober. And she wanted to hang out with me.

Mom elbowed me gently in the ribs, jolting me back to my sister and the Mucho Burrito staff waiting for a response. I made a sound somewhere between a grunt and a word, both of us uncertain of its meaning.

"Your poor sister," Mom said once we were in the car and she'd restarted the ignition. "It'll be hard for her to move up in the world now that she has a record."

Mom did not say *Because of you*, but she might as well have. I was to be held to account for breaking the family pact of silence. To staunch a rebuttal, I started in on my burrito. I ate the entire thing.

two

I rolled languidly onto my side and groaned. As the radiation continued its work, my hormones and emotions were still doing cartwheels, despite two weeks spent loafing at Mom and Dad's. I kept fantasizing about my life back in Vancouver with Joe, fearing that everything I wanted to germinate there would fail to sprout if I stayed away too long.

"Do we have to make tonight into some sort of event? I feel like crap," I croaked from the couch, ignorant to my own over-dramatization as I poked at my aching teeth with my fingertips. I'd been in so much pain that I couldn't chew, so I puréed everything, which wasn't helping me to regain the thirty pounds I'd lost to the illness. Most of my nails had fallen out too. Half my hair. I kept looking in the mirror and seeing Meghan at Santa's workshop four years ago, emaciated and pointlessly angry.

Mom was at the stove stirring spaghetti sauce—something I could safely chew for the family dinner she was clearly stressed about, if the taper candles on the table, which I'd only seen lit on holidays, were any indication. "I'm sure you'll be fine," she responded, not looking my way. *You'll be fine* was one of her familiar nursing incantations. Meghan and I used to joke that Mom saved her empathy for her patients and left it in her workplace locker before returning home each night. She had only recently retired, due to her advancing multiple sclerosis, but the change in job status hadn't resulted in a bank of sympathy from which to draw on.

"Geez, Mom, of course I'll be alright, but would it kill you to have some compassion?" I swiped sweat from my forehead with the front of my shirt.

Mom took a few awkward steps in my direction, her MS throwing her off balance, which made me inhale sharply, knowing that trying to help would only make her angry. She wobbled in place but righted herself, wagging the wooden spoon like a conductor's baton. "Kelly, have you ever considered you aren't the only one who suffers? Did you know your sister was crushing pills and snorting them? Snorting them! Her addiction ran deeper than any of us knew, but she turned it all around through hard work, and we should be celebrating that, as a family."

Even though this was true, it was not what I wanted to hear, and my face swelled with shame. Sadness clawed at my throat and then the pendulum swung to familiar acrimony.

"Why does no one ever talk about the fact that she only stopped doing drugs because a court forced her to? Thanks to me, by the way." Even as the words left my mouth, I recognized their ugliness and ignorance, but I couldn't be stopped. What was I even doing—taking credit for my sister's hard-won sobriety? But I was sick of heralding Meghan's wellness at the cost of my own, and frustrated that no matter what pain I experienced,

Meghan's trumped mine at every turn. What was worse was that it was so ridiculously childish, this feeling—which made me angrier still, even as the target of that anger kept transforming.

"You don't understand addiction." Mom stuffed noodles into the boiling pot of water and clattered a lid on top. I sucked my teeth and snatched the remote to turn up the volume. I was trying so very hard to understand—reading books, going to support groups—but still, I couldn't forgive.

There was a gentle tap at the front door before it swung open, a vacuum of air stirring the curtains. "Hello? Mom? Dad?" Meghan entered the kitchen, having come directly from work smelling of grilled chicken and Cajun spices, her hair still in its net and her visor looped around her neck like an oversized choker. It didn't escape my notice that Meghan had let herself in with a key. No one had given me a key, and I was actually staying there.

"Hi, Meggie." Mom kissed her on the cheek and gave me a stern look, a plea for me to not wreck this meal. Dad appeared at the top of the stairs, armed with china from the basement hutch. China. For spaghetti. On a Monday. There were even placemats and wine glasses set from their wedding crystal. He gave Meghan a kiss as he passed and, again, a jealous surge of anger rose within me. Whether due to cancer or addiction, Meghan had tottered towards death too many times, and that fear made Mom and Dad treat her like a delicate orchid. I hungered for some of that tenderness.

"Kell!" Meg rushed towards my spot on the couch and hugged me so tight I could barely breathe. Stubbornly, I let my arms hang stiffly at my side as though I were at attention on military parade, but Meghan didn't notice as she nestled her head against my collarbone. "I've missed you so much." I squirmed free to lean back against the couch, unable to shake my headache. "How much time do you have left in Ontario?" She sat beside me, the cushion depressing until I fell into her slightly. Parts of me tugged towards her like a sunflower head to sunlight. All the times she protected me from bullies. All the pretend weddings in the playroom. All the Girl Guide songs sung off-pitch.

"I'll go back in a few weeks. When I'm doing a little better."

"Oh, I'm so sorry you're not feeling well," she cooed, tearing up with compassion. I shifted uncomfortably, unsure how to respond to tears that weren't meant to absolve her of something—a familiar trick that in the past she'd employed on the regular. I regarded her carefully, not wanting to make myself obvious, uncertain if I was sitting with a stranger or the most recognizable person in my life.

"Dinner's up, girls." Dad filled everyone's glass to the brim with merlot.

"Fuck," I whispered as I wrestled myself between the chair and the tabletop, my bum sticking to the microfibre dining chair because of all the damn sweating. I was so overwhelmed with the need to cry that my ribcage constricted and I found myself fighting off another panic attack.

"Language, girls!" Dad clucked his tongue as he doled out the pasta, the deep crease in his forehead crinkling.

"Oh my God! I was in the military, remember?" I threw my arms around like a sassy teenager as tears formed, my heart raced, and I felt such a deep tide of anxiety that I could barely swallow. "I've been swearing for a few years. The jig is up." Maybe it was illness making me an asshole, but I just wanted one night of being a jerk, of feeling sorry for myself, of pointless pity that forgave my mistakes.

"Yeah, Dad. And she's a grown woman who can use whatever words she wants. Ever heard of feminism?" Meghan clinked her fork against my wine glass in solidarity. Even though I tried to stop it, a smile pulled at the corner of my mouth—my older sister rising to my defence. It was uncomfortable and unfamiliar but also, somehow, not.

"You're still Bill's Broads," Dad responded, but then he was grinning too. "So don't I get a say?"

Dad used to announce us as Bill's Broads as a joke, and Meghan and I would groan and pretend to hate his outdated, patriarchal ways. But we had liked it, this label, because it made us a team of women on the same side, something we must have sensed didn't always exist outside of family and might not even carry on between us. We were, always had been, Bill's Broads, now smirking like idiots as Dad loaded sauce onto dishes and wiggled noodles loose.

"You know, I could always take some time off work," Meghan said as she dug through the mound of grated Parmesan. "Help you out for a while? I know you have Joe, but he's so far away on the island. Google says with the ferry and everything it's a six-hour trip."

She was googling my address? "Meg, you can't afford that, but I appreciate the offer." In part, my words were lip service. I didn't want her there, and she knew it. But her cheeks were not sunken in and her hair no longer swallowed her whole and she was rosy and vibrant. Just maybe, she was Meghan again. Or I wanted to believe it, even though I knew that wanting might screw me over when this all went to shit.

You've got to be receptive but wary, Joe had said. *Do you want to go the rest of your life without your sister?*

"I would find a way to make it happen, if you needed me."
She reached for my hand, but I occupied it with my utensils,
pushed pasta into my mouth and washed it down with a gulp of
wine, emptying half the glass. I believed her, though. I didn't
know what to do with that feeling, so instead, as usual, I ate.

three

Less than a year later, Dad and I stood to the side of the April Point Resort and Spa honeymoon cabin while I pretended to hold a non-existent posey bouquet and waited to walk down the grassy aisle. I shaded the sun with a cupped palm against my brow to view the crowd of family and friends at the other end of the peninsula. My best friend, Nikki, was talking with the wedding coordinator to make sure the music was set to the right song, her long blonde hair catching on the wind and whipping behind her like a pennant.

"I feel stupid. Everyone is watching." I wiggled a rock out of my sandal and tugged my cardigan tighter. On the oceanfront in the shade, the September air was crisp, especially now that the sun was starting to dip below the mountains.

Dad patted my arm, which was looped in his. His forearm tattoo, blurry with age, was a familiar comfort, and I concentrated on the smeared lines of ink. "You're the bride. They're supposed to watch. Tomorrow my baby will be a bride."

"Gawd, please stop using the word."

The resort stretched across the edge of Quadra, a sleepy island sandwiched between Vancouver Island and British Columbia's mainland, which Joe and I still called home. Scrubby arbutus trees cracked red bark into the water below while a family of otters zipped through the waves nearby. It was like getting married in a leisure brochure.

"Nervous?" Dad asked, sounding anxious himself.

"No, actually." I could see Joe laughing with one of his grooms-men by the rocky outcrop next to the officiant, where a gaggle of other guests were waiting for the rehearsal to be over so we could have dinner. Meghan and Bernard sat together on a boulder, chewing on the ends of the cocktail straws in their drinks. She leaned into his ear and whispered, looking irritated as she stabbed her pointer finger as if poking air from dough. My stomach gurgled a dissent. I wasn't nervous about getting married, but having my sister in my wedding party was like peering over the edge of a cliff.

"Isn't Meghan supposed to be back here with us?" Nikki asked as she approached. She held a clipboard with the schedule on it and tapped the paper with her painted fingernail. "The music is about to start." Nikki and I both had oval faces, were almost the same height, and had similar builds. We looked more like sisters, I realized, than my biological one and I did.

"Have I told you how much your organization capabilities make my heart sing?"

She blew me a kiss. "Why else would I be maid of honour? I'll go get Meg." She walked at a clip towards our guests, waving for attention like someone calling a waiter.

Dad stiffened, his fingers tightening around my wrist. "This is probably a hard day for your sister."

"Not now, Dad."

Our parents hadn't hidden their disappointment when I chose Nikki instead of Meghan to lead my wedding party, but what kind of anecdotes could my sister offer to glossy-eyed grandparents when the closest thing we'd had to a relationship in sixteen years was me paying her dealer to stave off a threatened assault? All we had now was a ceasefire of amicability.

"I'm just saying. You know how she always wanted to get married. And being second place to Nikki, well . . ."

Across the way, Nikki was gesticulating towards the cabin and tapping at an imaginary wristwatch. In response, Meghan begrudgingly stood, drained her drink, and passed the empty glass to Bernard. He stayed sat on the boulder and remained focused on his cup and the ocean, which he regarded through oversized sunglasses with mirrored lenses. He and Meghan had been in a relationship for two years, but I was still struggling to know him in any real sense. I couldn't tell if this bothered me or not.

"Meghan and I don't even know each other, Dad."

"You've had plenty of time to make a start of things over the last year or two, no? You've been talking more."

I gritted my teeth. I hadn't returned to Ontario since recovering at Mom and Dad's the year prior—unable or unwilling, it was hard to say. My physical health had improved, but I didn't know how to mitigate the uneasy feeling of interacting with my family now that Meghan was sober, because we'd never examined how much had changed and how horrible we'd all been in survival mode. My resentment lingered like a bad smell but what was worse was that Meghan didn't seem to harbour any bitter feelings towards me beyond those of my marriage occurring before her own.

"Chatting on the phone isn't an actual relationship, Dad. She's barely said two words to me since we got here."

"Now that's not fair. She was a good sister to you, Moo. You know that. She always looked out for you."

"We're not kids anymore. She hasn't been a good sister for a really long time, so holding my hand on the way to kindergarten has been watered down by everything that came after that." I could hardly breathe. I willed Nikki to hurry up, for Meghan to join us so we could get this whole rigmarole over with.

Dad clucked his tongue and shook his head. "Why do you always spew such hate towards her?" His face was knotted in confusion. "We've all forgiven her, but you don't seem to want to. You have to let it go."

It. There was no single *it* that encapsulated all that we'd lost, and I didn't know how to define everything Meghan had done. And this moment felt even harder because in our approach to life, Dad had always been my family ally. Meghan and Mom were the emotional ones, tender-hearted and forgiving, whereas he and I were the veterans, practical overachievers, and epic grudge-holders. I felt abandoned by his new reasoning, his willingness to absolve her when he had always clung to lawfulness like a life raft. It was gross and uncompromising of me, but I wanted my sister to earn my forgiveness, or, at the very least, to be contrite— not for the addiction, but for how she treated us because of it.

"It's like we're supposed to pretend none of it happened because she was high when she did all this shit, but she still did it, Dad. And it still hurts." I swallowed repeatedly, tried to focus on my laughing fiancé and the peaceful ocean and the flutter of the gulls overhead. The next day I would be married and I was starting my MFA in creative writing in a week and I was moving on and making a new life. But my old life was a ball and chain I couldn't unlock.

"Try to understand," Dad muttered as Nikki and Meghan got closer. Meghan was wobbling on tall sandals, see-sawing across the lumpy grass. "Your sister has always wanted the things you have."

I squeezed my lids shut and stretched out a kink in my neck, hoping to stifle a scream.

"How much longer is this going to be?" Meghan blew a bubble of gum and swiped the burst web from her cheek, a plume of alcohol-tinged air escaping. As the sun dipped lower and highlighted her bouncy curls, she could have been mistaken for an underage drinker, even at thirty-one. "My ankle hurts. I want to change my shoes."

"So change them," I snapped. Behind Meghan's head, Nikki widened her eyes incredulously. *You okay?* I mimed a gag.

"You know I just twisted my ankle," Meghan whined, bending to rub at the injury. "It hurts to wear heels."

"Wasn't that three months ago?" I was fighting the tension that she seemed so keen on ratcheting up. "And you can wear whatever shoes you want. No one cares."

"I'll care when I'm standing next to you and I look like a stunted Smurf."

"Rehearsal will be however long it needs to be, right, Kelly?" Nikki nodded with satisfaction and signalled the coordinator to cue the music, then tossed her clipboard into a deck chair and smoothed her skirt. A Florence + The Machine song trilled, and Nikki nudged Meghan ahead. "You're first up. Don't forget to smile."

After dinner, Nikki, Meghan, and I surveyed our decorating work in the reception hall. The floor-to-ceiling windows looked out to blackness but come morning would reveal the calm Pacific inlet. The round tables that would seat thirty guests were dressed with vintage decor, and strings of sepia photographs were pinned to the exposed beams. Just outside the hall doors was the restaurant bar, where I could see Bernard sitting alone, leaning into a tumbler of amber liquid, and beyond him, the rest of our loved ones were scattered amongst tables in the restaurant, still finishing off their meals.

"It looks perfect," Nikki said as she adjusted a napkin to line up with its plate. "Laid-back and vintage."

"Kelly's never been laid-back about anything," Meghan said. "I think she was born with a stick up her ass." She snorted at this, then appeared to second-guess her audience in the face of our wide, gaping stares.

I tasted blood from gnawing my tongue. As a kid, I'd been a biter, but only of my sister, who so expertly stoked my temper. I would latch on until I broke her skin, feeling hot blood squish between my teeth. Hand, arm, back of the neck—the body part didn't matter, just the mark left behind, and my satisfaction would swell alongside the teeth marks that Mom would dab with iodine. *I don't know what makes you lose your temper like this, Kelly.* How to explain my rage, my jealousy over how Meghan moved so fearlessly within the boundaries of childhood? Anxiety had always controlled my every thought, every action, until lashing out at the person closest to me was the only response that made sense.

"So is there anything we have to do after this or are we done for the night?" Meghan fiddled with the fraying edge of a burlap table runner, which I'd carefully sewn just weeks ago. I wanted to slap her hand away. "Is there a girly bachelorette thing with penis necklaces or something?" She glanced between Nikki and me, assessing. I couldn't tell what answer she wanted: if she hoped to be included or was desperate to be released from her bridesmaid duties.

"Nope. I'm going to bed early. Have to look the well-rested bridal part tomorrow."

Nikki nodded in confirmation, far too exuberantly. We had a bottle of Prosecco on ice and a DVD to watch back in the honeymoon cabin. If Meghan knew I was lying, she didn't seem bothered.

"Good, because Bernard and I never really get a vacation, so I want to order some wine to the room and relax. Today has been *a lot*." I wondered if Bernard became animated in the right context, considering how earlier he had loped with disinterest behind Meghan as she chatted up the guests. He had mumbled a thanks to Joe and me for the free room, which I now assumed would come with unexpected charges, including the bottle of wine. "See you tomorrow for the big day. What time?"

"We meet at the spa at ten for mani-pedis," Nikki answered, having committed the schedule to memory. "So bring your dress to Kelly's cabin a few minutes before and we can all get ready together."

"Uh, that early? On a Saturday?" Meghan stared at us. "Fine. See you then." She waved and skipped out of the room to meet Bernard. Through the open door I saw her hop onto the barstool next to him and kiss him on the cheek. He wobbled a bit in place and signalled to the bartender.

"Ten is too early?" Nikki shook her head as she smoothed the drape of the runner Meghan had been fiddling with.

"Is it bad that I don't want her hanging out with us tonight?" I moved robotically, packing extra napkin holders and menus into Rubbermaid bins.

Nikki scrunched her nose in distaste. "After the way she's treated you for years, and now the cow she's been today? Hardly. If I have to hear her complain about her free bridesmaid dress one more time, I'll scream." We started stacking the empty plastic totes at the back of the room near the bar doors and flicking off the lights. "I hate to say it, but just pretend she isn't there tomorrow. She's making this a lot harder than it needs to be."

Meghan was in animated discussion with Bernard, hair tossing as she talked. Friends had approached me all day, folding me into hugs of congratulations. *I just met your sister. You two are so much alike!* I searched for that similarity but could not find it. "Thing is, we don't really know one another, after all these years, so I guess I'm wondering if it was the drugs making her unlikeable or if this is just her personality. I don't know what's more terrifying." Meghan laughed and I heard her snort. Reflexively, I smiled at her joy. "Sometimes I see glimpses of the old version, though, and I miss her."

"That Meghan might never come back, Kelly." Nikki snapped on a lid and gave me a kiss on the cheek. For more than two decades, Nikki had been at my side through all the things for which one craved a sister—the perfect stand-in. But still, she wasn't the person who had grown up sleeping in the twin bed next to my own.

"Better to make peace with that."

I carried the last two totes to the back of the room and drew the gold curtains over them so they'd be out of sight during the wedding. From that spot, peering through the crack behind the door, I watched as Meghan trailed her finger down the wine list, bottom lip pushed out in a pout.

"It's not fair, babe," Meghan said, reaching into Bernard's empty glass to snatch a piece of ice and pop it in her mouth. "She didn't even want a family, or to get married, and here she is, getting everything she wants. Again."

She couldn't see me, which made it easy to pretend I didn't hear, didn't care, didn't feel blood fill my mouth when she leaned into Bernard's shoulder and used his shirtsleeve to wipe her tears.

four

"I don't know if I'm supposed to ring the doorbell." Joe and I stood on Mom and Dad's porch, sheltered from the rain that pelted the spring grass. I'd worn a canvas jacket that wasn't warm enough, but I still couldn't bring myself to knock. Four years. I hadn't been back to Barrie since 2011, the year before I married, and it felt like an eternity.

With Joe, I'd forged a comfortable, happy life on the West Coast, having rid myself of the drama that came with Meghan and Bernard, Mom and Dad, and all the things I wanted to say but couldn't. I made up excuses when my parents asked me to visit. Said I was busy with finishing my MFA, or feeling ill effects from my thyroid treatment, both of which were true, but I could have made myself available. The reality was that I didn't want to leave the safe space I had with Joe, and anything outside of that secure bubble filled me with dread. Other than one visit from Mom and Dad for my graduation a year prior, I'd stuck to FaceTime as my sole means of communicating with them. Meghan had been making an effort, too, calling every few days to update me on her new life working in the registrar's office at a college, twirling around the room with her phone screen to showcase her desk, her nametag, her tidy cup of pens. Even from that distance it was getting easier to like her, to remember how fun she'd once been.

"Don't ask me. I've only been here twice," Joe said, his arms full of wrapped packages. "But hurry up, it's freezing. Looks like Meghan is already here." Her beat-up Chevrolet was dripping plops of oil on the driveway next to Dad's spotless pickup. There was a car seat in the back of Meghan's vehicle, a jumble of coloured sensory toys dangling from the headrest.

"I'll ring, I think." My finger hovered over the button too long, prompting Joe to lean in and press it first with a series of quick taps.

Dad threw open the door and wrapped his arms around me. "Moo! Joe! So good to see you both. What're you ringing the bell for?" We stepped inside, and Dad took the gifts and placed them in the chair by the window. "Presents?"

"For Sam. Plus something small for you and Mom from Vancouver. Chocolate." I used to see social media videos of lavish birthday parties for babies and wonder what the point was. The child wouldn't remember, certainly, and the pomp and circumstance seemed more like Instagram fodder for the parents. But I understood now. I'd brought a plastic dump truck and a set of blocks, wanting my nephew to hold these things and know me within them.

"Right! Okay, well come on in. Your sister and the baby are already here." Dad's grey moustache bounced above a smile that seemed uncontainable. He had always loved babies, but now he texted me a constant stream of pictures with his grandson on his knee, snuggled next to his cheek, having tummy time on the floor. I could hear the baby babbling from somewhere inside the house and my stomach did a dance.

The house still smelled the same—of Dove soap and Bounce sheets. My parents had updated the paint, though—another shade of off-white—and bought some new furniture. But otherwise, not much had changed. We shucked our coats and tucked everything in the closet, then wandered through the bungalow to find Mom on the couch, silhouetted by the lamp behind her head. Bernard was in an armchair with a bottle of beer resting in his lap.

"Hi, you two." Mom stood to squeeze us in succession, the effort seeming laborious with the stark advancement of her MS.

"Bernard, hey." I hovered in front of him, unsure of how to greet someone I'd hardly ever spoken to but who was essentially family. He didn't stand, so I sat on the floral carpet instead, which was prone to shedding wool fibres like tumbleweeds. "Where's Meg?"

"Feeding the baby," Mom answered. "In the guest room because your father is a prude."

"Am not!" Dad settled back onto the couch next to Mom. "A father should not see his daughter's breasts. End of story."

"She should be stopping by now," Bernard said in his achingly slow drawl. "He's old enough."

"I'm coming!" The door to the guest room flung open and Meghan emerged with the baby balanced on her hip while she refastened the strap of her nursing bra. She was flushed and nicely dressed in slacks and a patterned shirt, her hair dusting her shoulders and highlighted with streaks of blonde. She looked beautiful and impossibly happy.

And then my gaze settled on my nephew. Sam's eyes matched ours—greenish blue—but were set close together like Bernard's. His blond head was perfectly round, and he had teeth emerging from angry gums and pudgy knuckles dimpled with fat. Meghan grabbed him from underneath his bum and swung him in front of her like a football, bouncing up and down towards me, swaying left and right as the baby darted his tongue out of his mouth to release a stream of drool. "Sammy, this is your Auntie Kelly. Your only auntie."

The room was silent as she held him out to me. Nine months old. I'd been away for years, and in that time a whole new life had been created. Sam lifted his arms up like he recognized me somehow, and I gingerly took my nephew from my sister and brought him close, nuzzled and squeezed. He leaned back as if taking me in, trying to slot me into the family he knew. His chubby hand reached for my face and stroked it with an open, sticky palm.

"I'm your auntie, buddy. Do you know what that means?" Something had been set free inside of me. It opened its maw wide and took a calm breath.

"Whoa, Kell. This is weird to watch." Meghan sniffled, then drained a ginger ale and burped and hiccupped at the same time. "He's, like, your twin." She leaned in to fold Sam and me into a group hug, then wiped tears from her eyes.

I cupped the back of his skull and swung him down to the floor until his pale hair hung in feathery strings. He giggled wildly, trusting me to keep him safe as I nuzzled my nose to his belly. No one ever said Meghan and I looked alike, but here was my nephew, and he was mine. I felt it in my bones.

"Wait until you see the little vest we got him for our wedding," Meghan said, scrunching her fingers as if pinching cheeks. "Thompson tartan. I just hope it fits. Who knows how much he'll grow in six months."

I barely heard her, staring into Sam's upside-down face. I had resented Sam's birth because it created a permanent tie between our family and Bernard, and, as hard as I tried, what was there to like about someone whose quiet acquiescence belied apathy more than any other emotion? But holding Sam, I felt the tug of that tied string. We were a family now, and we would have to try.

"The good news is, now we'll just live a few hours away," Joe said, taking a sip of his drink. "We can have visits with the little man here." He craned his neck to jokingly nibble on Sam's feet, which stirred a bubble of baby giggles that loosened the knot in my chest. Everything I'd been holding on to finally dropped from my shoulders like a shawl slipping to the floor.

I'd been unhappy with Joe's new military position in Ontario. I didn't want to leave the West Coast, the thrum of Vancouver for the rural living of the Trenton air base. But this was military life, and we went where we were told. What I hadn't expected was to find myself holding a child and rapidly warming to the idea of family beyond the one I had made with Joe.

"I've got to get back home to do some work," Bernard muttered. He pocketed the phone he'd been staring at. "We should get going."

"So soon?" I held the baby tightly and he grabbed my bangs and pulled with shocking strength. "We just got here."

Meghan glanced between us. "We arrived a bit early because Sammy was getting some vaccines, so he's been a bit grumpy. Plus, Bernard's been doing some wiring on his friend's cottage.

Saving him lots of money. It's so nice of you, babe." Even though she was speaking to him, Bernard was already in the front hall putting on his shoes. Sam didn't seem grumpy in the slightest, and I didn't want them to go. It was the first time in a long time that I had wanted my sister to stay. "Things are going to be so different now that you're close by, right, Kell? Right?"

Now that you're close.

Geography had never been the reason our relationship faltered, but she knew that. Something else stood in the way, but in the absence of acknowledging that, there was love. I held that love in my arms and promised to call her next week. FaceTime, maybe, with Sam.

I called. And the week after that, and the one after that, too. From then on, I called every single day until Sam learned how to call me himself by touching my image on the screen.

five

Six months later, Meghan and I sat at a bistro-height table on the bar side of the local Milestones. She wore a flimsy Mylar sash emblazoned with *Bride* in script and a pink crown cocked to one side of her brunette bob, the plastic jewels stuck on with crusty adhesive. A stiff veil of tulle stuck out from the back of her head like a salute as Meghan slurped from her third fruity daiquiri with an umbrella dangling on the edge, the paper pleats gone soggy and limp.

We had gotten dressed at Mom and Dad's in the basement bedroom that used to be hers, now scrubbed to nondescript guest-suite status, and the space looked empty without her tacky decor dangling from every surface. The framed photos with inked hearts scribbled around Bernard's face were gone, along with the plastic Mardi Gras beads from bar nights that she'd hung from the dresser hardware. In their place were Wedgewood saucers holding nothing and pine furniture tart with lemon polish.

Between slugs from a beer bottle, Meghan had stood in front of the mirror scrunching waves into her hair and squealed when I tugged the hokey bridal accessories from my bag. For weeks I'd asked her to provide a guest list for her bachelorette, but other than one friend who was working, there was no one she was close enough to to ask. The party for two was a signifier of how even at thirty-four and almost five years sober, Meghan ignored friendships in favour of boyfriends with exhausting predictability. Out in public, the effect of the crown and sash languished, leaving a residue of loneliness.

"It's nice to finally be out without a baby attached to my boob!" Meghan clinked her glass with my club soda and spilled magenta slush across her chest, then dabbed at the stain with a napkin. "Gawd, can't take me anywhere." There was a reddish glob of chili sauce stuck to her chin, and it glimmered in the overhead lights of the dim bar.

"You haven't left him with Bernard at some point?" I had to holler to be heard over Taylor Swift's latest hit. Meghan was mouthing the lyrics. "He's fifteen months old!"

She went to speak but her phone screen lit up with Bernard's face, his shiny blond hair slopping forward and beard edging towards the wrong side of bushy. "Speak of the devil! It's my groom!" She waggled the phone at me, nearly knocking over our water glasses until I steadied them with open palms.

"Again? He's literally texted every ten minutes." Her phone had chimed endlessly all day—at our manicures, while we drove, while we dressed. *A little pre-wedding flirting with hubby?* the esthetician had asked as she painted a slipper pink stripe down the acrylic nails I'd thought were tacky. Meghan tapped out responses with apologies—*sorry I'm holding this up*—before finally answering his fifth call. The staff and I feigned deafness as he screamed at her for taking the wrong vehicle, for not planning lunch for their son, for forgetting to take out the garbage. When I mentioned, oh so casually, that he seemed irrationally angry, that his words were harsh, she fobbed me off with a wave of her hand and a stern look that told me to drop it.

My mouth felt like sandpaper and I slurped at my drink, gone bitter with lime. "Tell him you're busy getting your bachelorette on. No boys allowed!"

"I can't ignore him. He has Sammy." She held the phone close to her face while she read, her smile slipping.

"What does he want?" I leaned in, hoping that if I hovered, she wouldn't lie to me. Separating Meghan's personal truths from facts was like straining onions from soup—the flavour already tainted everything. I could handle the lies as they related to her addiction, when she was covering for herself, but her choices in men made for deception aimed to hide the treatment she withstood, and that felt more sinister. I wanted to trust her. Sometimes I did. But it was impossible to believe someone who always had something to hide.

"Uh, Sammy won't go to sleep. Poor Bernard, he's getting frustrated. I should call." She stood but forgot the raised table height and tripped, scrabbling after her phone that skittered under a nearby banquet seat. I grabbed her forearm to help steady her. Her crown had slipped from its perch, making her look on the brink of madness.

"Meg, come enjoy yourself. I think Bernard can handle one bedtime with his own kid." I knew it wasn't about Sam, or I'd have welcomed Bernard's interference.

Her knuckles whitened as she tightened her grasp on the phone. Despite the manicure, the skin around each nailbed was haggard from where she'd anxiously picked and chewed. She shrugged her shoulders in resignation and punched out a long text, sent it with a *whoosh*, then settled the phone face-up in her purse so she could pretend she wasn't waiting for his response.

"Sammy probably needs his blanket. Or Thomas the Tank Engine. Thomas solves everything in our house. Anyways." She shook her head, the topic dropped. "I can't believe that this weekend I'll finally be a married woman!" She shimmied in her seat and I laughed despite the knell of anxiety in my gut. She was a fun drunk, the few times I'd been in her company as an adult. But as I managed a smile, I pictured the marriage officiant asking for objections and Mom, Dad, and me standing up in unison.

I nibbled at our platter of deep-fried appetizers, the food gone cold and clammy. "You've wanted to marry every guy you've met since you were twelve." I left my meaning for interpretation but she didn't take the bait, instead swatting at me with her napkin. As kids, we played house, slipping into the roles in which we both felt comfortable—me, the parent with a job outside the home, and my sister, the aproned housewife with a brood of babies. Our mom didn't have an apron, so we knotted a makeshift version from ratty floral pillowcases. Sometimes we played "runaway," where we would tie up our belongings using our baby blankets, sling them on the end of a broomstick like cartoon hobos, and head off to our new lives. For these pretend futures, I packed the notebooks, pens, and books I imagined I'd need. Meghan packed dolls and the pillowcase apron.

She took a large gulp of her daiquiri, slapped her forehead at the brain freeze. "That's an exaggeration. Since puberty, maybe." She laughed hard then, freckled mouth wide and gaping, and in that rare moment I saw my face reflected in hers. Did people see us and wonder about how we were connected, just as I'd always searched for those links? Meghan plucked a limp battered pickle from the plate and popped the whole thing into her mouth, chewing with her freckled cheeks pushed out like a puffer fish. "I'm just glad you and Joe live closer now."

"So we can get wasted at a Milestones on a Tuesday like desperate housewives?" I couldn't stand looking at the chunk of sauce anymore and swiped at her chin with my licked thumb.

"You're the farthest thing from a desperate housewife." Meghan swirled the straw around the dregs of her fishbowl drink, clearly on a roll. "But we're finally getting along, seeing each other more often, part of each other's lives. I get to watch you do what you were meant to do, you know? I mean, you're writing a book, for Christ's sake."

"A book that currently has no publisher, or agent, or prospects, really." Since finishing my master's in creative writing the year prior, half of my classmates had been published. Meanwhile, I kept slogging over a manuscript that never seemed finished.

"Only a matter of time. You're my favourite author, and I'm not saying this because I'm drunk. You know that, right?"

"That's what everyone says when they're drunk."

"I mean it." She leaned across the table, showing off a bubble of cleavage. "I think you're amazing. I'm your biggest fan. Everything you've done for me, with the wedding especially. Even after all the things I've done to you."

A silence hung between us, even as other customers screamed at the televisions when a puck struck the net, with men in Leafs jerseys slamming fists on the glossy bar. Familiar tears sat weighty and glistening above her cheeks, but there was something different behind the irises. Something that was not a request for pity but, instead, a rawness. I bit into my lime wedge and squinted at its sourness as the waitress wordlessly delivered our cheque, then flitted back into the crowd with a pitcher of beer wobbling on a tray and her ponytail bouncing. Meghan faked a motion for the bill. I put my hand on hers and left it there a moment longer than seemed natural.

"I told you, I've got this, Meg. It's your bachelorette. Not that it's much of one."

"It's all I wanted. You know that." She tugged a light trench coat over her shoulders and knotted the tie at the waist. "Besides, I didn't do anything for you when you got married."

"I lived on the other side of the country then. It's fine. Really." I counted cash into the billfold. I had picked out my wedding dress alone at the shop across from my apartment in Vancouver. *Anyone joining you today?* the saleswoman had asked, dangling three champagne flutes between her fingers. She seemed disappointed when I said no, a potential commission drizzling down the drain. The woman didn't understand the nature of military life, how we scattered like dandelion seeds across the country and got used to pretending that solitary exis-tence was a choice. So I bought an off-the-rack gown that didn't fit, and slunk home feeling pointlessly angry.

Holding the bill, I couldn't concentrate. I fretted over the tip, did mental multiplication and addition, recalculated, then added another twenty, just in case.

"Well, and I wasn't your maid of honour, so it wasn't really my job." Meghan dropped her head at this, scuffing the floor as we walked towards the exit. Outside, our breath created puffs of condensation in the fall air. I shivered as we approached my Volkswagen, desperate for the short walk to dissuade her from taking the conversation further. Refraining from digging into the meat of what hurt us carried delightful sway, because if we were really to examine it, I worried we'd emerge more broken than before. We were talking. We had a friendship, even. For now, and after years of nothingness, that was enough.

"I deserved it, you know," she continued, trotting to keep up with me. "I deserved to be second best after the way I treated you."

Oh my God, please stop. I fiddled with the key fob and unlocked the doors with a lighted beep. Once inside, I started the ignition, blasting semi-warm air through the vents so our hair gusted into mushrooms clouds as Beyoncé bellowed through the speakers. Meghan quickly snapped off the radio, so that the only sound was the whirling of the fan and our huffing exhalations. "I was so horrible to you. To Mom and Dad. I missed out on so much with you guys because I was doing all this shitty stuff even though I had an actual, loving family. I hung out with a lot of people who weren't so lucky."

I didn't want to listen. A couple walked past the car, arms around each other's waists. The man pulled a tissue from his pocket and dabbed at his partner's nostrils, then kissed the bridge of her nose. *That is what love looks like,* I wanted to cry. *See that there? Why don't you know what it looks like?*

"At the end of the day, I'm alive because of what you told the judge. I needed the shock of it, to be held accountable, or I just would have kept going. I'd probably be dead. I'm just, I'm so sorry, Kell."

The moment crystallized like a Polaroid. I wanted to cry, I think, or laugh, or give her a hug, or shake her by the shoulders and ask where in the fuck this had been for the last twenty years, because I'd needed this—an apology not predicated on a want or an ask. I blinked over and over, my senses alight to the sound of the fan and the heat rising from my leather seat and the smell of Meghan's perfume. The car undulated like we were at sea, making me nauseated.

"You know what's worse than all the stuff you did?" I croaked, swallowing my heartburn down. "Sometimes, you messing up made me feel better. Like I was right about you all along."

The streetlight glare filled the car with a pale yellow sheen and condensation dotted the windows. Meghan smeared at it with her palm. "People are going think we're making out." She snort-laughed, producing a bubble of snot. She didn't look embarrassed as she dug through her purse for a tissue, eventually settling on a used one she had to unfurl. "I think I felt I deserved a certain way of life. And you were so . . ." She picked at her cuticles, drawing blood. "You were so *good*. I'd come home from some crazy bender and you were doing all these things with your life, and I was, I dunno, jealous."

I flexed my fingers around the steering wheel. Grip, release. Grip, release. "Hell, Meg. I've cheated, I've stolen, I've lied. I've made mistakes. You just weren't around to witness them." I was yelling, but she didn't shrink back, didn't turn away.

"Your mistakes didn't land you in jail."

"Nope, but some of them could have."

A grin spread from the side of her mouth before she blew another wet glob into her tissue. "Sounds interesting. I want to know more."

I joke-punched her arm. "So we've both fucked up at some point or another, but you pretending I'm perfect doesn't make this easier." I wrenched my body towards her so that we were really looking at one another, and our hands knotted and squeezed into a tight ball. We'd spent more time hating each other than being able to stand one another's presence, and that knowledge unspooled my defences. "You understand, right? That I had to pick myself over you? I didn't want to be a bitch." My tears slipped onto the console between us. I was shaking, but her grip steadied me. "I had to pretend to be one, to survive."

"I know you did, Kell. I know. It's okay."

I leaned forward and spontaneously kissed her forehead, and we both burst into strangled laughter. "Sorry, that was weird. I don't know why I did that."

"No, no, it was nice." She touched the place where my lip gloss had left a print, right above her left eyebrow. "Motherly, kind of." Meghan slapped her thighs and wiped her face, leaving a trail of mascara down her cheek. "Okay, we need to cheer up. We should go home and bust open a bottle of Mom and Dad's homebrew. Play some Monopoly."

"Do you ever *not* want to play Monopoly?"

She took her snotty tissue and dabbed at my nose and, for some reason, I let her. "Just remember, I get to be the shoe, and you better not cheat this time," she said, stuffing the tissue into her purse and pointing a finger in my face. "You always cheated. I saw."

Meghan was the only one who knew I snuck $500 bills from the banker's till when Dad wasn't watching. She was the only one who really saw.

six

On Thanksgiving Sunday, 2016, I woke at six in the morning and spread my arms over Joe's side of our king-sized bed. The coolness of the sheets signified his absence, as did the items discarded on his nightstand—his alarm clock, a dog-eared book on stoicism, and scribbled Post-it reminders that were no longer relevant. Since his deployment to Egypt in the summer, I still woke shocked to find him gone, and there was another nine months to go until he'd return.

While I stared at the popcorn ceiling, the previous night veered into consciousness even as I tried to bat the thoughts away. Meghan had insisted I shouldn't be alone for the holiday, said it was the chance to be the kind of sisters we'd imagined back when we were reading too many Sweet Valley High books. I suspected the suggested visit had more to do with my ratcheting depression, which seemed to be snaking tentacles into every element of my life, including our daily phone calls. Regardless, our parents chose to stay home, and I had pressed but then given up. *It'll be crowded*, Dad said. *You should bond with your sister.*

In the light of morning, it was hard to pinpoint just where our family dinner had gone so wrong. Bernard's third beer? Fifth? Or maybe it began with the plea for booze in the first place, even after promising Meghan he wouldn't drink for the weekend, wheedling platitudes on our way to the apple farm where we were taking Sam to pet horses. *Please, honey, please?* What was she to say?

The alcohol had loosened him at first, got him talking about his work, his love of music. He smiled while he chatted, actually smiled, reaching over once in a while to dab gravy off of Sam's chin, but as the empties stacked, so did his list of complaints: Meghan's parenting, her sloppy housekeeping, and, finally, her *wrecked* post-baby body. The night devolved into tears; Meghan's, then Sam's, and, once everyone was asleep and the cleanup was done, mine.

I rubbed my face to smear away the memory as Meghan and Sam's murmurs rose from the basement guest room, which motivated me to swing myself from bed and throw a robe over my pyjamas. My slippers made slapping noises on the stairs down to the den, where I found Meghan and Sam sprawled across the fold-out bed he slept on, the sheets mussed and pillows stacked into a fort. Upon seeing me, Sam leapt from the mattress and I snatched him mid-air, flopping on the springs and burrowing us under a pile of blankets. At two years old, he was looking more and more like my mini replica, complete with the bowl cut I'd had at his age.

"Happy Thanksgiving! How's my Piggy?" I poked his round belly, and he nuzzled into my neck. He wasn't verbal yet, but we always found other ways to communicate.

"Morning." Meghan looked wan, and her face was puffy from crying. She lay supine, cradling her baby bump as she edged towards the promised safety of the second trimester. I felt sick every time I thought of a second child, of more stress placed on this family that already seemed so precarious. Bernard's snores echoed through the guest bedroom door, which was still shut tight.

"I don't mean this as a slight, but you look exhausted."

"Well, someone has been up for two hours. You're lucky I managed to keep him this quiet because he kept wanting to come upstairs to see you."

"Coffee. You need coffee. Piggy, want to come upstairs and watch Treehouse with Auntie?"

"Mmm!" I led him up to the main floor of the bungalow while Meghan padded behind. My bull terrier, Pot Roast, wagged his tail and, after licking Sam's face, nestled into his bed by the window. We settled Sam on the couch with a show while Meghan stalked towards the kitchen, passing remnants of our hopeful Thanksgiving celebration: the autumnal centrepiece stuffed with succulents, the small gourd Sammy had fingerpainted with streaks of yellow and green, the pumpkin pie now covered in Saran— reminders of how it all went wrong. I set the kettle to boil while Meghan took clean pots from the drying rack and wiped them mechanically with a cloth.

"You're literally drying dry pans."

She regarded the heap of dishes through a haze. "God, I'm out of it. Last night was . . . well, you know."

I squeezed her shoulder. "You and Bernard didn't have a talk once you went to bed?" I whispered while cranking the bean grinder.

"Hard to talk to someone when they're in an alcohol coma. This was supposed to be family time, not like every other weekend he spends drinking alone by the bonfire until two in the morning." Meghan fiddled with a spoon in her mug, making metallic clinks against the porcelain. "I was thinking that maybe he's acting out because of nerves about the new baby, after all the miscarriages."

"Oh, come on, Meg. I've got issues, so I go to therapy and take my medication and work at getting better. If he's struggling, he could seek help instead of punishing everyone around him. Being ill isn't always a reason to be an asshole." Meghan kept her focus trained on her mug so that she didn't have to look at me. Her baby bump looked rounder since she arrived less than twenty-four hours ago, blurring at the edges of so much sharpness. "Being around all that anger can't be good for Sam, either."

She gave me a look of warning. Our bond was so pocked with scar tissue that this kind of blunt honesty was both terrifying and exhilarating. "Sam knows we love him." He jumped up and down on the cushions, grunting along to the song bleating onscreen, while adults in droopy foam costumes clunked into one another as if in a slapstick Stooge routine. Meghan had a fine talent for focusing on the details she wanted to see. A Norman Rockwell print used to hang in our shared childhood bedroom, the one of a doctor and a little girl. Meghan always loved it, while I thought the doctor looked lecherous, the girl as tender and afraid as the kitten at her heel.

As I poured our coffees and stirred in cream, Bernard emerged from the basement, yawning wide as he stumbled into the living room. Sam noticed his father's presence but didn't look away from his show. My whole body tensed, and Meghan's muscles mirrored mine.

"What is this garbage?" Bernard asked no one in particular, gesturing at the screen. He snatched the remote and Sam sniffled plaintively.

"Well, good morning to you too, Bernard. And Happy Thanksgiving." My saccharine tone didn't seem to register as he punched buttons on the remote. Meghan put herself between Bernard and their child and I stood behind Sam and the couch to grip his tiny shoulders. His hands snaked up to mine.

"I don't want to watch this." Bernard fumbled with the controls, slapping the plastic against his open palm like he was shaking ketchup from a bottle. "I want to watch that Pixar one. *Inside Out*. About the girl who has bi-polar or something. Was on the news." He started flipping through the Netflix cover images, each digital *boop* sucking the air from the room.

"Bernard." Meghan's voice was stern, a defensive warning.

"It'll teach him about his feelings, or whatever."

"Hey, you two." My tone approached sing-song territory. What had I expected? An apology? A calm, measured discussion between adults away from a vulnerable child? "Your. Son. Is. Watching." I stressed those last words so that every consonant was sharp and pronounced.

"Yeah, Bernard," Meghan said snidely as her voice rose a few decibels. "Maybe what you want to watch doesn't matter."

"I DON'T FUCKING CARE!" Bernard slammed the table, waking Pot Roast in his bed by the window and setting his tail into an anxious wag.

"Sweetie," I said, leaning into Sam's ear. His body was as rigid as a surfboard. "Why don't you go to Auntie's office and find her dolly. You can show Pot Roast how baby has breakfast? Then maybe we can feed Pot Roast his breakfast together, okay?

You stay there until I come get you." He nodded at me, face inscrutable, and then did as asked.

"You scared your son," Meghan barked.

"No, you did," Bernard fired back.

"Oh, real mature."

"Fuck you."

"No, fuck you."

They continued back and forth while I stood there like an idiot. The room was hot. Too bright and sunny for the feeling that cloaked us. No one had yelled in our home when we were growing up, and the absence of that kind of anger in my life meant that witnessing it, seeing how Meghan gave and took such rage, gave me goosebumps. And why did she always pick these kinds of men? There was the boyfriend who made her keep her clothing in baskets so he could toss her belongings into piles in the hall and make her sleep there when he was mad. Or the one who racked up debt with her credits cards and never paid her back. Or the one who kept cheating with sex workers. The ones who fed her addictions because it fed her dependence on them.

I clicked off the television. Everything was silent and noisy all at once.

"Hey!" I clapped like a kindergarten teacher to get their attention. My voice dropped to a whisper. "If you two can't sort yourselves out, then you're both failing here. Both of you." My pointer finger aimed at their heads. "Go discuss this somewhere private. I'll watch Sam." They remained locked in a staredown and neither moved. "Go. Now."

Once I heard them tersely snarking in the basement bedroom, I put Disney music on the surround sound and guided my nephew from my office to make us hot chocolate. We sipped our drinks while he sat on my lap at the island countertop, and I sang repetitive songs until he started to hum the choruses.

Less than thirty minutes later, Meghan and Bernard dropped their belongings in the foyer with a clatter. Their movements were sharp, the anger between them snapping like static.

"Kell," Meghan called out. I heard the phlegm in her throat, indicating she'd been crying. "I think we'll head home now."

I carried Sam to the foyer on my hip as Bernard disappeared outside to load the car. Meghan was surrounded by a pile of bags, items dangling from stuffed pockets and cords snaking out, everything smelling of cannabis. I wanted to tell her to stay, but then, what difference would it make? There had never been any point in standing between Meghan and what she felt she deserved.

"Already?" I asked. "A whole day early?" She winced, as if the decision was made and was non-negotiable. "You guys don't want breakfast? I was going to make bacon and Piggy loves bacon." I snorted like a pig until he laughed, his fingers twined in my pyjama shirt.

"We're fine. We'll stop at McDonald's for a muffin, eh, Sammy?" Meghan squeezed Sam's chubby thigh.

Bernard came to the door and reached for his son. "Pass him to me."

For a moment, I clung tight to my nephew. "Auntie loves you, Piggy." I blew a raspberry into his neck. Sam wiped his chocolate moustache on my shoulder before I passed him over and Bernard stormed outside again while Meghan and I watched from the open door.

"Thanks for a great weekend," she said, hugging me tight. She looked drained and defeated.

Bernard plopped Sam into his car seat before slinging himself into the driver's side of his Crown Victoria, which he'd outfitted with a trunk full of speakers that left room for nothing else. It was more practical than his other vehicle—the low-rider Chevy pickup with hydraulics that bumped the vehicle up and down mechanically.

"A great weekend?" I took a deep breath. "Meghan, I love you, but he's not welcome in my house if he's going to treat you guys like that. You get to make a choice to put up with this. Sam doesn't."

She pressed her lips together, angry. "Oh, that's great, Kell. What am I supposed to do with that?"

I held my breath and blew it out noisily through my nose. We enjoyed actual sisterhood now, and I didn't want to go back to where we'd been. "You're supposed to recognize that you've only been married a year and your life is basically a domestic abuse infographic. And besides you, Sam is surrounded by constant conflict. I'm worried about you and your kid, Meg. Kids." I patted her belly and she held me there a moment.

"You're making me choose between my husband and my family."

I hurt all over. A migraine coming on, maybe, or a giving over to this problem that never seemed to go away. Her lip wobbled, stoking my self-hatred. I hated myself so much for saying these words aloud, but I wanted her to hear them. *Abuse. Abused. Abusive.* They felt like motor oil in my mouth. "No, it's him making you choose. I'm just putting up a boundary. Don't you see how he's isolating you from us? How frightened Sammy is? How sad this all is?"

Her mouth formed words that seemed to dissipate upon reflection. I knew that when I tried to sleep that night, the look on her face would haunt me, as would the guilt burrowing under my skin. Was this a boundary? Or was this me walking away because it was hard, as I'd done so many times before? I didn't know anymore. I didn't know anything at all.

She left without responding, stopping to buckle Sam in before climbing into the front passenger seat. When Bernard drove away, my sister wiggled her fingertips goodbye while Sam's arm pumped back and forth with the kind of obliviousness that only childhood allows.

seven

The forest trail was soggy with mud that sucked at my boots. Pot Roast yanked on a gigantic branch knocked to the ground during the previous week's windstorm, his bark sharp and insistent despite the music piping through my headphones. I tried to smile and call out to him but stopped short, unable to engage. All I could focus on was the despair that had been circulating like fog for weeks with no rhyme or reason.

With the time difference, it was too early in the day to talk to Joe in Egypt over WhatsApp, so I trembled as I pressed the home button on my iPhone. "Hey Siri." The sniffles started immediately. "Call Meghan Thompson." As the phone rang, I tried to calm my breath. In, out. In, out. *Ground yourself when your emotions get out of control*, my therapist always said. *Notice things.* Chipmunk. Light. Leaves. Smell of decay.

"Morning, Kell," Meghan chirped over the sound of Sam playing in the background, his coos crackling the airwaves. "Yes!

Mommy sees it! Sorry. I'm being shown the same Tonka truck for the millionth time this morning. How're you doing?" Her voice was compassionate, turned up at the end like she was talking to a grieving wife. Had I been calling too often? Crying too much? This, too, panicked me.

"I don't know." A sob escaped and I swatted at my face blankly, my voice monotone. How was it possible to feel so much and so little simultaneously?

"What's wrong?" She sounded instantly serious, assertive, Little Miss Fix-It style.

I swallowed the lump in my throat. "It might not be any one thing."

Pot Roast caught up to me, the prized branch clutched between his jaws, making him stumble as it clacked between the trees. His beady eyes assessed me and he dropped the stick, flattened his ears, and licked gently at the cuff of my sleeve.

"I get it. Sometimes with depression, you just can't pinpoint a specific problem."

Breathe. In, out. In, out.

"This is stupid. What the hell am I even depressed about? It's almost embarrassing." My mind flashed back six weeks to Thanksgiving, to Bernard's sniping, Meghan's sobbing, Sammy's confusion. Compared to my sister, I had no reason to be sad. We hadn't spoken further about Bernard's behaviour that day, and I could feel her retreating to the comfortable charade of a happy marriage, although she'd still vent to me occasionally because her female relationships were limited and she'd never been good at keeping secrets from me. His drinking was escalating, she admitted, but her life was good and her husband was great and everything was fine, fine, fine.

"Geez, Kell, you of all people know that mental health is more complicated than that. Have you been writing much lately? That usually helps you." I heard the whirl of her Keurig as it sputtered a steaming drink into her cup.

I blinked in the sunlight. I had landed an agent for my military memoir manuscript, but progress had stalled in a sea of my own self-doubt, each typed sentence seeming more banal than the next. "I don't feel like it. I don't feel like doing anything, really."

My petulance was making me feel sick. I was a veteran, which provided me access to mental health supports. I could afford my medication. I had a pension that allowed me time and space to mentally heal. But all that privilege did was drench me in shame. Others deserved it more than me. Others needed it more than me. *Why am I so worthless?* "I just feel like I'm actually losing my mind. Like I need to go to the hospital or something. Everything feels ... dark." I choked out the last words like a cough.

"Kell, you're spiralling. Where are you right now?"

I steadied myself against a maple, its leaves scattered around the forest bed. "On a walk with Roast, so technically not alone, I guess. I should go home. I just want to be home." I twisted a damp leaf stem between my fingers so that it fluttered like a flag. Meghan and I used to assemble house floorplans from piles of leaves and mud, until we discovered I had allergies, with itchy welts to prove it. Forced indoors for much of fall, Meghan had sat inside to keep me company, dabbing on calamine while our dream world scattered with the leaf blower. "I tried talking to Mom and Dad about how I was feeling. It wasn't exactly helpful."

"Jesus, for sympathy? You know they mean well, but it's not exactly their strong suit. Should have come to me first."

I mustered a small laugh and stooped to pat the dog's head before throwing a stick, watching as he bounded towards it. "I'm being ridiculous. I shouldn't have bugged you." I tripped on a tree root and smacked to the ground. There was dirt smudged up my cheek, blood on my palm, mud smeared on my pants. Something deep inside my chest ached as I scrambled to locate my phone in a pile of termite-riddled sticks and fallen oak leaves. "Fuck. Sorry, I fell." Everything hurt—every cell, every eyelash, every finger-nail. How long since I'd tried to go off my depression meds? A few months? It had been a slow titrate that left me raw, and now, all I could think of was—what would it be like to not be here, on earth, in the sun on the path with my dog and loved ones on the phone? What was the point, really, of getting up and repeating it all over again come morning? I shook my head, the tears falling and making wet streaks on my boots. "I need you, Meg."

"Listen, I'll be there tomorrow, okay? First thing in the morning. Mom and Dad can take Sam and I'll come straight to you for however long you need. We'll get you through this."

"You can't. You're pregnant and you've got a family. It's too much for me to ask." Even as I tried to talk her out of it, I knew she wouldn't listen. Holding that knowledge was the most com-forting feeling in the world.

"Hey, it'll be nice to support you for once. Finally, some payback."

I wiped my nose on my sleeve. "You're still in emotional debt up to your eyeballs."

"Then you can deduct this one from my bill. I'll see you tomorrow. I've gotta go. Sammy is stuffing animal crackers down his pants."

I hung up, brushed off the dirt, and inspected the torn hole in my jeans, then pocketed my phone and ruffled Pot Roast's ears. "We'll be okay, eh, buddy?" A squirrel caught his attention and he zoomed up the trail, and I found the strength to follow.

eight

Sam was napping in Mom and Dad's upstairs guest bedroom, so Mom, Dad, Meghan, and I stared at the television with the volume turned low. The channel didn't matter because we weren't watching, the emotional atmosphere as dour as the early December weather. Meghan sat in the armchair by the window, her shoulders hunched, staring out to the backyard where the season's first snowfall frosted the lawn like a coat of icing. She was now almost four months pregnant and so her baby bump bulged from the waistband of her jeans, but she looked fragile and elfin, like a child having a child.

She had called me and asked me to meet her at Mom and Dad's, where she planned to stay for "a while," claiming she and Bernard were taking a few days apart. She needed me there, she said—as confidante or child-minder, I still wasn't sure three days in. Since I arrived, I'd been coordinating activities for Sam like a recreation director on a cruise ship—decorating sugar cookies, doing arts and crafts, putting puzzles together, and playing endless games of hide-and-go-seek—hopeful that a happy, busy child might boost Meghan's spirits or encourage her to chat about whatever it was that had brought us here. But she was perpetually despondent, half here, half somewhere else.

The gas fireplace was roaring, so I had stripped down to a T-shirt that was covered in dog hair and lint. I stretched across the carpet taking large slurps from a glass of wine that I had balanced on my chest. "Hey, you know what we should do?" I rose up to my elbows to look between Meghan and my parents. No one turned their attention to me. "We should put the Christmas tree up while we're all here." Meghan, above all, was a stickler for the tradition and nostalgia of Christmas decorating—the laying out of our matching ornaments, placing them on the tree at the same time, all to the rhythm of carols playing on our worn-out CD player. Even in the deepest days of her addiction, she required all family members present and participatory, often stumbling drunkenly through her own routine. I used to begrudge her this, hating the ceremony of it when we skirted around meaningful conversation, but considering our current stress level, I understood the appeal of something known. "How often do we get to be together as a family these days? Sam would like it, too."

Mom and Dad stared through me, and Meghan folded her arms tight across her chest. "We're not all here though, are we?" she mumbled. Bernard's absence was palpable, even if welcomed.

I didn't know if I should press, if this was an opening to ask the questions we'd been stifling for days. *Why are you here? What happened?* Once Meghan had gone off to bed each night that week, Mom, Dad, and I would drum up theories. *Does this mean she's leaving him? Maybe he doesn't want another kid? Money problems?*

But if we even tried to ask, she snapped that she didn't need to share all the details of her private life, that some things were between husband and wife. She had always been like this—you had to wait for her to come to you.

"Well, Joe isn't going to appear anytime soon," I said, keeping my tone light. "Egypt is a little far to pop by for tree trimming." Mentioning his name was a reminder of my daily countdown to Joe's return, which I marked on a calendar with a red marker, striking off days with bright streaks. But in my rush to get here, I'd forgotten the calendar at home, which stirred my anxiety—all those days unchecked. *You're fine, Kelly. Everything is fine.* Since last month's emotional meltdown, I'd started some new medication and was now tottering on a thin balance beam of sanity, nervous each time I wobbled closer to sadness. I couldn't bear returning to that dark place, so I focused on Meghan and Sam and doing and playing. "We might as well do something cheery, no?" Meghan and I were operating in a weird sort of support pendulum, and that week, she was the one with the greater need.

"I'm not exactly in the holiday spirit," Meghan muttered. She pressed a fingertip to the window and left a perfect bud of a print on the glass. Mom watched and I felt her desire to clean the mark as much as Meghan's need to make it, but since Meghan's arrival, no one had dared to challenge her on anything she wanted to do.

"It's a nice idea, Moo," Dad said airily.

"I'm just saying, Meg's having another baby, and who knows where Joe and I will get posted next. One day we'll all wish we'd taken this opportunity to do something nice together." My family regarded me sullenly, saying nothing. I squeezed the bridge of my nose and thought of my peaceful home hours away. The cozy throw blankets. The office. The stacks of books. The absence of stress like this. I took their continued silence for the answer it was. "I'm going to get another drink. Anyone want anything?"

Mom and Dad shook their heads and turned their loose attention back to the television and Meghan followed me robotically to the kitchen, sidestepping Sam's toys along the way. She twisted the ends of her hair into a rope, then twirled it back and forth with a nervous twitch.

As I filled a water glass at the sink, she pressed so close to me that I stumbled into the countertop. "What?"

"I need a favour," she said, her voice hushed. She licked her lips, which were dry and peeling, then leaned up on tiptoe so that her breath tickled the hair around my ears. "Can you lend me a couple hundred bucks?" She reached behind me and snatched an orange from the fruit basket and rolled it back and forth across the granite.

I took a step sideways, hoping to create space between us, then drained my glass in one chug. "What for?"

Her face darkened, as if a curtain had fallen. "Why can't anyone in this family ever just do something nice for me without needing some kind of explanation?" Her fists tightened in fury and the veins of her neck strained. "I'm an adult. I don't need to show you my fucking bank account whenever I need some support."

Even after years of bracing myself for it, it was still shocking how quickly my sister could flip to hostility. She was like a cornered animal—if confronted, even if she was in the wrong, Meghan lashed out, blamed, pointed fingers anywhere but at her own chest. Familiar anger of my own sparked alongside memories of this exact conversation held too often to count.

How many times had I fuelled her addiction with money, leaving me to question if I was preventing harm or encouraging it? I didn't know anymore.

"You think because we love you that we don't have bills of our own to pay? So sorry if I want to know what the money is for so I can determine if it's worth me going without." Back when I was in the Forces and Meghan was deep into drugs, she'd often made midnight calls to beg me to wire cash. I'd make a late-night trip to Western Union, or Money Mart, or whatever was closest at the time, shuffling into the fluorescent lights in my pyjamas with dark circles under my eyes, knowing I was already in overdraft, too. She said the money was because she couldn't afford to eat, didn't have electricity, would lose her apartment. I never voiced how close I was to those things as well; I just signed the form and sent what I could manage. "You're thirty-five, for Christ's sake. A little old to keep having this temper tantrum."

"Girls?" Mom glanced over, her face furrowed with concern.

"It's fine, Mom." I lowered my voice and took a breath, hating how easily we slipped into these ugly versions of ourselves. We were so good at finding the juiciest wounds in which to grind the salt. "What do you need money for?"

Meghan slapped the orange back and forth between her palms like a baseball, jaw set. "Just some toiletries and stuff. And Sam needs things to eat. Mom and Dad have seven million cans of tomato paste in the cupboards and that's it. No snacks or kid stuff. You know, I need everyday living stuff until I go back home."

Go back. She said it like returning was predetermined, and I bit my tongue. She'd been here so many times before, full of empty threats in the hopes that Bernard would be so frightened to lose her that he'd leap towards change. But then Meghan was a font of forgiveness. It was me who was so good at holding grudges and keeping score.

"You said you and Bernard don't have any money problems." Meghan always championed his ability to provide, as though a steady income was its own love language. She seemed to forget how on her wedding day she hadn't had enough gas or money to get her to the ceremony. I had paid without question, but wondered how Bernard afforded the two-fours of beer that were stacked four high on their front porch. "It's understandable if things are rough. You've got another kid on the way. Are you guys okay, financially?"

"It isn't that. We're fine." She picked at her cuticles, staring down at her feet. "I just don't have my debit card with me."

"Oh hell, that's all?" My body sagged with relief. "I'll go to your house and get it for you. You just don't want to have to see Bernard while you're fighting, right?" I stepped towards the row of hanging keys and slung my purse onto my shoulder, grateful for an easy solution.

Meghan reached out to stop me, chewing on the inside of her cheek. "It's not that." I felt the heat of her desperation, the shame in her hung head. And I wanted her to stop talking because I didn't want to hear the rest. But I did, I did. "Bernard took my card from my wallet before I left." This part she said so quickly I was convinced I'd not heard right.

"What, like a punishment?" I choked out the words, trying to disguise my horror. She shrugged as tears brimmed, moving so quickly between bravado and mortification that I was dizzy. "So, you have your child, and he left you with no way to care for yourself or, I don't know, feed that child?"

"I mean, he has a point. I'm the one leaving instead of staying at the house to work things out. I just needed some time."

"I don't give a shit what the reason was, Meghan. He's controlling your finances to control you, and that's messed up. Especially when it affects your children."

She squeezed the orange so tight I worried it would burst, the juice flexing against dimpled rind. "I'll pay you back. I promise."

"Fuck the money, Meghan. I need you to tell me what's going on." I tried to picture Joe withholding our money, leaving me pregnant and vulnerable, but the image would not come. Maybe I was lucky for that kind of surety. "Don't you think it's scary that he's denying you access to any of your income? That's bullshit, Meg. That's scary, abusive bullshit."

"What are you girls whispering about?" Dad hollered. "It's rude to whisper."

"Nothing, Dad. Geez," Meghan said, rubbing her face with open palms. "We're just talking about Christmas presents, okay?"

She steered us into the privacy of Mom and Dad's bedroom while I surreptitiously searched her for indications of different forms of abuse that I'd not witnessed. But I had no idea what to look for, because it was not any one thing but rather a collection of moments that totalled the person in front of me. I couldn't shake the image of one of Meghan's first boyfriends at the annual fair, beer garden guests milling nearby with their watery keg draught. He'd stood menacingly over her, screaming that she was a whore and a slut, and she said nothing back while staring down at her worn sneakers. She hadn't seen me watching—thirteen, cotton candy melting sugary crystals on my tongue, shocked and paralyzed because she was so different when she was with me. So strong and determined. Brave.

I stumbled backwards and landed on the bed, which made Meghan loom over me, our height difference reversed. "Do you need somewhere to stay longer term? There's lots of room for you and Sammy at our place, plus the baby, when it comes." Even as I said the words I was unsure if I wanted her to take me up on the offer. It was obvious how easily our oil and vinegar personalities could wreck all the delicate work we'd been doing to reconnect, and I could barely maintain my own precarious mental health. But there didn't seem to be any rational alternative. I wanted to save her. Even when I knew I couldn't.

"I don't want to leave my husband, Kelly." *My husband.* Whenever she didn't want to defend Bernard and the choices she made that were associated with him, she awarded him her most powerful noun, employing it like incantation. She used the word as a reminder of her vows, even as he broke his.

"I'm just saying. If you needed. It's always an option." *Run*, I wanted to beg her. I had to bite my bottom lip to keep the word from spilling out.

"I just need some cash to tide me over. Sam needs it." Her hands rested on her hips, her stance wide. She looked so powerful and sure.

Mom and Dad had joked that I was the quickest study in learning to resist Meghan's manipulation, which had often centred around finances. We'd all given her money, or she'd stolen it from us, but I was the first to stand up and say no more, to cut off contact for self-preservation. *It's harder*, Mom said, *to deny your child.* But Meghan was deeply aware of my new loyalties to Sam and the soon-to-be-baby, and this request felt so different from all the others. I reached into my wallet and pulled out whatever cash was there. "I'll get more tomorrow." I shakily extended the fan of twenties, ignoring the sense of déjà vu.

She squeezed me tight around my shoulders. "Thank you. Thank you so much." She flipped on a smile and walked away before I could ask more questions. It was a convenient Meghan tactic that I knew well.

nine

Sam peered into the glass display case at the hospital gift shop, his face pressed against the pane. "Mmm." He pointed at a single rose arranged with sprigs of baby's breath. I hated baby's breath.

"That one, Piggy?"

"Mmm hmm."

"Excuse me?" I called. An elderly volunteer looked up from the cash register and smiled at Sam, smoothing her blue Royal Victoria Regional Health Centre smock as she approached. "Can we have that one there?"

"Sure you can, dearie. Your son is adorable." She whooshed open the cooler door to grab the vase, then caressed Sam's cheek. He leaned into her touch like a kitten.

I kissed his other cheek and gave him a squeeze. "He's my nephew. We're here to see Mommy, aren't we?"

After ringing in the new year three weeks ago, Meghan had called Mom and Dad at three in the morning, asking for a drive to the hospital as she wailed in pain. None of us asked why she didn't have Bernard drive her because the question had seemed moot when she was in such agony.

"Oh, you must miss her!" The woman rang in the flowers and pushed a pen across the counter. "Do you want to sign a card?" A stack of cards, all of them overly feminine and floral, sat near the register on a plastic rack. *Get Well Soon! Congrats! It's a Boy!* On the back of each one was the hospital stamp, which made me want none of the stupid cards.

"Thanks." I picked *We Love You* because nothing else seemed appropriate. Sam wiggled from my arms and, in the corner of the gift shop, found a pink stuffed pig that he squished to his chest.

"Should we get that for Mommy too? A pig for my Piggy?" I wiggled the snout of the stuffie into his armpit until his laugher echoed into the atrium. "This too, please."

Sam and I found Meghan in her room, propped up in bed with worn sheets folded across her belly and white haze filtering in from the north-facing window. She didn't look like she belonged in the maternity ward—her face was gaunt and white, and her small stomach could have been mistaken for a big lunch or a case of bloat.

"Knock, knock. Brought you a visitor."

She straightened when she saw us, pushing greasy hair from her face. Sam ran towards her bed with the stuffed pig in his arms, winter boots slapping the linoleum. "Sammy!" Meghan swooped her son into a hug and tried to haul him into the hospital bed, but her arms were too weak. Instead, Sam held the toy to her as an offering. "For me?"

"To keep Mommy company, right, buddy?" I said from the darkness of the doorway. If she saw me cry, she wouldn't be able to stop herself.

"Mmm hmm." Sam was two and a half, not yet verbal, and a tide of guilt swept over me. Since Mom and Dad and Bernard's mom were all rotating caring for Sam during the week, we'd not been working with the flash cards or encouraging speech or any of the other things Meghan had been practising with him. It was like we were all treading water, trying to keep our heads above the rising levels.

I watched them embrace and girded myself. "He picked these out too," I said, arranging the small vase on her crowded wheeled tray, amongst tissues, phone charging cords, books in a haphazard stack, and a slew of other junk.

"I bet you loved the baby's breath," she responded, smirking at me as she tickled Sam into a fit of laughter.

"I can't help that I have taste. Your son clearly needs a floral education."

Sam snagged the television remote from the tray and Meghan set him up with a show. He nestled into the crook of her arm, his head resting against her breast, and sighed contentedly.

"He's missed you." I leaned in to kiss her cheek. "I've missed you too."

She turned away from me towards the window that was shrouded from view by the curtain separating her and the other patient and waited for the threat of tears to pass.

"You're such a drama queen," I said, reaching for her. "You and your complicated little lady in there." She laughed, then brought my hand to her stomach and held it there until I rubbed back and forth. Somehow, at thirty-two, I had never felt a pregnant belly before, except in Meghan's early stages, before the fluttering of movement. My niece kicked and a burst of emotion rushed through me, the movement like an air bubble trapped under ice. "Look who's getting saucy in there."

"Just saying hello to her auntie, aren't you, little girl? If I didn't have this TV I think I'd be losing my mind. Dad bought me the pass. Some crazy price, like fifteen dollars a day? Fifteen bucks for a couple wobbly cable channels."

"Well, if we're looking for comic relief, you're the only person I know who gets hospitalized because they are actually full of shit."

"Oh, you're hilarious." Still, she snorted a laugh. "Bowel obstructions are no joke though. Feels like someone is stabbing me." She brought her shoulders to her ears and let them drop. "I thought I'd be out sooner, not sitting here for weeks on end. In and out, like I was with Sammy." Meghan's first pregnancy had also involved a week-long hospital stint with a nasogastric tube stuck down her throat until the obstruction, the result of the baby pressing against the scar tissue from her childhood kidney cancer, passed.

"Well, for now you're where you need to be. Safe and sound to give that bun a cozy oven-proofing."

"Yeah, but now they're moving me to Mount Sinai in Toronto because they specialize in high-risk and geriatric pregnancies. Geriatric. Seriously," she said with a chuckle. "That's what they call it when you're over thirty-five and giving birth. They're putting me on IV nutrition until she's born, and stupid bed rest. Four more months laying around like this. All I want is a hamburger."

"Oh please, you love lazing around and doing nothing. Look at it as a vacation to prep for life as a mother of two." I hoped so badly she couldn't hear the nervousness in my humour.

She squeezed Sam's knee and took a sharp breath. "I'm worried about her in there, Kell. Like, she'll be sick because I couldn't keep her fed. And once I'm in Toronto I'll never get to see Sam and Bernard." Tears slipped down her cheeks, some landing on Sam's head. He didn't seem to notice, his focus so squarely on the television that was inches from his face.

Sensing her fear brought me so close to falling apart that I bordered on panic. I could no longer ignore the medical alarms alerting, the too-bright lights, the stench of overcooked food and unwashed bodies. How did anyone rest in here? "Meg." I tucked the sheets tight around her legs like Dad used to do when we were little, snugging us into blanketed cocoons. "You aren't doing anything to her. It's happening to both of you, and the best doctors are on the job. Plus, Sam has me to keep him entertained, and a bunch of other family who are pitching in, okay?"

"And his father. He has his father," she said insistently.

I forced my lips into a tight line. "Oodles of love from oodles of people."

"You're right, I'm just moping. Mommy will be home soon, right, Sammy? Once Mommy's done growing your baby sister." Then to me: "But you can't be coming here every weekend. You've got too much going on."

"Hey, the writing life is a relatively flexible life. And it's not like I have Joe waiting for me at home." I knew it would be hard though. If she was in hospital for the next few months, the weekly drive back home would be exhausting. But the alternative—my sister lonely, afraid, and pregnant in a hospital room—was too much to bear.

"Good," she said. "Because honestly, if you weren't here, I'd go insane. So hurry up and finish your book already so I have something to read. I'm bored as ..." She pointed at Sam, mouthed *fuck*, then flopped back into her pillow. "You know, my mood would be greatly improved by a Popsicle. Can you grab me one? And one for him? It's the only thing I'm allowed to *eat*." She snarled her upper lip in disdain.

"Sure. They have them down in the food court?"

"I'll show you," a voice said from the other side of the curtain. A woman appeared, long wavy hair tucked behind her ears. She was heavily pregnant, yet small like Meghan. "I'm waddling that way."

"Kelly, this is Beth, my roommate."

"Oh," Beth said, giving my arm a knowing squeeze. "The writer, yeah? She never stops talking about you."

"That's me." I rolled my eyes.

"What?" Meghan threw up her arms like she'd been caught committing a crime. "I'm proud of you."

"You're really working it for that Popsicle, eh? We'll be right back."

I followed Beth towards the nursing station. "Are you sure you're okay to walk?" I gestured at her protruding stomach.

"Oh yeah. I'm on bed rest but allowed to shower, get something to eat, that kind of thing." She led me to the patient lounge, which held a fridge, coffee machine, kettle, plastic cutlery, and cups. She pulled back the freezer door and I picked a few frozen banana-flavoured ice pops from the pile. "I'm glad to catch you alone, actually. I always try to talk with your parents but it's awkward."

"Oh?" I held both Popsicles with consideration. There was a printed sign on the fridge in bold, large font. *PATIENTS ONLY.*

"Your sister's husband," she whispered, as though Meghan might pop out from behind the door. "What's his name?"

She knew his name, likely because Meghan said it a million times a day, but Beth was testing something. I didn't answer, nervous to fan flames. Instead, I raised a brow in encouragement, a hint at my role as her ally.

"He just, well, he's not really been here. I know he commutes to Toronto for work and everything, but doesn't he only work four days a week? Your sister's been asking on the phone to see Sam, but then I ask her about it, and she basically brushes it off. The husband stopped in once for, like, two minutes. Acted like it was some kind of chore."

It was oddly validating to have someone outside of our family notice this. "That's par for the course for their entire relationship." I tore open the package and bit into the Popsicle sending a frozen jolt of pain up my neck. "Sadly."

"Ah, that's too bad." Beth steepled her fingers as the kettle sang. She plunked four herbal tea bags into her obscenely large travel mug. "I figured it was something along those lines. Your parents are here every single day, and my husband, heck, you can barely keep him out of here. I have to remind him we have two other daughters who need their love and attention as much as this little one." She rubbed her stomach and seemed to drift somewhere else, then return. "Meghan's lucky then, to have a sister like you. She said she screwed it up for a long time, between the two of you. Owns that it was her fault and everything."

I looked out the window at the other patients, families, and staff milling in the snow-crusted parking lot. Orderlies hovered outside a back entrance and hauled on cigarettes, puffing frosty nicotine clouds. "Sisters come back to one another, I think. When they're ready. It wasn't just her fault though. I was judgmental. Harsh. I'm still like that, I think."

Beth patted me on the back like we were long-lost sisters ourselves. "Look after her in Toronto, eh? I know the drive is long for you, making this trip. But she appreciates you, the light you bring." Beth left, shuffling towards their shared room.

I ate three Popsicles in silence before following, brandishing the treats, a strained smile on my face, willing myself not to make this harder for my sister by asking for answers she didn't have.

ten

My doctor's office was in a century brick home in downtown Belleville with hardwood floors that cracked like arthritic knuckles. The exam room stank of antiseptic and was painted a buttery yellow that bordered on fluorescent. I settled into an icy metal chair and played endless games of Candy Crush for distraction.

"Kelly, nice to see you." Dr. Hartland sat in front of the computer and turned so our knees nearly touched. As my general practitioner, her scheduled bimonthly mental health check-ins were a familiar routine, but their regularity didn't dull the uncomfortable bareness I felt when discussing my medications, my moods, my pointed despair. And this appointment had an unexpected additional purpose—to go over results of recent tests. "Let me just pop today's details in here. Goodness, April already, eh? How're things going?"

"It's going." I punched at the last digital candy and watched as it zapped the others in a cascading wheel of light.

"How's your sister doing? The baby?" she asked hopefully. "That bowel obstruction finally clear?"

My cheeks were wet with tears before I realized what was happening, and I leaned forward onto my knees. "A little girl. Born yesterday, almost six weeks early."

The night before, Meghan had called—one of many chats throughout the day to help with the tedium of bedrest. Her latest symptom had us snickering. *I'm so swollen. My whole lower body is, like, four times the normal size.* We cracked jokes about it, the edema so obvious that when she sent photos, she looked like a crime suspect composite with different parts of the body slotted in to make a whole, except her top and bottom halves didn't fit together. But when she called hours later, she was breathless, her voice faint but simultaneously shrieking. *Kell? Kell, they're inducing me right now. Now. Oh my God. Bernard will call when I'm out.* Bernard never called, and hours later Meghan dialled instead, groggy with exhaustion, and relayed the news. *Her name is Lily.*

"Six weeks. Premature, but still viable. Congrats!" The doctor spoke hesitantly, unsure of how I seemed to be taking the news. Her mouth curled into a half-smile, half-wince. "Baby and mom are doing well?"

I picked at a hangnail. If I focused on this crust of peeling finger skin, then I could ignore everything else and pretend Meghan's call last night was some kind of nightmare.

"She gave birth to a baby and then they found a six-pound sarcoma." I emitted a strange sound somewhere between a sob and a laugh. On the seat next to me, the candies still sparkled in their colourful void. I could not bear to darken the screen and find nothing there except my own thoughts.

"Cancer?" Dr. Hartland's mouth hung open. "That's why she's been in hospital all this time?"

"Yeah, not a bowel obstruction, it turns out. The baby was hiding the tumour in her scans."

"Oh my, I'm so sorry to hear all this. Sarcomas are quite rare." Dr. Hartland shook her head. She didn't say what we both already knew; the rarity of sarcomas wasn't as frightening as their deadliness. I'd been up until two in the morning researching, disheartened at every new webpage that didn't give the answers I wanted.

"I'm headed to see her this afternoon at Mount Sinai." A weird laugh emerged. At least, I thought it came from me, but it was hard to tell when everything felt hollow and unsure, like the jumpy reel of a B movie.

"Well, they have excellent doctors there, so she'll get top-level care." We sat in silence while she searched for words of comfort. Realizing there were none, she clicked open my chart and pretended to read it, but clearly, she already knew the results. "Well, I wish I had better news, considering everything else you've got going on, but I think it's safe to say, as you suspected, that you're dealing with polycystic ovary syndrome. PCOS, we call it." The month before, I'd scribbled a list of symptoms, just as I'd done with the Graves' disease, and then presented the list to Dr. Hartland: deeper depression, erratic and painful periods, difficulty losing weight, a spray of cystic acne across my jaw and back, and, best of all, a cluster of wiry chin hairs. "Considering your Graves' and celiac disease, both being autoimmune, it's not overly surprising to have other hormonal issues. Not serious or life-threatening, though, so that's good news."

Good news. I blinked back at Dr. Hartland, trying to stem my agnostic prayer for non-cystic ovaries when I should have been expending all my good wishes on my sister not dying. "So, what does this mean?"

"Well, it's definitely another large barrier to pregnancy."

Another. Large. Barrier.

I pictured Joe in Egypt and something inside of me cracked. I thought of our plans to start a family upon his return. If he were home, he would have assured me that my health didn't change anything, that we'd get through it together. But he wasn't home, and I felt like a failure. "What do I do to treat it?"

"Well, we can get you into an ob-gyn if you want to talk a bit more about fertility treatments. Since you're—what, nearly thirty-three?—we'll want to get that ball rolling quickly. Other than that, sadly, the only other thing you can do is go on birth control to manage the symptoms. There are some blood pressure medications that can help ease the hirsutism and acne, but with your low blood pressure, you might not tolerate them very well."

I snorted. "So, I go on birth control to manage a condition that makes me mostly infertile?"

The doctor gave a sympathetic tilt of her head. "Bodies are strange," she conceded, typing some information into her chart. "In the meantime, I'll renew your Cymbalta prescription for the depression. Once things settle down with your sister, come back and we'll chat about alternatives for the reproductive side of things, okay? And take care of yourself. I know you give a lot of support to your family, but you might need some too, especially with Joe gone. This is a lot to take in."

I left her office in a haze and stuffed the prescription into my purse. Once I slumped into the driver's seat of my car, I punched a text to Joe on WhatsApp. *All done at doc and on my way to Meg in Toronto. Will call later.*

I started the car and let the engine rumble, as I took deep, gasping breaths. *PCOS is nothing, considering your husband is in a war zone and your sister has cancer and a newborn and your mom has MS and your dad is a prostate cancer survivor and this is fucking nothing.* This was what I told myself as I veered onto the highway and headed west.

───────────

I got to the hospital in less than two hours and wound my way through the maze of hallways in Mount Sinai to the maternity ward nursing station. The nurse told me Meghan had been given a private room even though her benefits didn't allow for one; someone had taken pity on her while she awaited transfer to the oncology unit. Meghan's daughter, weighing just a few pounds, had been assigned to the neonatal ICU.

When I peeked around her door, Meghan was in bed with her eyes closed. She had a towel wrapped around her head like a turban, the two inches of grey roots in her widow's peak serving as evidence of months in hospital. She looked older than thirty-five, and she'd grown so thin that she practically disappeared under the striped flannel sheets.

"Nice digs," I called gently so as not to startle her, placing the gluten-free brownies I'd made on the bedside tray. There was no room for the snacks except for next to the breast pump that sat like a monolith.

Meghan's lashes fluttered. "Well, a little cancer gets you the royal treatment."

I took her hand and we pressed our waiting tears down somewhere deep. Visiting Meghan in hospital was becoming a stark new norm, holding her hand in my own and trying to settle into new realities. "Now why didn't I think of that?" My thumb rubbed back and forth on her palm and I swallowed hard. "This is all total bullshit."

"The bullshittiest. Is that a word?" Meghan wiped her face as tears escaped.

"Nope. But we can make it one. Where's Bernard?" I looked for signs of his vigil—empty Styrofoam coffee cups or a blanket and pillow for sleeping next to her bedside. I found none of these things.

"Oh, he went home to get some sleep. He's so tired. This has all been so stressful for him." I pressed my lips into a firm line and said nothing. "I can't believe this, Kell." Her voice was barely audible, and she leaned back into her pillow until it wrapped around her ears. "Why is this happening?"

Were there reasons? Could someone be a reformed jerk but still earn themselves punishment for whatever had come before? That was the thing about illness and suffering: kindness didn't earn you a guarantee. We'd always joked about our family's propensity for illness—Mom's MS and breast cancer survival, Dad's intense battle with prostate cancer, Meghan's history of hell—and wondered if we'd all been next-level jerks in previous lives. When strangers heard us relate our medical histories and commented on how unlucky we were, I would think of how we'd always come out on the other side, alive, which seemed lucky enough to celebrate. Meghan worried the ties on her gown, and I knew that no matter how horrible she'd been in the past, no amount of karma could lead to this. If providence relied solely on a life of goodness, half the population would die young.

"I don't know, Meg. But I know we'll get through this together."

"I know. I know we will. Hey, I beat cancer once before, right?" She sounded hopeful, like my assurance would change the outcome. I'd done this too—sought guarantees—when we were little. *I won't be sick, right, Meghan? I won't throw up?* She'd shush me, press a maternal cheek to mine. *You're not even warm. You won't throw up. You'll be fine.* I always believed her.

"Sure did, tough ol' broad. Speaking of which, congrats on producing another line of said toughness. All this cancer talk is distracting us from your baby girl."

She sparked at this, coming to life. "She's perfect, Kell. So tiny. Want to go see her?"

"Absolutely."

We acquired a pushchair and then wheeled slowly to the elevators to access the NICU, where Meghan scanned her thumbprint like Miss Moneypenny, the electronic lock disengaging and revealing a medicinal-scented space lit with gentle wattage. After washing our hands for the required amount of time, we entered the room where baby Lily was stretched out under a bluish light. She was motionless, wearing a mini sleep mask to block out the brightness, and in a diaper so minute it looked fit for a doll. For a brief, glimmering moment, I allowed myself to wonder what it might be like to make a life and literally hold it in your arms.

"Hi, baby girl. It's Mommy." Meghan tightened the belt of her robe, then wrangled her arms into the incubator to rub Lily's foot.

"She's beautiful, Meg." She wasn't, particularly, as newborns, preemies especially, so often aren't. And yet it wasn't a lie, this underlying beauty of grit; the proof was right there in the miraculous lighted box.

"She is." Meghan's face was soft in the blue light. "But look at these friggin' gun boats." She waggled the baby's leg at me. Lily's foot was like a surfboard attached to a stick.

"Good Lord. Hope she grows into those things." We snorted under our breath as nurses strolled by in cartoon-printed scrubs.

"I can't believe you made this," I said, reaching in to stroke a slender arm, even though it was against the rules. Only parents could touch the baby, but Meghan angled her body protectively between me and the nurses. "Auntie loves you." I whispered the words towards the plastic case, swallowing over and over as pain and joy coalesced. I would never have this experience with Joe. I would never have my own lit box of grit, and the only person I wanted to tell, aside from my husband, had no capacity for the news.

"I need to go back to the room," Meghan said, clutching at her belly. "Getting sore."

I was grateful for the distraction, quick to whisk Meghan back to her room several floors down and ease her into bed. She looked completely undone.

"Want me to let you have a rest? I can go have a coffee somewhere and come back."

"No way. I want you here with me."

"Well, in that case, I brought goodies." I pulled items from my tote with dramatic flair—celebrity magazines, books, my Netflix password, sheet face masks, and a drugstore box of chestnut hair dye. "Thought I could at least ensure you stop looking like a cancer patient." I rattled the box's contents.

Meghan pressed her palms together as if in prayer. "Thank fucking God."

"You sure you're up for it?"

She reached for the plastic cup on her tray, which held two white pills. She popped them in her mouth and slurped some water. "Give me five minutes with these suckers and I will be."

We set to work in the large room, sun pouring in the windows. I draped her shoulders with a cheap hospital towel, scratchy with bleach, and sputtered dye from the mixing tube.

"You should take off your shirt," Meghan said, gesturing to my white tee and the stains on the towel. I did, looping it over a chair. We wrapped Meghan's head in plastic wrap and watched an episode of *Call the Midwife* while we counted down the minutes.

"Alright, let's hose you down," I said, gesturing to the bathroom.

"How am I going to keep my pyjamas clean?" Meghan tugged at her loose flannels with the gown overtop.

"Just go in there naked," I said, already taking off my own clothes. "I'm your sister. What do I care? I'll be in my bra and underwear anyways. Don't want to get soaked."

She shrugged. Motherhood, giving birth, and illness had scrubbed her of modesty. She gingerly stripped down to reveal a padded Depend, convenient after having a child. Her breasts were pendulous, full of milk, nipples white with colostrum. I could not take my eyes off them. "Well, at least your boobs look great."

She gave her chest a gentle shimmy. "Yeah, I'm a regular porn star." We giggled at this as I helped her shuffle into the bathroom, shocked at how she was rail thin yet simultaneously puffy. She sat on the supportive bathing chair and then leaned forward as I set to work with the extendable shower head, releasing a stream of inky brown from the tendrils that dangled over her face. That is, until I dropped the shower handle, cracking off the cover and sending water everywhere in a zealous spray, cascading splotches of dye across the walls, Meghan, and the bathroom. The incontinence brief hung limp with liquid and mascara ran down my face, pooling within the brown sludge at our feet.

"There's a porn movie in this somewhere," Meghan said, laughing so hard she was gasping and clutching her misshapen stomach.

"What's with you and porn today? Besides, I don't think anyone in porn is wearing a diaper." I was laughing too hard to control the shower handle, so I dropped it to my side to squirt out a dollop of conditioner to work into her silky hair.

"Oh, you'd be surprised," she said. And then we laughed even harder. We laughed so hard that later that day, when her tumour ruptured after I had gone home and she was rushed into emergency surgery, I worried it was me and our shared sense of humour that had caused it to burst.

eleven

The international arrivals area of the Toronto airport was chilly inside despite the blazing July heat outdoors. I smoothed wrinkles from my dress while hovering near the swooshing double doors that led to the baggage area as crowds of people buzzed nearby. Dad still remembered what Mom had worn when he returned from his deployment to Egypt more than thirty years ago, and as I waited for Joe to come back from the same sandy place, I fretted about my plain linen shift and whether it would create an equally lasting impression. I wore heels, too, and plenty of makeup to distract from the fact that I'd shaved my head for a cancer fundraiser. Two weeks on, my reflection still shocked me whenever I glanced in the mirror.

A text from Meghan buzzed in my palm. *Where the hell is he?*

I glanced at my watch. Joe's flight was forty minutes late, and Meghan was in my car in the airport parking lot, running the air conditioning for her and Pot Roast. She'd insisted on coming when we learned the airport didn't allow pets, certain that Joe would want to see his dog the moment he arrived. She had dropped Sam and Lily off with Mom and Dad, and I was overwhelmed by the amount of inconvenience I was causing.

Likely stuck in customs, I responded, thumbs tapping out the message. *Sorry.*

I can wait a while longer but I'm getting kinda desperate to empty this fucking bag.

I gripped my phone tight, anxiety ratcheting. When Meghan's tumour ruptured, so had parts of her intestines, spreading bacteria and cancer cells throughout her abdomen. She woke from the anesthetic devastated to find that they had placed an ileostomy bag to allow her gut to heal, with a plan to reverse it in six months. Her meals seemed to trickle into the pouch as quickly as they entered her mouth.

An undiscernible announcement boomed over the PA system just as a bald head emerged from the crowd that had disembarked from the Israel flight, obvious amongst women in tichel and men in yarmulke. Joe grinned when he saw me, his face dotted with stubble, bags slung on both shoulders and another wheeled behind him. He was both precisely the same as when he left and yet entirely different. My heart sat in my throat as he folded me into his arms, his breath smelling of sleep and mint gum.

"I missed you so much," he said, his words stifled in my neck. "A year is too long."

"Never again. Right? Never for this long." I felt the former distance between us stretch like a sleepy giant. Overhead, speakers continued to blurt names and locations and destinations, but I heard only the sound of Joe's breathing in my ear, the rustle of his hands up and down my spine.

"Quite the 'do you have there." He rubbed his palm across my fuzzy regrowth, the shorn ends bristling under his fingertips, then kissed me deeply, not caring who was watching until I pulled away. "Hey," he said, pursing his lips into a theatrical pout. "I wasn't done enacting our Harlequin romance."

"I know, sorry, but we have to get moving." I grabbed one of his bags and slung it over my shoulder. It was heavier than I expected, and I stumbled in my wedge heels. "Meg is in the car and really needs to use the bathroom."

"Doesn't she have a, um, you know . . ." He pointed at his stomach, where the ileostomy bag would be.

"Yeah, well that thing doesn't empty itself. We have to hurry." I was frantic now, struggling with the bag. The air conditioning made me shiver, and Joe took the duffle from my shoulder and forced me to stand still.

"I'm home to help you through all of this now, okay? Home for good." It was this line that let me sink further into him. Since Meghan had landed in hospital at the start of the year, I'd barely paused long enough to consider the toll it had taken on our family, not to mention Lily and Sam; the reality of what we were wading through was too horrific to withstand. I was so, so tired that I didn't know how to remain vertical, to keep functioning in the face of all this devastation and uncertainty.

"We'll get through this, okay?" He kissed my forehead and swatted my bum. "Let's go get your sister. And Pot Roast! I can't believe she drove all the way here to sit in the car with a dog."

"Sisterly dedication runs deep with us these days," I called over my shoulder as I walked towards the parking garage.

Joe trotted behind me to catch up. "How's she doing?"

The moment he asked, anxiety stood the hairs on my neck to attention. "Hard to say. Healthwise, things seem, I don't know, stable? But it's like Mom, Dad, and I have all these questions about the future, and she never really asks the doctor what the prognosis is or anything."

"Maybe she doesn't want to know."

I quickened my pace, felt my heart lurch. Meghan had always been the type to stuff her bills under the seat of her car, unopened, as if they might pay themselves through osmosis. Whereas I armed myself with information—too much of it, really—because at least then I could prepare. Struggling with anxiety is, by its very definition, a constant fretting over what may be. And that's what I wanted now, to prepare for what might come.

"Her main concern is the ileostomy and having it reversed in the fall. Feels like she's treating the small matter of survival like an afterthought." The weekend prior, I'd taken her out to a fancy restaurant to celebrate our birthdays, only days apart. The place had been mostly empty, but she kept pulling her shirt away from her stomach, making a tent with the fabric. *I'm so disgusting. I can't wait to get rid of this thing.* I'd paused, champagne flute halfway to my mouth. *Are you kidding? You're a fucking warrior, and that's beautiful.* And she did look stunning, the soft focus of the pendant lights falling on the sweep of blush she'd applied to brighten her cheeks. We ordered another round of champagne, toasted to being alive.

Joe and I crossed the glass-encased pedestrian overpass that danced with light, wheeling his luggage over the tiled floor, and were met with a humid bank of air. *Almost there, Meg.* I couldn't decide if I should stop to text her, tell her we were seconds away.

It was like a dream where my legs wouldn't move, time expressed in slow motion—a helplessness that made my body sluggish and my mind frantic.

"I imagine if her husband didn't constantly remind her how gross he found it, then it wouldn't be as much of an issue," Joe said snidely.

There had been small indicators that Meghan's relationship was in a tailspin, although she'd been revealing less to me, and I couldn't tell if it was because the instances of abuse were escalating or her reserves of strength were draining. But she hadn't been able to disguise her tears over Bernard's drinking, the ensuing anger, how repulsive he found her. *He can't even lie to me to spare my feelings*, she whispered over the phone, sobbing. *Just leave*, I snapped, frustrated that she declined my offer to move into my basement with the kids, or of money for an apartment security deposit, or to pay for a divorce. *If not for you, then for your kids*. She said I didn't get it and hung up just as Sam started wailing in the background. It was only then that I noticed all my offers of help were financial, as if money were the reason she stayed.

"I just wish she'd appreciate life more." I lowered my voice as we approached our parking space. "Smell the roses and all that or, for Pete's sake, find someone worth smelling the roses with."

The moment we came into view of our red Golf, Pot Roast burst from the car and charged towards Joe, sporting the yellow ribbon Meghan had tied around his neck. My brain was overloaded with both serenity and apprehension as Joe nuzzled into the dog's fur and Meghan approached from behind, clutching her purse to her chest like a security blanket.

"Meghan!" Joe threw his arms around her. She was nearly half the weight she'd been when he deployed. Her thin hair fell ethereally to her bony shoulders and she was hollow now in all the places she should be round. There was an eerie resemblance to when she was an addict, and that knowledge made me dizzy as I watched from the sidelines. "It's so good to see you."

"I'm so glad you're home safe," Meghan said, sniffling. "We've really missed you." She honked into the tissue like a goose, the sound echoing in the garage. The air smelled of oil and exhaust and I felt sick, unable to place my rising jitters. My husband was home and my sister was moving towards wellness and this was a time for joy.

"It's been a rough year for the Thompsons," Joe said, an arm slung around her. "I'm sorry I wasn't here."

"God, stop being so nice!" She playfully batted at him. "I can't take more emotion."

"You're a walking ball of emotion," I said, laughing as I hugged her too, my chin sitting atop her head as she leaned into my chest. Joe loaded his bags into the car while having an animated, squeaky-voiced conversation with Pot Roast, who was a flurry of tail wags and face licks. "We can wait while you go to the bathroom," I whispered to her.

"Oh." She blushed, leaning into my ear. "I had to, um, take care of things in the car."

"I'm really hoping a bag of your shit isn't in my front seat right now."

She looked bashful as she bit down laughter. "In a Ziploc bag. But I threw it in the garbage. I guess that's one benefit of walking around with your own poop pouch."

"Fuck, Meg, I'm sorry. I'm sorry you had to do that." I wanted to cry, looking to my sister and Joe and the dog and back again, loyalties and anxieties pulled in so many directions that my throat felt like it was closing and a bead of sweat gathered at my temples. "That must have been embarrassing for you."

"Don't worry about it. I said I'd be here for you and Joe, and I wanted to be."

"I just feel so . . ." I swallowed a few times, gawped like a fish hungry for more oxygen. Joe was here but also was there, and what if we didn't work anymore because he had seen too much and, here at home, so had I? When he'd left, things were easy and we were happy and everyone was alive and healthy and now none of those things felt true.

"Kelly. It's fine. Really. Everything is going to be fine. You. Me. Joe. Everyone. It's going to be fine. Look at me. Take a deep breath." I listened, bug-eyed, as I inhaled through my nose, heaving on my diaphragm. Meghan mimicked the motion and I saw the plastic ileostomy bag crinkle under the fabric of her T-shirt.

I swiped tears from my face. "How are you the one consoling me right now?"

"It's my job. I'm your big sister. Today is a big day for you guys."

"What if he decides he wants kids and I'm defective wife material? And what if he's different now, after deploying? Like Dad was?"

"Then you'll figure it out. You two always figure things out. Together." We looked over to Joe, who was planting kisses across Pot Roast's face, laughing as the dog's fat tongue lapped at his cheeks. "Although, your husband's a total dweeb, so, that's a problem that can't be helped."

"I love you, Meg."

"I love you too." She said it with such conviction that my nerves softened, tension eroding. For years, I denied her those words, like I wanted her to earn them—as though love was something to earn. And I'd always looked down on her for the way she gave love so freely, always willing to risk getting hurt if it meant a chance at a family. That judgement was so foolish in the light of everything we faced now.

I waved as she climbed into her truck to drive in the opposite direction from us, before getting into the Golf with Joe and winding our separate ways home.

twelve

I arrived to pick up Meghan from Mount Sinai Hospital to find it decorated for the holidays with garlands of fake pine and plasticky loops of dollar-store wreaths. I was an hour early, flustered, sweating even in the cold. All week, every action had been an overreaction, panic giving way to the terrifying reality of the return of Meghan's cancer. After her initial diagnosis eight months ago, hope had felt possible, but in the wake of this second surgery, each moment was spiked with underlying hysteria.

Since Lily's birth, our family had trundled through life in survival mode. Meghan was in remission, and that was everyone's sole focus. Everyone except me. But whenever I pressed my medically educated mom for information—*What stage was the cancer when they found it? Sarcomas reoccur most of the time, no? How come she's not having any treatment?*—I'd get a blank stare, because we couldn't push Meghan to face down what she didn't want to acknowledge or to ask the questions that came with unwanted answers. So while Joe and I had settled back into our lives together, I'd also spent those months consumed by Google research. When my vision went grainy with wide-eyed nervousness, I would shut my laptop, blinking back panic.

When Meghan had finally been scheduled for the ileostomy reversal, she was sent for what was supposed to be a routine CT scan. Instead, it revealed countless hungry tumours filling her abdomen, nudging organs aside, and so the surgery plan had been radically altered from rerouting her intestines to excising the cancer. At one week post-op, the entire family was anxiously anticipating a prognosis and course of treatment.

Despite having visited Mount Sinai several times when Meghan was in the maternity ward, the maze of hospital hallways and waiting rooms was still dizzying. When I finally found her in the gastrointestinal unit, she was in the bed by the window, her face bathed in grey light from the sky darkened by a threatening storm. The room was quiet except for the murmuring of televisions on low volume, moans of pain from the other three patients, and the occasional beep from an IV alarm.

"Finally!" Her face lit up when I peeked around the curtain that encircled her bed and leaned to give her a gentle hug. "Oh my God, I'm so glad you're here."

"You get a discharge! And you get a discharge! Everybody gets a discharge!" I boomed in my best Oprah voice. She smiled weakly. "You ready for me to spring you loose, or what?"

"You have no idea. Just waiting on the doctor to sign the release paperwork."

"Well, your personal recovery palace awaits Chez Sister."

"I better get spoiled. Waffles and daily massage therapy." She extricated herself from the cord of her IV so she could reach for a plastic cup of water. The cup was tan, as was the food tray and the utensils and the food left on the plate—everything the shade of sun-beaten wood.

"Your healing locale options are limited, so spoiled or not, it's my place or parenting two kids while attempting to get well at the same time."

"Bernard would have looked after me." She didn't sound sure, and she fussed with the blankets. He hadn't planned any days off work to help her recuperate, and I craved the job of protecting her under my roof, where I could make her organic chicken broth and rub her back and paint her nails when she got bored. Above all, I knew that with me, she'd be safe. Meghan had played it off like I was first choice anyways, and Mom and Dad had promised—at Meghan's request—not to bring up Bernard's complacency again. Thankfully, Bernard's mother, Phyllis, and a host of volunteers had offered to care for eight-month-old Lily and three-year-old Sam. I kept thinking of the days stretching out before this family—the recovery, the treatment, the ending—and had to shake the fear away, like snapping dirt from a rug.

"Has he come to see you lots?" I already knew the answer. "Doesn't he work down the street from here?"

She turned her head away and blinked, the silence heavy. Then she tugged the sheet down to her pubic bone. "Wanna see?" Her face pleaded for me to lean into the distraction.

"Stupid question."

She lifted her gown, baring her belly and three distinct scars. The first was a three-inch enclosure of buckled skin from the ileostomy, the area now sealed like an envelope. Harder to ignore was the line from ribs to pelvis where the doctor had gone in to carve away the latest tumours, the scar wobbly, as if he'd been drunk while operating. The childhood scar, from belly button to back, was white with age but made an uneven cross pattern across her stomach.

Since Meghan had designated me as next of kin, I was the one who called the hospital nightly for updates, waiting on hold for half an hour at a time. *Stage-wise, it's very, very advanced,* the surgeon said. *But we have to wait on pathology before I can say with more certainty.* I sat in my kitchen, listening with polite words of understanding until the surgeon's pager beeped him to another emergency. *My sister is going to die,* I wrote in my journal, cursive huge and looping. Half the letters were blotted out by the fountain pen ink that had seeped out where I lingered too long. I stared at the words on the page, crushed by how sure I was of this.

Now, in the hospital room, I looked from Meghan's stomach to her face, waiting to see grief or anger at the cancer's return, but there was only glee at being free from the ileostomy. "Any word yet? On a prognosis?"

"We know it's the cancer; we just don't know how bad yet. But hey, I'm not wearing my own crap like a fashion accessory, so there's that." She patted her belly gently, as if she could pat the denial into place like parging on a leaking dam.

"Only you would find a way to work up two of the rarest cancers in the world in one lifetime."

"I'm special like that."

"Why do I want to touch it so bad?" I reached out a finger with a joking threat to poke the wound and Meghan swatted at me but then cried out in pain, clutching the surgical site.

"God, are you okay? Want me to get someone?" I dug frantically through the blankets for a call button. I had talked to my sister three or four times a day throughout this hospital stay, finding new reasons to be devastated with each chat: she'd lost control of her bowels or thrown up on herself or gotten her period and bled all over the sheets. I pictured her in these moments—wet, embarrassed, helpless—and a tight ball formed in my gut. I could not stand for it on my watch.

"No, I'm fine, but that was weird. I haven't felt that pain before." Her grip on the bedrails was white-knuckled. "They gave me something a while ago, said it was the last dose I'd have before discharge. I just want out of here. God, where is the doctor to sign the stupid paperwork?"

———

An hour passed. Then two. Four. Meghan's face went from pale to ashen around the temples where her skin bunched tight with each wave of pain.

"Good news!" chirped a nurse as she entered the room, shaking a sheet of paper like a New Year's noisemaker. "You're free to go."

I looked out the window. The forecasted winter storm was in full swing with massive clumps of snow falling, plops hitting the window. "We could have been home by now," I said sharply, and then immediately regretted my tone. I was never rude like this, never this pushy, but desperation electrified me. "And she hasn't received anything for pain the entire time I've been here." It was two in the afternoon. No way to make it out of the city before rush hour.

"It's fine, Kell," Meghan whispered. "Let's just go." It wasn't fine, but her expression begged for my silence.

"So, is there a porter or something?" I asked the nurse as she turned to the next patient, stethoscope poised. I wanted someone with trained qualifications to manoeuvre my sister's chair, since the smallest movement hurt her and sent my heart rate soaring.

"You'll have to go find a wheelchair," the nurse said, gesturing vaguely towards the hallway. "I think there's one down the hall."

I bit back a retort and returned ten minutes later with a wheelchair that had questionable stains and a tear in the padded seat.

"Where have you been?" Meghan was childlike, her body disappearing under the thin sheet. I said nothing and helped her into the only clean clothes she had—grey Uggs, a grey robe, and plaid pyjamas, as though we were headed to some sort of outdoor slumber party. The process of getting her into the chair was Herculean, and I manipulated her like a marionette, bending her legs and placing her feet on the foot pads. Finally, I slung her duffle and countless reusable Costco bags over my shoulders, packed full of incontinence briefs, paperwork, and medications, and we set off in search of the way I'd come in.

We found the elevators and crammed into the first car, large enough for a cartwheel and yet densely packed with people. It reeked of sweat and snow melting on moth-balled jackets. Classical music piped through the speakers, audible in concert with Meghan's low murmurs of agony.

When the elevator arrived at the main floor, I surged onwards, but the chair wheels caught on the open lip between the elevator and the flooring, lurching Meghan forward. She screamed, and the sound scraped at my insides, filling the lobby and all the space in my head.

"Jesus Christ, I'm sorry, Meg."

She sobbed openly as strangers helped me manhandle the chair across the barrier. "Oh God, oh God. Oh my God," she cried over and over, rocking slightly in place, clutching her stomach. People looked at her with pity, and then at me—I was convinced—as though they questioned my ability to provide care. I questioned it, too.

"What can I do?"

"Hurry up." Half growl, half plea.

"Just wait here while I grab the car, okay?" I arranged her by the entrance.

"Where do you think I'm going to go?" she snapped.

I ran until my lungs burned, down the street and up three flights of parkade stairs, half crying and half gasping for air. It was mere minutes until I wheeled into the entrance amongst ambulances and police cars, dashed into the hospital, and pushed Meghan to the vehicle, then eyed the impossible task of tucking her inside.

She cried in pain for the entire fifteen minutes it took me to get her into the car. When I had swaddled enough blankets and pillows around her, we set off into the storm towards home.

———

Meghan fell asleep as I drove. I kept the radio on low so I could hear her lungs empty and fill and reached out occasionally to keep her head from bobbing against her chest. After a few hours, Oshawa's traffic reached a pinnacle, the car puttering at a maddening pace as the snow dropped, building up on the windshield in the whiteout. Slops of salt and sand formed thick sludge and I gently tapped the brakes as a transport truck's back tires slipped into my lane and we skidded sideways before I righted us. Meghan stirred and squinted, clutching her stomach, pressing her palms to the stapled incisions. I dialled up the seat warmers, adjusted the car's temperature control so that a vent gently hissed air on her face.

"How're you doing?"

"Miserable." She licked her papery lips and I passed a bottle of water. She took a small, tentative sip. "Where are we?"

"Not even halfway. Storm and traffic are both being assholes."

She groaned. "Go figure. I have to go to the bathroom." A gurgle emanated loudly in the enclosed space. "Now."

"You're in luck, milady," I said, gesturing to the side of the highway. "Behold." Blessedly, the highway rest stop lights blinked through the storm, promising bathrooms, fuel, and a few fast-food joints. I parked in the packed lot as close to the entrance as possible, which was still more than a hundred metres away.

"Help. I need help. Hurry." She tugged on the door handle without effect, and I dashed to her side of the car to extract her from the pile of cushioning I'd stuffed in hours earlier. She took my arm and hobbled through the snow in her robe, step after laborious step, as crowds taking refuge from the storm parted or rushed to open doors for us. *Please let us make it. Please.* A toileting accident would be one too many indignities.

When Meghan was safely in a stall, I leaned into the finger-printed mirror and assessed myself in the overhead lights that cast eerie shadows. I looked older than thirty-three, full of knowing I didn't want. I washed my hands over and over in scalding water until Meghan exited the stall and grabbed at my sweater.

"Home, please," she croaked, her voice a whisper. Her skin was the colour of eggshells.

We waddled towards the exit, even slower than when we'd arrived, but she stopped just before the doors and hunched forward to grip her knees, crying out a sound that echoed around the vaulted ceiling. Groups of travellers stared, more doors opened, more thanks were murmured. Outside, the car was so very far away. Snow had piled like white clouds, masking the footprints we'd made only ten minutes before. "Meg, let me grab the car, bring it closer. We can get someone to help. I'll just . . ."

"Stop talking." She gripped my arm tightly and took a few more steps, then stopped and moaned in pain. I couldn't stand it.

"Meg, I'm going to pick you up, okay? Don't flex your stomach muscles because that'll hurt like hell. Just trust that I can hold you. Fall back into my arms." I offered, despite being unsure if I physically could manage, and then what? What then?

"No, your bad knee. You'll hurt it." But even as she talked, she slung her arms around my neck and stopped protesting, her legs giving in to me. I lifted her as if I were carrying a newlywed over the waiting threshold, surprised to find she was both heavy and light. Then I shuffled towards the car in the slip of slush, Meghan's head tucked into my armpit, one arm looped around my neck, the other sagging in her lap, and deposited her into the Volkswagen.

While walking to my side of the car, I paused and looked into the sky, taking a grateful breath. We had made it this far.

thirteen

The next morning, a moan jolted me awake while Joe snored softly next to me. Five a.m. blinked on the alarm clock. Then the sound, again—deep and braying, like an animal. I threw back the sheets and sprang from the bed in my underwear and pyjama top, then tore down the stairs to the guest room where I found Meghan curled into a fetal position in the centre of the mattress, clutching her gut. Pot Roast was beside the bed anxiously wagging his tail in tight figure eights.

"Hurts. So. Bad."

"I'm sorry, I slept through the alarm," I sputtered, wiping sleep from my face. "You're due for your meds."

After the disastrous drive home, we'd eased Meghan to the guest bedroom and I'd shifted into control mode, sending Joe out to fill her prescriptions while I made chicken soup and set on a load of laundry to clean the stink of illness from her clothing. She slurped the meal from a mug and then was so delirious with pain that she'd snatched the bag of drugs the moment Joe came in the door. Worried she'd accidentally take too much—or maybe not accidentally—I lined the medications up on the windowsill, labels facing outward, with firm instructions to let me mete them out according to my handwritten timetable. I'd then punched the schedule into my phone, complete with alarmed reminders that tinkled like a bell. The night was a blur of lifting, soothing, cooking, and panicking, and I'd been unable to fall asleep under the new weight of responsibility. It was my job to keep her alive, even though I had never been seen as the caregiver of the family. Meghan was the kind, gentle one and I was the fixer, and this flip-flopping of roles felt all wrong, proven in the fact that I'd somehow fallen asleep before the four a.m. reminder. My stomach churned with guilt as I wrestled with the childproof lid of the opioids and managed to rattle two tablets into my palm. Her mouth hung open and I dropped them directly onto her tongue, then wiggled a straw to her lips, which she pushed away. She swallowed the pills dry without lifting her head from the pillow.

"Those will take effect pretty quick," I said as I fussed around the room, hoping to make enough conversation that her keening would dissipate into the background. I twisted open the blinds to reveal a view of the backyard that glistened under the streetlamp and then folded and refolded the blanket that was usually draped at the end of the bed. With Christmas just over a week away, Joe had decorated the guest room with a small pine and light strings, which I flicked on so they sparkled a soft warmth. Even lit, Meghan's face was white with pain. "Going to be nice today, once the sun finally rises. Six degrees. Half that snow from yesterday will probably melt."

"Be quiet," she said, but not unkindly. "Just come here."

I went and stood beside the bed to rub her back until her breathing eased from tight spurts to gentle sighs. "How're you doing? A bit better?"

"Holy mother of Pete. That was horrible." She pointed to the water glass, and I held it as she took a long pull on the straw, some colour returning to her cheeks. I smoothed hair from her face and brought the sheets over her shoulder. "I woke you up," she said finally. "I'm sorry."

"Jeez, Meg. That's what I'm here for. You could have rung your bell if you needed me instead of letting it get this bad." The bell was meant as a joke, sort of—the tiny cow bell we used to tie around Pot Roast's neck remained untouched on the nightstand.

Pain had given way enough for her to smirk at this. "There's no way I'm ringing a bell for attention."

I gave it a jingle and Pot Roast leapt onto the bed with an agility incongruous with seventy-five pounds of muscle. I positioned myself protectively, worried he'd accidentally stomp on a surgical wound, but he laid down in bizarre slow motion and rested his head on Meghan's thigh. She stroked his velvety head until his eyelids sagged. "Good boy. He's been down here sitting with me all night." As if sensing he was part of the discussion, he wagged the tip of his tail a few times before he slipped towards sleep.

"Really?" I rubbed his freckled stomach. "He literally never comes down here. I think it's too cold for him or something. Guarding your auntie, buddy?"

"He just laid over there the whole time." Meghan pointed to the corner by the window. "It was a bit creepy, to be honest. Those beady eyeballs can really give a staredown." She wrestled herself out from underneath him to lean against the headboard.

"How's your pain now? Ready for breakfast?" The doctor had provided me with a list of approved foods: Vegetables were to be cooked to mush. No skins. No seeds. No whole grains. Limited fibre for a while, at least, until her intestines knitted back together. "I thought I'd make you some French toast. Load you up with syrup and butter. It's weird that everything you're allowed to have feels insanely unhealthy."

"How do you always know what I need?"

"Because I am a domestic goddess. I'll bring it down to you when it's ready, okay?" I laid the bell and the television remote in her lap. "Ring if you need me. Seriously. It might have made me panic less than you moaning like you're two seconds from death."

She reached up to pat my cheek, cupping it tenderly. It hit me then that almost everything I knew about caregiving came from her. She had brought me to that moment in her illness, but she was also the person who'd prepared me to survive it.

"How about I just text?"

"Deal."

Once upstairs, I set to making her tray and punched out an update to Mom and Dad while the tea brewed. *Pain is managed. She's in decent spirits, I think.* I hadn't wanted to tell them how bad it had been the night before, so had said she was uncomfortable but it was under control. Everything was under control.

The response came instantly, despite the time of day. *Thanks, Moo.* I wasn't the only one not sleeping.

───────────

A few nights later, I balanced bowls on my forearm as I joined Meghan and my dog in her bed, the TV lighting her face with a blue glow. The television had run endlessly since she arrived, with one Netflix series cued up right after the other. I wasn't even sure she turned it off at night, since murmurs of dialogue were always floating up from the basement while I fought off nightmares.

"Ice cream? Pooh. What's a movie night without popcorn?"

"You're not allowed to have popcorn. Your guts are like tissue paper right now, remember? I will not be the one who sends you back to hospital. At least it's Ben & Jerry's."

She stuck out her lower lip but took the bowl I offered. Pot Roast perked at the clink of the utensil on the bowl, and Meghan fed him a mouthful directly from her spoon. "Don't judge me. He's become my little therapy animal."

"You don't see either of us complaining. What movie did you pick?"

"*Pitch Perfect.* There's singing. Comedy. No one dies, as far as we know. Checks all the required boxes."

"Sounds good. Move over."

She lifted the sheets to let me climb in and I felt heat radiate from her. It was in moments like this where I obsessed about filling the blank space with all the things we'd missed out on. I wanted to share in everything now but didn't want to spook her into sensing my rising tide of fear: that we were running out of time to share these stories. I opened my mouth and closed it again, settling into her familiarity.

"Kell?" Meghan nudged me, mouth agape and her phone stuck close to my face. "Wake up. My report is in."

"What?" I rubbed knuckles into my sockets, trying to place myself. The cast of *Pitch Perfect* crooned on stage, their harmonized tones a gentle purr, clearly smooth enough to sing me to sleep.

"My medical report. From the surgeon. Pathology and all that." She vibrated as she held out her phone, the screen scattered with tiny font. "I don't know if I want to read it."

I blinked again and again. I didn't know if I wanted to read it either. Pot Roast had moved to the end of the bed, too far away. I wanted him closer and Meghan closer and *fuck don't make me read this document.* "You want to just put it away for now? Maybe look at it tomorrow? Or we can call Mom and Dad and read it together, if you want." We called Mom and Dad each day, often on speakerphone, but there was a sense we were jointly protecting one another, as though no one wanted to make known the depth of their fear. Meghan's recovery was spoken of with light positivity before moving on to discussing the kids, Christmas approaching, or another topic that was less likely to veer towards melancholy.

"Can you read it now? Not aloud or anything. Just read it to yourself and let me know."

"Let you know?"

"Yes," she said impatiently. "Like, if I'm dead meat or not."

I tried to mask my own tremor as I took the phone and zoomed in on the text. It was several pages long, attached to forty pages of her medical history since the cancer diagnosis. I scanned the dates and times, the hospital admissions and treatments, and wondered how in the hell someone could survive so much and have it annotated to such a succinct amount of type. Half of the report was written in medical jargon I couldn't or didn't want to understand, but some of it stood out as though streaked with highlighter. *We resected at least 150cm of small bowel . . . Diagnosis: metastatic leiomyosarcoma stage 4.* I searched the forty pages of dispassionate writing for the "but," even though I knew it wouldn't come. When I turned to face her, Meghan was hovering over my shoulder, silently taking in every word.

"Kelly, am I going to die?" Her voice was so tiny I barely heard her. I expected it, this question, but had hoped she'd seek advice from someone with professional insight or experience in counselling. Or Mom, perhaps, whom we called each time we had a weird rash or an infection because she was a nurse and a mom and therefore should have answers for moments like this. All I had was this knowledge and a painful nodule of love in my chest.

I swallowed the bitter taste in my mouth. "The oncologist will be the better person to answer that, Meg. It says that you'll hear from them before the new year, likely with chemotherapy to start right away." I darkened the phone screen and blinked and blinked. I couldn't erase the image of my sister on an operating table, innards exposed and doctors shrugging gowned shoulders. *Nothing else we can do here*, then putting her body back together like Humpty-Dumpty. "We'll figure it out." Sammy, Lily, Mom, Dad—how would we survive it? What would our family look like when she was no longer a part of it?

"Right. Okay." She cleared her throat and fussed with some Kleenex but didn't actually blow her nose.

"Do you want me to call Mom and Dad? Or Bernard? I can call for you or we can dial together and I can stay here with you."

"Can you leave me alone for a while? I'd like to be by myself to think."

"You sure, Meg? We can finish the movie. I'll stay awake. Promise. I don't want you alone after reading that." I didn't want to be alone after reading that. She shook her head back and forth, trying to stop the sobs from escaping but it was a fruitless pursuit. I was frozen in bed next to her, wanting to fix things and knowing I couldn't.

"Please, Kell. Go."

I kissed her cheek and extricated myself from our basket-weave of limbs. As I closed the door behind me, Pot Roast stood to take my place in the warm spot I'd left in the bed. He flopped down beside Meghan and craned his head to her face, offering gentle licks. I tiptoed upstairs to join Joe in bed and curled in unnoticed behind him. It was hours before I fell asleep, unable to tune out her crying.

fourteen

A week after bringing Meghan home from the hospital, I spread a terrycloth towel across my bed and Meghan lay on it, holding her shirt to her chin, staring down at the exposed zipper of staples, now moistened after her shower. She smelled of my bath gel and body lotion, vanilla with a hint of lavender, and her wet hair made a splotchy imprint on the pillowcase. Next to her was another towel with some rubbing alcohol, a staple remover in a sterilized sheath, and, because it seemed like the thing to do, a stress ball for Meghan to squeeze. She flexed her fingers around it and the material squished between her knuckles. "I feel like a pregnant woman told to bite down on a piece of wood."

I snapped on blue nitrile gloves with a confidence I didn't feel and sat next to her, the mattress sagging towards me. "I can find a leather belt if you prefer. Wait, should I be wearing a mask or something? I don't want to breathe bacteria over your scab."

"As long as you avoid coughing directly into it, I think we're fine. Besides, you were made for this. It's like the excitement you get from popping a zit, but a hundred times over. Thanks for doing this. Saves another trip to the hospital."

"I am nurse, chef, and sister all rolled into one. Ready?" There was no averting my gaze from the incision, no denial I could cling to. I peeled back the protective film from the removal tool and laced my fingers through the handles. The device looked like a pair of clunky safety scissors from a kindergarten class.

"Do I have a choice?"

I inched my face close to her belly. Some of the staples were deeply imbedded, and a fear of causing harm lurched up my throat, making the room feel small and dark. I paused, gloved hand hovering over her abdomen. "You sure you don't want to wait until you get home tonight? I can take them out for you there instead. Nice and cozy in your own house."

"Nah, do it now. It'll be comfier sitting in the car for three hours without my stomach full of metal. Plus, I'd rather Bernard see me looking less like a patient." She tucked her top underneath her bra band; a fancy bra with lace, so different from the stretchy sports bras she'd been wearing all week. I thought of her packing this piece of lingerie in preparation for the hospital, like an outfit for leaving a wedding reception, and it stung like a slap.

I set to work. The nurse had told me to count the staples as I pulled them out and to lay them on a piece of paper towel to ensure I had every single one of the eight across the ileostomy closure and sixty-five up the abdomen. I nudged the remover underneath each staple, squeezed the handles to release them, and, one by one, dropped the metal pegs onto the paper towel while Meghan counted aloud.

"You're enjoying this too much," Meghan said. She stuffed another pillow under her head for a better look, and despite how painfully thin she was, her neck wrinkled into several chins.

"I'm concentrating." I pried another staple free, amazed by the body's capacity to close tight around such trauma. "There." I dropped the final one onto the paper towel and we counted them together all over again. "All soldiers present and accounted for."

We fell silent, taking in her decimated body. A cross of healing like some messed-up stigmata, flecked with plasma and blood crusted between incisions. It was both beautiful and horrific, miraculous and seemingly innocuous. Had Mom and Dad regarded her in the same way when she was a toddler, split open from belly button to back? I'd told them the result of Meghan's medical report the night before, fighting to keep my voice even in the face of such news. The speakerphone crackled and Dad coughed a few times while Mom openly sobbed in the background. *Oh, our baby. Oh God.* I couldn't save any of them from the news and the reality that came with it.

I smeared Polysporin across the trail with a cotton swab. She looked so tender and small lying there.

"Buddhists say that life is suffering. If that's the case, then I think you've lived the nine lives of a cat."

"I look hideous." She sniffled and poked a finger at a loose piece of scab. It tumbled onto the towel and she picked it up, this piece of herself, and rolled it between her thumb and forefinger. "Who would want me?"

The question wasn't who, but *will he?* She and I had spent nearly every waking moment of the week in each other's company, and from what I could tell, Bernard rarely made contact, either because he had to work late or he was tired. He rang once at eleven at night, rousing her from a medication-infused sleep, and she groggily stirred into conversation but couldn't stay awake. When I called Mom and Dad to offer my daily updates, they asked if she'd spoken to the kids, if she'd had some nice FaceTime chats with them. I never knew how to answer. Often, I lied to protect everyone involved.

"Meg, be kind to yourself. You've literally been through hell, and I'd say you're looking pretty damn good."

She traced the line of the cross on her stomach and released the T-shirt from her bra band. "I look like Frankenstein."

"If it helps, Frankenstein was actually the mad scientist, not the monster." The moment the words left my lips, her face darkened and I flooded with regret. In light of the medical report, I struggled to balance the scale of humour in our usual quips.

"It doesn't fucking help, Kell. It doesn't help at all." She swung her legs over the side of the bed to a seated position and turned away from me, but we were in my bedroom, with nowhere for her to escape to.

"That was stupid. I'm sorry." I tucked her hair behind her ears, then gathered the evidence of our medical procedure into the terrycloth towel and furled it into a ball. "I get wanting to look nice. You haven't seen each other in a while. Want me to do your hair and makeup? You can borrow some clothes if you want. I mean, you're a kazillion sizes smaller than me now but maybe a nice sweater? Some earrings?"

She considered this, anger abating. "You never let me borrow your clothes."

She remembered, just as I did, the day I'd vowed to never lend her anything again. She was sixteen and used her newly minted driving licence as a reason to borrow my favourite

Empire-waisted shirt, the one with tiny violets and a royal-blue ribbon at the chest. That night, after a few too many wine coolers, she crashed a car for the first time—one of many, the start of the drug spiral—crushing in the ceiling of the family Toyota. When the cops reported to Mom and Dad, they insisted she was lucky to be pulled from that farmer's ditch, saying if she'd been tall like me, she'd be dead. Hospital visits, concussion, glass tugged from her skin. But all I could focus on, thirteen years old and angry at what I perceived as abandonment as she lived her new grown-up life, was my prized shirt cut off her in the ambulance.

I choked the guilty memory down and pulled a blue paisley cardigan from my closet and a pair of delicate pearl earrings that dangled like pendulums. "This would look nice with your leggings. I can straighten your hair." She begrudgingly lifted her arms so I could guide the cardigan sleeves over her shoulders, then turned this way and that in front of the mirror. "You look great," I said, reaching to hug her from behind. We watched one another in the mirror, so starkly different.

"Yeah? What about my weird lumps?" Through her T-shirt she poked at a fold of skin from the childhood cancer, then the newer lumpy incision line that was still healing.

"We all have weird lumps, Meg."

"But I'm not symmetrical. *Cosmo* says that men like women to be symmetrical. They're naturally wired to want it and I'm all lopsided." She turned to the side, lifted her shirt and then let it fall and the material caught on her new scar.

"*Cosmo* also had an advice column that told me men like to have their eyeballs erotically sucked on, and I've never met a partner yet who seemed game for it."

She sputtered a laugh. "Okay, doll me up and then take me home to my babies." She stretched to kiss my cheek and followed me into the bathroom, sitting like an obedient child on my toilet seat while I streaked liner across her lids, swept brown shadow in the creases, and dragged a mascara wand through her impossibly long lashes. I blew her hair dry and she leaned into the gusts, euphoric at being fussed over. When I finished, she shone with a confidence so ebullient that I wanted to cry.

After a three-hour car trip with Meghan doped up on Gravol, I pulled into her poorly plowed driveway that was littered with choppy patches of snow. The bungalow windows were dark. No sounds emanated from inside the house or the garage. Sammy's swing tied to the maple tree hung lank, its basin holding a seat of ice. A sadness took hold and froze me in place, convincing me I couldn't open the car door to get out.

"Where's Bernard?" Joe asked from the back seat, leaning forward over the console. Pot Roast snorted awake from Joe's lap and sat alert to lick the window. We were packed to the headliner with gifts for our family's Christmas celebration, Meghan's luggage, and our own. "He knew when we were coming, right?"

"Oh." Meghan's voice was fairy-like; tiny and distant. She fumbled for her phone as though checking messages. I glimpsed the screen and saw there were none. "He's just picking the kids up from Phyllis's house. He'll be home any minute." She stepped out into the wintery temperatures and lifted her arms in a

salutation. "Ah, it's good to be home. Not that I haven't appreci-
ated staying with you guys."

"We get it," Joe responded as he followed, keeping his tone
light. "When you feel like crap, it's nice to be in your own house
with your own stuff." He popped the trunk and carried her bags
while Meghan swatted at my attempt to steady her by the elbow
to cross the treacherous path up the porch stairs. Joe tested the
doorknob, and in finding the door unlocked, carted the bags into
the living room. "Well, Meghan, I guess we'll see you and the
rest of the Montaignes tomorrow for the Thompson Christmas,
eh? You're probably sick of us by now."

"Thanks so much for having me to stay, Joe. For everything
you did."

He gave her a hug and took careful steps back to the car
while I lingered in the cold, stamping my feet. I hadn't bothered
with my coat and I regretted it in the biting wind that swept up
the open meadow.

"I don't want to just leave you here alone." I peered behind
her to look for a sign of Bernard having made an attempt to make
her feel welcome—a warm light on, a show she liked playing on
TV, dinner prepared. Nothing. She swirled her keys in a loop
around her finger, clacking the metal together in a way that set
my teeth on edge.

"It's fine, Kell. They'll be home any minute. Go. I'll see you
tomorrow at Mom and Dad's."

"You sure?"

"Didn't you say you had lectures to prepare anyways? You
have," she pretended to check her non-existent wristwatch, "two
point five weeks until school is in session and twenty-four hours
until I see you again."

I had been hired by Trent University to teach a first-year creative writing course, to start in January. Commuting from Trenton to teach in Peterborough had seemed like a good idea, but the drive would suck up long Friday hours and, if I made the trip to Barrie from Trent for Meghan's impending chemo, would stick me in rush-hour Toronto traffic. I had accepted the job before the surgery, the diagnosis, the planned treatment. What if she needed me? What if?

"Joe!" Meghan called out and he rolled down the window. "Take your wife with you!" She made a lame attempt at a laugh, but I saw the hint of disappointment and felt my breastbone crack in two.

"Okay, okay." I backed away with a bow of surrender. "But I'm going to make you the best dinner tomorrow. Enough gravy to drown in."

Meghan leaned against the porch railing while we manoeuvred the car around the slush and she called out to us, waving the whole time. She was so grateful for our care. She couldn't wait for family Christmas. She was so excited. All of these things said in an inflection that hinted at the opposite emotion. When she thought we were out of view, the smile dropped from her lips and she turned to go into the house, her shoulders slumped forward with something akin to dread.

fifteen

The next day, the smell of roasting turkey and sage filled Mom and Dad's house as steam wafted from the oven. I drizzled the crisping poultry skin with a line of fat from the baster, added some more salt, checked the temperature.

"Late, as usual," Dad said with a huff from his recliner, dramatically assessing his watch.

"You know if it was up to Meghan, they'd be here first thing," Mom quipped. "She loves Christmas."

"Can't be on time, even once. For her." Dad's decibel level rose with Mom's support. They shared a look while I rattled the turkey back into the oven, then uselessly fiddled with knobs on the stove. The food, at least, was on schedule. Joe kissed my shoulder as he passed and poured me a glass of wine.

"I just want to give her a nice, final Christmas," I whispered as I took the pinot. Meghan's surgical report lingered in my inbox, where I still marked it "unread" despite having nearly committed it to memory. Nausea floated up at the thought.

"Deep breaths," Joe said, wiping the counter. "Let's just get through today." I blew out through pursed lips at the exact moment the doorbell chimed.

"About time," Dad muttered, but still, he pushed up from his chair to help Mom walk to the front door. She'd been moving so much slower lately, her MS clearly affected by all the stress. But this was a worry for later. Joe was right: the focus had to be on getting through the day.

We collected in the entryway and saw Bernard looking miserable on the other side of the glass front door with the children. When I flung open the door, he shoved Lily at me, her body a puffy snowsuit sausage.

"Merry Christmas, Montaignes! Hi, Pudding! Hi, Piggy! I missed you guys so much!"

"Auntie!" Sam circled my legs with his arms before fleeing to his grandpa, who scooped him into the air and zipped him airplane-style through the foyer. There was a murmur of *hello*s and *missed you*s, squealing baby noises, and the clanking of hangers as jackets were hung. Meghan ambled wearily up the driveway. As she got closer, it was clear she'd slathered on too much makeup and hairstyling product in an effort to disguise the melancholy underneath.

"How're you doing?" I asked, leaning in to kiss her cheek while Bernard wordlessly piled packages into my arms alongside his daughter. I'd helped Meghan do her Christmas shopping before she went into hospital, and, with forethought, she'd wrapped them before her surgery. It was unlike her to plan so far ahead.

"Alright."

"Well, come in so we can load you up with food and presents." The entryway became a trove of boots and mittens, melted snow making puddles on the tiles. Joe and I helped the kids shuck the rest of their layers and eased Meghan out of her coat and into a chair to catch her breath while Sam darted into the living room to play with the trains Dad always set up for him. Our parents hovered at the top of the stairs holding one another to brace against the shock of Meghan's appearance, having not seen her since she went into hospital weeks ago. I should have prepared them, but how was one to prepare other loved ones for the starkness of that suffering? I didn't even know where to begin.

"I'm frigging hungry," Bernard muttered, his first words since arrival. He had not taken off his outerwear and stood like a hunched bear by the door. "Gonna go get a bite."

"Oh, we're eating in an hour." I nodded towards the kitchen with my chin. Lily had begun to whine and I jostled her like a maraca to stave off a meltdown. "I baked cookies if you want something to tide you over. Maybe my Lily wants a cookie too?" I kissed her all over until she bared her mottled gums.

"Cookies! Treats!" Sam had appeared at Dad's side, clinging to the leg of his jeans.

"I need to eat now," Bernard wheedled to Meghan, without looking at the rest of the family. "I'm going to go grab a burger."

"We were going to open presents first," I said, bouncing Lily with more fervour now that her bottom lip was trembling. When no one rose to the defence of my perfectly laid plans, I hefted Lily farther up my hip and made a point of assessing the grandfather clock. "You're two hours late."

Bernard ignored me and walked back to their vehicle, revved the truck engine, and then raced out of the subdivision. Meghan watched from the window, tears glistening.

"Hey," Joe said to Sam. "Why don't I take these little minions down to check out the tree and see what Santa brought, eh?" I gave him a grateful kiss as he lifted Lily from my arms and ushered Sam downstairs.

Mom, Dad, and I stood, waiting for some kind of explanation, even when the point seemed moot. It wasn't the first holiday they'd nearly missed for tardiness, but surely even Bernard knew this Christmas was different.

"What the hell is Bernard's problem?" I blurted.

"Kell," Meghan grunted as I stooped to tug off her winter boots. "Not now, please."

"Let's just have a nice day," Mom chirped. As a habitual people pleaser, she was keen to keep us on the right side of polite. But her mouth trembled as she fought to keep herself together. "Meggie, we missed you so much." Meghan went to Mom and Dad and leaned into their combined hug, looking so tiny and in need of the kind of comfort only parents can give. Dad caressed her hair and squeezed her tightly and their chests collectively heaved with stifled tears while I fussed with the remaining outerwear and sopped up melted snow with the dog towel. I was armouring myself in some way, determined to immunize myself to the ratcheting levels of anguish.

"I'm okay. I'm okay," she said, pulling away finally. "I've got to keep it together, for the kids. I want today to be nice for them."

"You look tired." Mom reached out to pat Meghan's curls. "Did you get any sleep?"

"All I do is sleep, Ma. It's all I do."

"Well, let's get you settled downstairs then," Dad said. "I thought you'd be comfiest on the rocker, and I put out an extra blanket for you. And the fireplace is going." He took Meghan by the elbow like a gentleman leading a fine lady, but their bodies bottlenecked on the turning staircase and he was forced to watch her descent with his grip tight on the banister. He rushed to follow and helped her into the rocking chair, his arthritic knees popping like bubble wrap.

"We're like the lame leading the lame," Meghan said, kissing Dad's cheek as he tucked a blanket around her legs. His tenderness towards her, considering his lifelong military career in which he was known for toughness, made my chest ache. Mom flopped into the leather couch like a baseball hitting a catcher's mitt, her face already tear-mottled. Everyone looked worn out, and it was barely lunchtime.

"Mum! Presents!" Sam jumped up and down pointing at the tree, while Lily lay on her stomach, rattling one of Pot Roast's dog toys before bringing it to her mouth.

"Lily, oh no, Lily, drop that. That's dirty." I tried to pry it from her hand but her screams paralyzed me.

"Oh, who cares." Meghan's tone was deadpan as she pulled the blanket up around her neck. "I mean, can it really be that bad? Some dog slobber? Won't kill her."

Mom clapped her hand over her mouth, like she was the one who'd spoken, then turned to stare into the gas fire that danced behind the glass. It was impossible to withstand the recognition that there were things that could kill, silent things so much more sinister than germs.

I sat on the floor near Meghan's feet, Dad squishing in close next to Mom on the couch. My focus had been so squarely on Meghan that I only then considered how Mom and Dad had aged this past year. It showed in their stiff joints and drooping cheeks, in their necks folding in like worn handbags. But we were together, and I wanted to hold the memory close. I raised my phone to snap some photos, then dropped it—a push-pull between keeping and letting go.

"Mum, we open? We open now?" Sam sat by the tree with Joe, holding out various packages that glittered in metallic paper.

"Are we waiting? For Bernard?" Mom asked tentatively.

"Do we know when he's even coming back?" Dad couldn't keep the growl from his throat.

"Fine. It's fine," Meghan said, her lids half open. "Let them open their stockings, I guess. It'll keep Sam busy. Baby, ask Uncle Joe where your stocking is."

Joe and Sam passed out overfilled socks and we feigned interest in rolls of Life Savers and tubes of hand cream, but the feeling of celebration had been sucked from the process. It helped to focus on the kids instead, as Lily zeroed in her concentration on Pot Roast's toys, joyless in the actual gifts she was given, and Sam rushed to show us each treasure he wrenched free from his stocking.

An hour later, a waft of marijuana marked Bernard's arrival as he wordlessly joined us, flopping into the chair in the farthest corner of the room.

"All better?" Meghan called out. She didn't make an effort to hide the annoyance in her voice, and I loved her for it. He shrugged as Sam rushed up and placed a gift gingerly in his father's lap. Bernard turned the box around in his hand like it might explode, then patted Sam on the head like one would a dog.

"Thanks, bud."

"Open, Daddy!"

We watched silently as Bernard unwrapped a set of long underwear from Joe and me, holding them between his pointer finger and thumb. "These are great, thanks. They'll be good for work."

A hush fell, with not even Lily squealing or paper rustling. The awkwardness was painful, like something stuck between my teeth.

"Hey, Sammy," Joe called. "Why don't you pass out the rest of the presents, eh?"

On cue, Dad stood to hover at the ready. "You done there?" he barked each time someone finished opening a present. Before we could say thanks, he snatched the wrapping and balled it into a construction-grade garbage bag, as per every other Thompson family gift-giving event. It was something Meghan and I had always joked about—his unease with celebration if it came with litter, mess, disorder. We called him the Garbage Nazi behind his back.

"Hey, Dad," Meghan said innocently. "I think you missed a piece over there." She pointed to the opposite corner of the den, warbled her wrist generically.

"What?" He whipped around to face us, head on a swivel. "Where?"

"Over there," Meghan repeated airily. Dad stomped to the corner to peek around furniture as Meghan continued to gesture non-specifically. "Keep searching. It might have blown under the chair from the furnace fan." *Same old, Dad*, she mouthed to me, only a foot away, and we stifled smirks. I could smell her laundry detergent, the essential oil–based soap I'd bought for her, her hairspray: these things that reminded me that she was still here, in this moment. And just for a second, I tried to imagine life without her. No one else—absolutely no one—would share in this joke with me, this history, this knowledge of our family and its complicated inner workings. The Garbage Nazi joke would die with her, and all I wanted for Christmas was to stop time.

"Where, Meg? Where's the paper you saw?" Dad's bum wiggled from behind the armchair, where he'd stooped to peer under the skirt of its cover.

I wanted to laugh with her, out loud and noisy, but I also wanted this silence, this perfection, to remain a private thing. *I love you*, Meghan mouthed to me. I patted her legs, swallowed so many times that my throat felt raw.

Utensils clacked against dishes strewn with smears of gravy and apple pie. Our meal had been hilariously silent and fraught, making me grateful for the distraction created by Sam narrating each item he put in his mouth.

In the few hours since her family had arrived, Meghan's energy had wilted like a flower. Joe, Dad, and I began clearing the table while Bernard settled into the recliner in the living area and Meghan worked at freeing the kids from their highchairs.

"Let me," Joe said, gently touching her arm to stop her. "You're not supposed to be lifting anything, remember?"

"I know, I just . . ." Meghan started to cry as she glanced at each of us in succession—Joe. Mom. Dad. Me. Her children. Finally, she turned to Bernard, who was either sleeping or pretending we weren't there. From the dining table, it was hard to tell.

Sam reached for Joe's neck. "Gunco Joe!" Joe swung Sam from the chair and held him upside down, comically bouncing to some unheard beat until he had a child in each arm, galloping around the living room.

"Why don't you go lie on the couch?" I said to Meghan as I reached across her for her plate. "You look tired."

"It's pain, actually." Her face bunched into something between anger and sadness. "But I don't want to dine and dash."

"My God, Meghan, we're family. We don't care. Go home and have a rest." Sometimes it was easy to forget that just over two weeks ago, she'd been in surgery, the incision a foot long. And only a week ago, I had carried her to the car like a princess and it hadn't felt like we would ever make it to this dinner.

"You guys sure? Maybe you're right. Babe?" she said to Bernard. "Do you think you could gather the kids and gifts? I'm in a lot of pain. Think I've overdone it for the day." Bernard's lashes fluttered open, but he didn't answer.

"Babe? Did you hear me? Can you get the kids? So much pain." She pointed to her abdomen for effect, in case any of us had somehow forgotten.

"Yeah, yeah." He blinked a few times and waved dismissively. "My back hurts. I just want to chill a minute." He stretched lazily, the leather crunching under his weight.

I gritted my teeth while aggressively scrubbing pots and hustling plates into neat stacks. Dad made a concerted effort to create as much noise as possible—clattering pans on the gas range, bonking dishes as they were rinsed and thrust into the dishwasher. Meghan perched on the edge of a couch cushion, leaning forward to stem the pain.

"I can help you load the car, Meghan," Joe said cheerily, Sam still dangling from his arm. He gently lowered Sam to the floor. "Hey buddy, why don't you go collect your new toys for Mommy?

But I'm going to time you to see how fast you run, okay? One, two . . ." Sam made for the basement, a grocery bag tucked under his arm.

"No, no, you've done enough, Joe. Bernard, please. I'm hurting so bad."

I willed him to move, not just because my sister was in agony but because I could feel her shame over his inaction.

Bernard leaned back farther in the recliner and gripped the armrests, his face blank. He didn't bother rising from his seat. "WHY DON'T YOU GET OFF YOUR OWN LAZY ASS AND DO SOMETHING!"

Dad didn't hear Bernard over his own racket, but Mom, Joe, Meghan, and I sat stunned, mouths agape. Lily, nestled in her uncle's arms, looked unfazed as she sucked her thumb.

"BECAUSE SHE CAN'T!" I screamed, startling everyone, even myself. I leaned in, my face close to Bernard's. "You realize she just had half her insides excavated, right?"

The room froze. Tears threatened and I was hot all over, sweating, and so wildly, impossibly exhausted. Bernard looked through me and into my sister instead, hate dancing across his expression, nose scrunched. I searched for something in his being, for the elusive root of Meghan's love for him. He was part of my niece and nephew, the two people I loved most, but I couldn't find anything in Bernard to hold tenderly. And just like Meghan used to, he brought out a part of me I disliked even more than him, one who rose to ribbing, who became an abuser in the face of abuse.

Dad paused, holding wet dishes that dripped down his arm. "What? What just happened? What'd I miss?"

"Kelly," Meghan said, putting herself between me and her husband. "It's fine. Bernard, let's go. *Now.*"

He left the house quickly under the pretense of getting the car warmed for the kids. Joe and Dad delivered the children to the truck, no words exchanged with Bernard, as if everyone knew the ice was cracking. Meanwhile, Meghan sat on the chair in the front hall and I helped her put on her boots, like a parent would a child. As I eased her coat around her shoulders, a plastic card fell from the pocket and rattled to the floor.

"Whoops." I passed the gift card to her. It was emblazoned with an image of an overcooked pizza printed in primary colours. The *To* and *From* sections of the card had not been filled out. Meghan sheepishly shoved it back in her pocket as a blush flooded her otherwise pale cheeks. "Meg?"

"Kelly." She said it almost as a warning, through gritted teeth.

But the words formed anyways. "Did he get you a fucking pizza gift card? As your actual Christmas gift?"

She shrugged and zipped up her coat. "It's thoughtful, really, so I don't have to cook. We don't have a lot of money for each other this year."

The whole scenario kept getting worse, and I didn't know how to stand it. On my dining room wall in Trenton was a photo of Joe and me at our wedding. In it, my mouth is wide in laughter and Joe holds me close, with love crinkling around his eyes, and whenever I looked at it, I was reminded of that joy, unfaked for the camera. *Not everyone has what you do,* Meghan had said to me once as she stared at the picture, scrutinizing it so closely she could have seen my pores. By contrast, in Meghan and Bernard's wedding pictures, Bernard appears to be in a perpetual state of unease, which Meghan said was because he hated wearing a suit. But his eyes never met hers, and his smile didn't reach beyond his mouth. Now, holding the gift card, I wanted to give her a shake. I wanted anything but this. I wanted her to want anything but this. "Then how about cooking a meal himself or giving you a home pedicure or something? It's not about the money. It's about making an effort."

She bit her lip to keep from crying. But she couldn't hold it in—the embarrassment, the anger, the sadness—and I was suddenly responsible and sick with myself over it. I always had to be right on the side of my sister's wrongs.

"God, I'm sorry. You okay, Meg?"

"I'll be fine. Everything is just sort of . . ." She let her words trail off and watched exhaust plume from the idling truck.

I wanted to fix it. I wanted to fix everything. "I can come out to the house tomorrow if you want. Help with the kids and give you a break before we go back to Trenton."

"I'll be okay." She waved her palms in my face and shook her head. "Bernard and I just need some time together, I think. Sorry, Mom, for wrecking everything. Again."

"You didn't wreck anything, Meggie," Mom squeaked. "We love you." Both she and Meghan were blotchy and red from the strain of holding their emotions close.

Meghan waved goodbye as Mom and I stood in the front entryway, letting cold wind gust through the home like a poltergeist. Out at the car, Dad kissed Meghan as he helped her climb into the cab, his voice a positive chirp for the kids.

When Joe and Dad came back inside, we gathered in the living room and tried to occupy the void that the tension had left behind.

"And to think," Mom said. "On her very last Christmas." And then she began to cry.

I cried too. It was the first time anyone other than me had voiced the truth.

sixteen

Meghan waved frantically as I pulled into the parking lot at Trent University, as if I could miss her in her bright red winter coat, the fake fur trim fluffed around her cheeks and the loops of a thick scarf coiled around her neck like a purple python. As was typical for Peterborough at the end of February, it was twenty-five below zero, but she stood outside her car wearing oversized sunglasses even though the sun was hiding behind thick cumulus. I pulled into the parking space beside hers and killed the engine.

"You made it." I slung my leather messenger bag over my shoulder and hugged her with my free arm.

"I am so stinkin' excited. My little sister, the creative writing professor. Can I record your lecture? I wanna record it."

"Instructor," I corrected her, then passed her a steaming travel mug. "Tenured profs would be pissed hearing you promote me. Here. I brought you a coffee."

"Oh my God, thanks. I'm so thirsty." She slurped noisily from the cup, then jumped from foot to foot, stomping out the cold with winter boots that were bulky like a child's.

"Coffee isn't exactly a thirst quencher. Did you bring any water? You're supposed to be keeping hydrated, remember?"

The oncologist had said that chemotherapy would require her to eat well and drink lots of water—whereas Meghan preferred McDonald's and orange juice. Since the start of the new year, she'd received weekly treatments, with Mom, Dad, and I rotating both to keep her company at the hospital and watch the kids. *Thompson sisters, reporting for duty*, I said to the receptionist at the hospital on the first day, giving a mock salute. Except technically we weren't Thompsons anymore, both of us married, grown women with new last names. Still, I'd made us matching white T-shirts with black block letters. Meghan grinned at hers—*Making Cancer My Bitch Since 1983*—and donned it like a suit of armour. Bernard hadn't been to a single appointment.

The corners of her mouth tugged into a triangle. "I had a bottle of water, but I forgot it on the counter. Bernard says I have chemo brain, which is apparently an actual thing. I should have grabbed something at Mom and Dad's when I dropped the kids off, but you know what their pantry is like—a bunch of canned beans and some saltine crackers. I'm all over the place, but can you blame me? It's my first day of university!" She danced a little jig that made me inhale coffee up my nose. "Okay, so not technically. But I've never been on a university campus before."

I gathered the rest of my things from my back seat, taking longer than necessary, trying to decide what was worth pressing her on. Bernard had a four-day workweek with Fridays off, so why weren't the kids with him? Whenever I arrived to take her to treatment, fresh off another three-hour drive from Trenton, he wasn't at home. Instead, he'd be in the garage with rap music blaring, doing electrical work for someone, or out running unspecified errands. If he was there, a mood lingered like smoke, and he couldn't be bothered to look up from his video game.

Mom, Dad, and I had discussed these rising tensions, unsure of how to approach them. Did you let someone die in peace, or recognize that ignoring the abuse made us complicit in it? And when we did question Meghan, she threatened to leave us in the same way Bernard threatened her. It was clear who she sided with. To push her was to lose her.

I passed a cooler bag for her to carry. "Some water in there. And I made you some lunch. We won't be back at my place until later in the afternoon and, somehow, I figured you'd forget to bring anything." I donned gloves, wrapped my fingers around my own coffee mug, and started walking towards the lecture hall.

"You take such good care of me." Meghan skipped after me, two steps for each one of my own. I bit back the pointless buzz of irritation. Bernard couldn't make some ham on rye for her three-hour drive, or devise weekend plans for her one-week break from chemo before the next round began? "I've told all my friends I'm going to watch my little sister teach. Then it's girl time. Will you give me a manicure? I want pink, or neon. Do you have any neon?" As adults, we'd only had a handful of nights alone together, but my favourite memory was her first visit to Trenton when Sam was just a year old, in which Meghan got drunk on sangria and danced to Michael Jackson hits on the Wii. She kept pronouncing it *sang-dra*, her teeth stained cherry red, and slurred over and over that *This is the best night ever. You're the best. Isn't this the best?* I wanted more nights just like that.

We crossed the parking lot towards the library and started up the long flight of outdoor stairs. "You're full of beans today. You'll be even more jaunty when I tell you my news." It was so cold that my lashes crystallized together and my teeth ached, but I couldn't stop smiling.

She halted mid-step. "What do you mean? What news?"

"Oh, nothing big." I paused to dramatically clear my throat. "Just that my book sold to a publisher last week. In August 2019, I'll be a published author!"

We screamed and bounced up and down on the steps holding one another, slopping coffee all over ourselves. The students who passed seemed indifferent to our joy, edging themselves to the opposite side of the flight to avoid us. "Holy shit! Holy shit. I'm so proud of you I could pop. I always knew. See? I always knew." A bubble of emotion broke as Meghan's grin melted slowly from her face, a realization dawning—she might not be alive to see the following summer. But she shook her head side to side and squeezed me tight again. "I can't believe you didn't tell me before now. The moment it happened."

"I had to tell my biggest fan in person, no?"

"This is huge, Kell. The hugest news." She sniffled a few times and swiped at her nose with her mitten.

"Shit, we have to get a wiggle on here. We're going to be late." We jogged the last hundred metres to escape the cold, and I pried open the door to the lecture hall. Inside, more than a hundred students waited with open notebooks or laptops glowing before them, and a buzz of chatter echoed. Our lecture hall was draughty with a perpetual leak in the back ceiling, which plopped a wet rhythm into a metal pail, but Meghan gawped at the nondescript features of the 1970s building, admiring the ceiling, reaching out to touch the railing as though it was sculpted by an artist.

"It looks just like I pictured it would," she whispered.

"Worn down and tired?" Still, I liked that she liked it. "Morning everyone." I flicked on the overhead lights by the podium and geared up my slides. Meghan followed me like a lamb and sat at the front, offering a wobbly grin, waving like she had when sending me off to kindergarten. Back then, I had been too shy to peer out from behind Mom's skirt, much less to let go of my sister's hand. She held on until her own teacher called her into second grade, and I had cried until I almost peed my pants. "Glad to see at least half of you are awake today."

I rubbed my palms together and blew warmth into them as the projector slid down with the press of a button. "I see they still haven't fixed the heat in here. Before we get started today, I want to introduce you all to my sister, Meghan." She stood and did a small curtsey, her face bright red with the attention. "Believe it or not, despite being a tiny fart of a thing, Meghan is my older sister, and she wanted to come hear what a lecturing badass I am, so make me look smart and pretend you're super interested, capiche? Let's get started."

———————

While they were generally an attentive bunch, as we approached the end of the two-hour lecture, even the most dedicated amongst the students were fading. Meghan, however, looked like she was in a posture lesson at finishing school, still alert and nodding at every sentence that left my mouth.

"So, what do you think of the tortured artist model?" I asked the class, snapping off the projector and stepping off the stage. I flicked on all the lights and wandered the aisles. "Is writing life one that lends itself to suffering, since Andreasen notes writers experience a higher rate of mental health issues compared to other professions? Or is it the other way around? Do we make art in suffering? Or is it all a bunch of bull?"

Arms shot up and various answers rang out:

"The textbook is full of shit!"

"No way—lots of writers are happy and still make great art."

"We glorify suffering in society, and so writers feel a need to cater to that vision of them."

"To write is to suffer."

And then Meghan lifted one pointer finger upwards, tentative and shy.

"Ooh, listen up, all. My big sister is getting her university on! What do you think, Meg?" She suddenly looked close to crying, too embarrassed to open her mouth. I dug the heel of my right boot into my left toes until I felt the sting. Why did I poke fun? Why did I make her feel small?

"Do you think, maybe, um . . ." She fretted, feeling for a hangnail to pick. I nodded to encourage her. *Go on.* "Maybe that because writers look at what it is to be human, that they're just, you know, showing us who we are?" She swiped at her blushing face like she could rub away the colour, but I could tell she was fighting tears. Under the harsh fluorescent light, the hollows of her cheeks looked like bruises. Her hair, thinning with treatment, was cut into a pixie that didn't suit her face. I wanted to shield her from all of it, from the knowing gaze of teenagers.

"Yeah, Meg," I said, palm to my heart to rub at the tenderness there. "That's a great point." How long did we stare at one another? Was it one minute or ten? She tugged her sweater over her fists and kneaded the material like bread, straddling sheepishness and pride. Another student reached across a row of chairs to pat Meghan on the forearm, and I steadied myself against one of the folding auditorium seats, then gratefully noticed the clock. I cleared my throat to bring back my voice. "Well, everyone, you're saved by the proverbial bell from not one but two Thompsons sobbing at you! I'll see you all next week, and don't forget your first short story is due next Thursday. I want to see you stretch your writing muscles. Thanks for another great class."

The students gathered their things and the room filled with the sound of backpacks zipping closed and laptops snapping shut. They shrugged on winter coats and chattered amongst themselves as they filtered out through the various exits. The next class lingered in the hallway, their faces pressed to the glass as they waited for me to leave.

"Kell, that was awesome," Meghan said as I loaded my bag. "You were awesome. I sat there the whole time so proud I thought I'd die."

It was my turn to be shy, and I focused on buckling my bag. "Thanks, Meg. And turns out you're a secret creative writer at heart—you made a good point in class. I have to stop at my office for a few things before we go, okay?"

"Sure thing. As long as you get me home in time for that manicure." We walked down the hall to the faculty offices with Meghan talking the whole time at breakneck speed. "Notice how well I'm moving?" She spun in a quick circle and without missing a beat, kept her step with mine. "It's this new oil I've been taking. It's making me feel so much better."

"Oil?"

"Yeah. This new cannabis oil that Bernard found for me. The guy cured his own cancer with it because it shrinks the tumours by, well, I don't know how, but it does. Bernard's been watching all these YouTube videos about it and there's a lot of science and studies about everything it can heal. Not just cancer, either. Epilepsy. Other, um, brain problems, and depression too. It's expensive as all get out, but worth it. I can feel the difference."

The hallway shrunk into tunnel vision like the aura that precedes a migraine. I sipped from my empty mug and jostled files from one arm to another. It was scary to trust the knot of hope that Meghan was attaching herself to, because while I wanted to share in it, I had a sense it couldn't hold both our weight.

"It's called Rick Simpson Oil, and Bernard reads about it for hours. He didn't come to bed last night until, like, two in the morning. He's been up late every night this week, which is insane because he has to wake up so early to commute and gets maybe two hours of sleep, but that's love, right?" She swooned, squeezing her fingers into a tangle at her chest.

That's love. This analogy was too indistinct to make sense of. We started climbing the stairs towards my office. "That can't be healthy, Meg. Is he sleeping at all? You both need rest right now."

She ignored my question and kept prattling on. "It tastes like shit, and I have to hold it in my mouth a while, which makes me feel like barfing. I don't know how we're affording it, but if it helps, then . . ." She raised her palms upwards, as if money would have a magical way of sorting itself out. They'd been spending so flagrantly lately that Bernard had asked me to help them write a GoFundMe page, but I couldn't stomach lending my writing skills to help them—a couple who had plenty of money—to buy more cars, a camp trailer nearly as big as their house, or countless other things that didn't support a real future for their family.

"Have you told your oncologist you're taking this stuff? And honestly, how is Bernard surviving on two hours of sleep a night? He's going to crash."

She looked at me like I was a complete moron. "You're missing the point. The oil. He's researching for ways to help me."

"I know, Meg, but he's an electrician. It's dangerous work, and he has to be totally aware of what's going on around him. Not sleeping so he can google stuff online seems a little, I don't know, manic." I swung open the office door to the stark room that smelled of plywood and a garbage can that never got emptied. Meghan shuffled in behind me and peered out the tall slit of a window to the Trent River. Minutes passed as I loaded textbooks into a tote bag.

"Maybe I only have a couple years left, so I'm willing to try anything. *We're* willing to try anything." She blew onto the glass until frost formed, then scraped her and Bernard's initials in it and a heart looped around the letters.

A couple of years. I didn't want to steal this dream. She watched a cluster of students three floors below us run up and scare the ducks onto the water, coats undone to the frigid temperatures, fingertips snipped off their gloves in grunge-like coolness. They wore black and dramatic makeup, all four of them at the delicate age nearing graduation—adults only by legal definition. Meghan opened her mouth when they passed a shared cigarette. She was still smoking, despite the cancer diagnosis, despite never admitting to me that she'd started as a teenager. It was another thing we never spoke of.

"Well, if the oil makes you feel better, Meg, then I'm glad you're taking it." I didn't care if it was a sham or a miracle drug, because she seemed happy, and she deserved that. But I suspected it was less so her clinging to it as a cure and more to do with the fact that she saw Bernard's hyper focus as a symbol of love instead of anything sinister.

"You'll feel stupid, Miss Education, if I end up tumour-free after a year of this stuff. Bernard can send you the links so you can learn more."

"I'd happily embrace being dumb as a stone if it meant you were healthy, Meg."

She left the window and came to kiss my cheek. Her breath was foul from the chemo, but the smell was immediately replaced with the floral scent of her body cream.

"Speaking of education, now that you're a university student…" From my desk drawer, I produced a forest-green Trent sweatshirt in a child's medium. Holding it up to her, it looked too big. "Now you're officially one of us."

"Oh my God, I love it!" She snatched the sweater and pulled it right over the shirt she was already wearing and spun and spun. When we were little girls, we'd picked dresses by their spinnability—a necessary height to be reached with equally necessary ruffles. Anne of Green Gables wannabes with puffy sleeves. I watched my sister, thirty-six and spinning, and knew exactly what she was dreaming of.

seventeen

The end-of-April air had a chill even as tulips pushed through mulch and robins scratched at snow-flattened grass. I checked the time and watched the main entrance of Royal Victoria Regional Health Centre from my parking spot, where I sipped a Tim Hortons iced coffee that was laced with sweetness, despite having requested sugar-free. I didn't need the caffeine, much less the sugar high. I felt like an overstretched elastic threatening to snap.

My phone blinked.

Meghan: *All finished.*

I threw my car into gear and zipped towards the hospital entryway, then leaned across the console to push the door open for Meghan. "All good?"

"Yup." She settled in, pressing on the tiny bandage that sat like a bull's eye in the crook of her arm. Five other bandages were scattered nearby where the phlebotomist must have struggled to find a vein. "They'll wait for my blood test results to come in, then I'll meet with the oncologist. Anywhere from an hour to longer, the receptionist said—which, by the way, is an awfully loose timeline when you're literally waiting to find out whether or not you're going to die. I'll lose my mind by then." She put her face in her palms while I drove and tried to summon a response.

Google had informed me that her specific chemo medication was a last-ditch effort for advanced ovarian and pancreatic tumours—cancers that communicated time in months or weeks, not years. Meghan approached this oncological checkup like an ostrich, just as she had all the others. Our parents had wanted to come to the appointment, as support, they insisted, but Meghan wanted only me and begged me to stop Dad from pushing his way into the car as he called out promises we knew he wouldn't keep. *I won't ask any questions! I'll stay quiet the whole time!*

I can't stand it, Kell, Meghan had said as we drove away. *I'm too tired and scared to make them feel better.*

"How about we keep busy at the mall? A little retail therapy." I eased us into highway traffic.

"There isn't enough retail therapy in the world to make me forget all this. Especially when I only need new bras because I look like no one feeds me."

We were beyond pretending she didn't look sick, laughing when we used her haunted look to skip a line or get a free latte from the gullible Starbucks barista. *The burls on those trees are bigger than my tits. Look on the bright side, at least you'll go out as the skinny sister.* We snickered, looked around like teenagers caught smoking during free period. But in the space between breaths, a palpable knowing strung between us like a tether.

"Don't take Cundles, for Christ's sake," she screeched. "We'll be in traffic forever. Watch out for that pedestrian. God, you're driving so slow." She pointed this way and that.

"Did you want to drive, Miss Crazy Town? Or can I master my own vehicle?"

"Sorry. I'm being controlling. I'm just . . ." She looked down into her lap, picking at the cupid's bow of her lip. So much had changed and so much had not.

"You get a free pass to moodiness today."

She flipped through messages on her phone until I swerved into Georgian Mall. Our last time here together had been for the failed Santa photo eleven years earlier, the one I'd stuffed to the bottom of a drawer and never wanted to see again because now Meghan was as thin and ghostly as she was back then, in both instances edging towards death. More than a decade. It felt like a lifetime.

"What are you waiting for?" Meghan snapped. She hopped from the car, her legs moving like hummingbird wings so I had to jog to catch up as she stalked towards Victoria's Secret. Inside the dimly lit store, everything smelled of the saccharine floral scent they piped throughout, fake and pungent. Within minutes, Meghan had wordlessly looped a collection of bras over her forearms, three cup sizes smaller than her previous versions, and was frowning as she checked price tags. We used to share bras, stare at our 34Es and wonder who in the family had gifted us with them when Mom could barely fill an egg carton.

"My treat," I called to her. The last few months, everything had been my treat, or footed by Mom and Dad. The visits to nail salons, the hair appointments, the clothes she didn't need and sized out of the following month, the endless loop of coffees during visits, after-chemo snacks, during-chemo snacks, parking.

Neither she nor Bernard ever offered to pay, and we never asked. The financial cost of death seemed so unworthy of discussion. And who could deny her?

"Is that just because of my Big C?"

"Why else? You think it's because I love you or something?"

"Well, I guess I'm ready to try them on." Meghan clutched the throng of lace and microfibre as we entered the change room area.

"Hi, ladies!" The saleswoman sauntered close, smiling wide while she adjusted the headset resting at her temple. Like the rest of the staff, she was dressed in black, perfect red lipstick circling her crescent mouth, youthful breasts hefted high. "You let me know if you need anything, okay?" she said as she unlocked a room, the smell of lilacs wafting behind her.

Meghan closed the door and called out to me. "Kell, stay close in case I need advice."

"I'll be right out here." I sat on a tufted pink cushion in the hall and turned away from the overhead lights.

"You two having a nice day out together?" the saleswoman asked as she snapped her gum—a trait I generally found annoying, but there was something about her that was comforting, affable. Her curves slithered left and right as she folded undergarments into tidy squares.

"Well, yeah. Kind of." I didn't know how to explain our purpose. *She's lost her boobs to cancer.* No, no, not breast cancer. *We're wasting time until we can find out if her chemo is working and how long she'll live.* No, that wouldn't work either. *Please, distract us because we can barely breathe.* Yes, those were the words I could not say.

"Kell?" Meghan called gently from behind the closed door. "What do you think?" She cracked the door open and I slipped in behind her. The ridge of her spine was like a knotted tree root, snaking from absent glutes to the nape of her neck, sharp bone after sharp edge, tendons taut and stark. Then I saw her front on display in the mirror, ribs mummified, deflated breasts slinking lazily in the fabric cups.

She watched me, waiting. I observed all of this in mere seconds and gathered my thoughts with military precision. "Hey, that one looks great!" There were moments when I could lie to her so well, I hardly recognized myself.

"Yeah? You sure? I'm worried I look a little saggy." She jiggled a finger between her breasts as evidence. The flesh wobbled back and forth like jelly.

"Christ, Meg. Give yourself a break. You've lost, what, fifty pounds? That one is super flattering. You look beautiful." She twisted and turned in front of the mirror and I watched the scars, one running from belly button to back, the other cutting her from ribs to pubic bone. I bit down on the awareness of all the years when I'd refused to tell her she was loved, beautiful, funny, weird—practically choking on regret.

"Yeah, okay." She shrugged noncommittally. I suspected the bra could have been adorned in diamonds and she still wouldn't have been interested. "Can you see if they have more colours? Black just feels sort of . . . you know." She passed the tiny bra to me.

Outside the changeroom I found the saleswoman, who was folding another stack of frilly panties into a perilous tower. "How's it going in there?"

"We need some other colours," I squeaked. "Ideally not black. She doesn't want black because, because she . . ." And then I could not stop the tears, deep and consuming in a way that made me nauseated, combined with an ache in my chest from stifling the sound. "I'm sorry," I gasp-whispered, gesturing with a thumb at the door where my sister waited for petal pink or sunshine yellow. Anything but black. "She's so thin. Cancer. It's cancer. I didn't expect . . ."

"I just said goodbye to my mom to the same damn thing, sweetie. You let it out." She tugged me close and my body fell into hers, and I let this stranger hug me, her perfumed skin tart in my nose. My arms wrapped around her back and I rested myself there, in the Victoria's Secret change area, choking back sobs.

I snorted up my tears, fumbled awkwardly through my purse for tissues. "God, I have to sort my shit out. She needs me."

The woman gently released her hold and tenderly smoothed my wild pixie cut. "You can't change the outcome, so what she needs, and what you need too, is to look after *you* a bit." I swallowed hard and nodded at her sage advice. "Now," she said, all matter-of-fact, holding bras by their foamy cups. "I have this style in white, pink, and orange. Take your pick."

We chose orange. Bright. Hopeful. Impossible to wear under a white shirt, but Meghan and I were women uninterested in practicality.

As I passed my credit card to the cashier, the oncologist's office called. The caller informed Meghan that her blood work was in, so she could come for her appointment whenever she was ready, and could she hurry? Dr. Lim wanted to leave for his weekend holiday. I strained to hear, trying to discern results based on the tone of the receptionist's voice. Meghan popped the Ativan I offered and was silent the entire ride back to the hospital.

———

At the RVH cancer centre, Meghan tapped on the kiosk screen to register, familiar with the routine, her fingerprints one of thousands of smeared and gummy identities on the touchpad.

Since your last treatment, have you had:
- ❑ *Any sweating or dizziness?*
- ❑ *Any flu-like symptoms?*
- ❑ *Any fever?*
- ❑ *Any aches or pains?*
- ❑ *Any mouth sores?*

She tap, tap, tapped, each push of her finger angrier, and I swallowed the upset over the fact that she was so familiar with the questions. We silently approached chairs in the waiting area and sat for barely a moment before a nurse called out and directed us to an exam room. The space was not light-filled and shiny like the chemo treatment rooms or the waiting area. I had imagined major medical news would be delivered like it was on television, with the doctor behind a large oak desk with a panel of supportive family members lining the other side. But this was a regular hospital room with a computer, exam table, and sink, plus two uncomfortable plastic chairs against the wall.

"Jesus, they can't spruce this room up a little?" I muttered. "It's depressing in here."

"Guess they figure you're already pissed to be in the Cancer Centre, so you don't give a hoot about decor."

"I like a nice dose of feng shui with my cancer experience, thank you very much. Tea would be nice."

"It'd probably be fucking radioactive." She laughed but her

face quickly returned to sombreness. "You know, Mom and Dad hate our death jokes."

"Yeah, I've learned that the hard way. Had some good zingers that have fallen pretty flat the last few days."

"Well, they don't get it."

I took my sister's hand as the door popped open with a soft click. Dr. Lim peeked in, unsmiling, looking barely old enough to vote, much less relay important medical information. He wore New Balance sneakers—not the hipster suede kind but the sporty running kind—pleated khakis that broke over the shoes, and a plaid shirt with pens tucked in the pockets. If Meghan and I had seen him in the mall twenty minutes ago, we would have shared a secret smile at the sight of the actual pocket protector hovering near his heart.

"Hi, Meghan." Then, to me: "Kelly, right? The sister."

"Yup. Nice to meet you."

"Nice to see you have support, Meghan. Your husband coming today?"

"He couldn't make it," she said quickly. We left it there, this pregnant awareness of his absence. Meghan was horrified when the chemo nurses thought Dad was her husband. I didn't say it was because she had listed "married" as her marital status but hadn't produced an actual spouse for a single appointment.

The doctor sat on a wheeled stool in front of us, rocking slightly back and forth. He pulled up Meghan's latest scan on the screen, blinked repeatedly, cleared his throat. Meghan and I leaned forward, waiting, barely breathing.

"I'm afraid it's not good news," said Dr. Lim. And then he stopped. Clicked a few more times around the screen.

"Oh God." Meghan hung her head to her chest. These were the words I'd expected, yet still, a hot flash bloomed. I squeezed her fingertips twice. *I'm here.*

"And?" I finally said to prod him on, angry that I had to do so. I needed to stay calm. Stable. My sister needed this, and I needed her. "Is there more information?"

Dr. Lim spun his monitor around to show us Meghan's CT scan, side by side with the one from five months before—just after surgery, before chemo. "The entire abdomen is full of cancer, I'm afraid. It's spreading quite rapidly. The chemo hasn't effected any positive results."

"Which parts are the tumours?" Meghan asked, squinting at the screen. The scan results were hard to discern, shades of grey blending into snowy static. A lung could have been a liver, for all I could tell.

"All of this." The doctor used his pen to point out a general area that covered from rib cage to pelvic bone. Everything was filled in with dark masses that I could not stop comparing to orb-shaped fruit. A grapefruit in the pelvic bone. An orange over the diaphragm. A plum on the kidney. A goddamned melon where her intestines should have been.

"I'm going to die," Meghan whispered. No one argued.

"How long?" I asked. It was the practical question asked in all those movies, so the words sounded trite and clichéd.

"Well." Dr. Lim stretched his lips into a nervous grimace, and I wanted to slap him and his healthy insides, his oncological education. *Spit it out!* "Taking into account how fast it's spreading, and judging by how full your abdomen is currently, I wouldn't expect you'd see Labour Day." He didn't seem to notice his distasteful phrasing. It was April 27, 2018. Four months. Meghan's fingers tightened into a vice. "But if you're not having symptoms yet, then it could be longer." He sounded unsure and squinted again at the screen, as if it would give him new answers.

"I don't have any symptoms!" Meghan said in a positive chirp. "So, I probably have more time, right? If I don't have symptoms yet?" Her pitch rose, her body vibrating. "What should I expect to see when I'm going downhill?"

Dr. Lim looked to me uncertainly, then back at his patient. "First, we'd expect that you'd lose some of your appetite or start vomiting."

"I'm still hungry. So that's good, right?"

"Meghan," I said gently. "You haven't been able to keep food down for a while now."

She turned to me with wide eyes, like this hadn't occurred to her. "Yeah, I guess that's true. But it might just be the chemo, right, Dr. Lim?"

"Probably not. Vomiting isn't a typical side effect of Gemcitabine once you adjust to the treatment."

Meghan wilted. "What else?"

"Another symptom we would expect would be for you to start having some acute pain. But we can manage that for you as things progress."

"See?" Meghan threw her arms up in the air triumphantly, like the doctor and I were full of shit. "I haven't had any pain."

"Meg." My voice was pleading, borderline desperate. I needed her to hear this. Really listen. "You've been complaining about back pain all week." During my last visit, she'd asked me to rub out a muscle knot, which looked like a deformed bulge poking out between her ribs. She couldn't tolerate even the lightest pressure, and I had known I wasn't pressing on muscle as I rubbed warming oil into her side.

"That was just a strain from lifting Lily. Right?" She turned to the doctor. "Right?" Her panic filled the room like water in a glass. I wanted to tear out of there, run to my car, drive too fast down the highway. Be anywhere but there.

"Why don't I take a look?" Dr. Lim invited Meghan onto the exam table and she climbed up deftly. *See?* her face seemed to say. *Could a dying person move like THIS?* She lifted her shirt and winced as he pressed down her spine, then prodded at her abdomen. "I'm sorry. That's definitely the cancer. I can feel the tumours all over."

Time froze. Meghan's mouth hanging open, shirt still held up around her withered breasts, material gathered at her neck. The doctor, awkward and unmoving, staring at the floor. I watched hope drain from her face as if she were waking from a dream, and it was that moment, not the dying, that I couldn't stand—the complete absence of possibility. Meghan sat there, blinking her huge eyes, the same colour as mine but infinitely more beautiful in the way they protruded beyond the brow bone, the way the lashes curled up and out.

"So, there's nothing else that can be done?" I asked.

"We're kind of out of options," Dr. Lim said as he washed his hands. "I'll talk to Dr. Baratta in Toronto and see if there are any experimental studies you can be a part of."

"So, that's it? Experimental stuff?"

"Afraid so. I'll be in touch when I hear from Dr. Baratta, and we'll set you up with a pain treatment plan. I really am sorry." He looked at his feet, genuinely sad. I wondered how many people he'd relayed this type of news to. "I know this wasn't what you wanted to hear."

Out in the hall, Meghan wailed as she walked, awkwardly leaning her head into my shoulder while I robotically wrapped an arm around her and we made our way towards the exit. An elderly couple walked past arm in arm, the husband evidently bald from chemo, his face scabby and blotchy. He looked to Meghan, who could barely walk for crying, and shook his head in sympathy. And then I could not hold it in and the tears lurched forward, my sister and I stumbling like drunken bar mates, snot dripping, tears staining. The automatic hospital doors rotated and swept, directing us out into the sunlight where we found ourselves standing beside my Golf, stunned.

Meghan folded into me. "I'm dying, Kell. I'm going to die. Labour Day." She cried so hard into my shirt that when I pulled away, I had a stripe of damp down my front.

I nodded, over and over, my chin bonking her hair each time. "I love you, Meg."

We drove home in silence. I wanted to offer a grocery shop, on me. A tub of shared rocky road. Maybe another shopping trip. But there was nowhere we could go to buy the one thing she wanted most: time.

eighteen

"Oh my God. I want one of everything." Meghan fanned out her menu and ran a finger down the page, talking so loudly that other spa guests turned to stare. "I can order anything?" The dining room was surrounded with windows that opened onto the rolling hills of Grafton and bees buzzing in the nearby garden. The brightness of the room only served to highlight Meghan's rapidly yellowing skin, the colour of a healing bruise.

"It's an inclusive package deal. Whatever you want," I responded, taking a sip of ice water. It hit the nerves in my teeth with a sharp rap. All I could think of was how we shouldn't be here pretending. After the oncologist visit three weeks earlier, I'd helped Meghan make a bucket list. Then I'd gotten into my car and wept over the humility of it. Camping with her children and Bernard. A date with her husband. A trip to a spa. I could only actualize one item on the list and had booked the spa get-away with urgency. Her decline in the short period of time since had been dramatic and terrifying.

"Mom, what are you having?"

Mom hung her cane on the back of her chair and tugged the tie of her spa robe closer around her body, which was pointless considering she was clothed underneath. She still shaved her legs every day, never left the house without makeup. It was a commitment to beauty I couldn't muster, especially in the wake of all the mounting stress. "Not sure. It feels strange, eating lunch in a robe. Improper."

"Ma, literally every person in the room is wearing their robe," I said. "It's part of the chill factor."

"Still." She popped the terrycloth collar up and gathered the material around her neck. "It doesn't seem right." She had refused to put on a bathing suit, insisting there was no need because she didn't intend to use the hydrotherapy pools or saunas. But really, it was because the effort to wrestle her unco-operative limbs into the stretchy fabrics embarrassed her. I pinched my thighs until I left indents in the skin, enjoying the pain it brought. I'd assured her this place was accessible, no stairs, that her MS wouldn't be a problem, and watching her struggle was making me feel like another iteration of failure.

"Hello, ladies. Welcome to Ste. Anne's Spa." A waiter stood next to the table, young and handsome, dark hair sweeping across his forehead. He scanned the table and produced a small pad of paper and pen from his apron. "My name's Matthew, and I'm going to be serving you today. Now you three just have to be related, am I right?" He pointed with his pen at each of us in turn, as if he were assessing our shared features. It wasn't something we normally heard. Mom and I, yes, but Meghan's looks had always skewed towards the Thompson side. "Having a girly trip, are we?"

"My mom and sister brought me here for my bucket list," Meghan said proudly, not a lick of shyness. "I have cancer. I'm dying."

Mom looked caught somewhere between horrified and humoured, while Matthew held his pad of paper to his chest in shock. I spat my water out on the table, inhaled a little up my nose. "Subtle, Meg. Real subtle."

"Sorry. Yeah, I guess that's a lot to take in," Meghan said dreamily into her bread plate. She leaned so close her nose touched the ceramic rose print.

"Morphine," I whispered to Matthew. "Makes her a little, um, forward." I'd injected her with the drug back in our room, trembling as I drew the liquid from the glass vial. She'd only recently needed the pain relief, carrying around the syringes in an old makeup bag. *You're the nurse, Ma. Can't you do it?* I'd asked, feeling helpless as I held out the needle. Mom shook her head and lifted the cane dangling from a string on her wrist. *My hands are numb. I might put it in too deep.* We both glanced at Meghan then, arse bared and waiting. Mom stood by giving orders and, as instructed, I snapped off the glass vial tip but sliced open my thumb, dripping crimson across the hardwood floors. After wrapping a chubby wad of gauze around the cut, I managed to push the needle into Meghan's glute and press the plunger. A sigh of relief puffed from her open mouth.

"Well, gosh, I'm just, I'm so very sorry," Matthew said. "My boyfriend was sick recently, and we thought we were going to lose him and it's just . . . it's just that . . ." He stopped to fan his face with the paper pad to keep his emotion at bay.

"My husband is sick too," Meghan said. She grasped at Matthew's shirt. "He's in the hospital right now."

God, please don't elaborate. I drained my water glass and wished it were filled with wine instead, wincing as the iciness burned my throat. It was impossible to process the ways in which Meghan's life kept unfolding with soap opera–like plot twists. The previous week had been so filled with turmoil that the trip to the spa felt even more ludicrous.

Bernard's behaviour had become increasingly erratic and manic but had reached a crescendo days before the spa trip. They'd been fighting about who knows what, but he resorted to throwing Meghan up against the wall and threatening to kill her and himself. I'd been witness to half of it on the phone when she hid in the bedroom and dialled me in a panic, her words hard to discern between her sobs and his fist echoing against the door. *I don't know what to do, Kelly,* she shrieked. *What do I do?* There was only one response that made sense, that assured the safety of her and the kids. But when she called the cops, Bernard evaded them all through town despite the sweep of red and blue lights behind him, the spike belt thrown across the busy highway, and the endless attempts to coerce him off the road. He ended the ordeal by crashing into a bank of police cruisers that waited for him at home in a blockade. Bernard was hauled off in handcuffs in a high-risk takedown while Meghan, Phyllis, and the kids watched from the living room window. He'd since been released from police custody and admitted to hospital.

We all knew he was battling a major mental health crisis and jointly worried about one more layer of pain heaved onto this family. But the car chase was so dramatic, almost laughably over-the-top, that I'd suggested we cancel the spa date, do it another time. *There won't be another time,* Mom said sadly. And if all the other bucket list items were going to prove unattainable, didn't we owe her that one perfect day? So Phyllis took the kids for the night and we loaded bags, meds, and bathing suits and pretended the spirit was still there. Hearing the snippets parroted back to this stranger made me realize how foolish we were to think it was possible.

"Listen," Matthew said to Meghan, "we're gonna make sure you have such a good time here that you get the right send off to heaven."

Meghan turned a grateful face to the server, but her pupils were dilated, lids droopy, mouth slack with medication. "I'm going to eat a lot and make it worth my while."

I took a gulp of air, pushed it down. Her appetite was there, but once food was in front of her, she found it repellent, or she would manage only a few bites before pushing it away in disgust.

"I'll make sure there's extra love in every serving, doll." Matthew gave Meghan a sassy wink and she tried to return it, looking instead like a drunken sailor.

"Do you think I gave her too much?" I whispered to Mom while Matthew helped Meghan through the menu. "She seems real out of it."

Mom shook her head at me sadly. "No, the dose is right. It's just her body adjusting to it. It's a powerful drug."

Our meals arrived adorned with edible flowers from the gardens. Meghan took two bites and then dropped her spoon with a clatter into her bowl of Thai curry. "This is all I wanted. Time with my mom and sister." She raised her arms up and up, like she was addressing an adoring audience, then pushed her plate away and tucked her chin to her chest.

Mom and I ate wordlessly as Meghan remained semi-conscious, even as desserts arrived in multicoloured slices, chocolate truffles arranged in couplets. The silence let us pretend this really was all she wanted.

———————

That evening, back in our suite, I poured three pinot grigios and sat them on coasters in the living room. The glasses instantly beaded sweat as heat radiated from the gas fire. When I popped the cork, Mom argued that Meghan shouldn't be mixing alcohol and her meds, and Meghan shot back that she was dying anyways so what did it matter if she overdosed. To appease everyone, we settled on small glasses that I only filled a quarter of the way, secretly chugging half the bottle before stashing it in the fridge.

Meghan held her phone mere inches from her face, tapping out message after message as digital pings alerted her to new responses from Phyllis, with what I assumed were updates on Bernard. I watched my sister, tried mapping her constellation of freckles, desperate for memories and bonding and karaoke. I wanted to do all the things we hadn't had a chance to do from my own sister bucket list, and I wanted Mom to see her daughters together, actually loving one another in real time.

"Anyone need anything else?" I called out, scraping dinner leftovers into a garbage can. Meghan was in too much pain to go to the main inn for the meal, so we'd ordered room service. She'd eaten a tiny portion of chicken before pushing her food away in favour of her phone, so I ate her dinner and mine, knowing I'd feel sick regardless.

Mom limped in from one of the bedrooms and settled into an oversized armchair closest to the fire. "Heck, you could get lost in this place. It takes me five minutes to walk from one side of the room to the other." This had been the only remaining suite that could accommodate all three of us: two king bedrooms, two bathrooms, and an open kitchen and living room with an extra twin bed for me, all of it in a building set away from the main spa facilities.

I plopped onto the opposite end of the couch from Meghan and she gave an irritated squint of her nose. My neck was knotted like macrame. Despite the spa treatments, I'd never felt so unrelaxed, tiptoeing around Meghan and her tides of anger— related to medication or the contents of her text messages, it was hard to say.

"Have you had a nice time, Meggie?" Mom asked. She tucked her feet up under her on the plush chair, a posture that made her look far younger than her early sixties.

"Sure," Meghan responded, tone flat. "It's been great."

I gritted my teeth until the enamel felt close to chipping. "How's Bernard doing? Everything okay?"

"Oh, like you care?"

I opened my mouth and closed it again, shocked by her nastiness but also hopelessly accustomed to it. Two hours earlier, she had accidentally stepped on my heel and sent me sprawling across the tiled floor of the gift shop, snarking that I ought to watch where I was going. Then she bemoaned the cost of some rubbery sandals that reminded me of our jelly shoes from the eighties, and when I pointed out the resemblance, she said I should fuck right off and mind my own business.

"Okay, okay. We're just worried about you."

"And what about my husband, huh? Do you worry for him?"

Tension rippled through the suite like a sonic boom. *It's the medication. Yes. Just the medication.* "Considering you're the one dying of cancer, Meg, sorry if I'm struggling to have as much concern for Bernard as I am for how you and the kids are coping."

She squinted at me and her expression quickly softened into another emotion I couldn't track. "I know. God, it's all too much, all of this happening," she sobbed, grabbing handfuls of tissues from the box on the coffee table. I moved closer so I could curl my toes around the tops of hers, locking on like a monkey. "I have to go through Phyllis for everything because Bernard doesn't want any information given to me because I called the cops. I'm his wife, for Christ's sake." She scrolled through Phyllis's texts to summarize. "He's been moved out of jail and into a mental health facility so he can get some care. I mean, clearly they recognize that the way he was behaving was illness-related. Apparently, they're going to change his meds."

"Well, that's good news, right? He clearly needs help and now he'll get it." Mom's voice was gentle, encouraging.

"But he was sick, and I should have noticed. He wasn't sleeping, barely eating, pacing all the time. Why didn't I notice?" Meghan bonked her forehead with her palm.

"Go easy on yourself," I said. "You've got a few issues of your own to manage, plus you have the kids to think about."

"Uh. That's the worst part. Sam saw all of it. You should have heard him, crying for his Daddy while Daddy gets arrested. It was horrible." Despite the box of tissues nearby and the ones balled up in her hand, Meghan wiped snot on the sleeve of her robe. She'd been crying and wiping so much that there was a permanent crease across the cartilage of her nose. "He's taking everything away from me, you know? I don't get to just die in peace with my family. I have to deal with his shit, too." She gulped her wine and then immediately spat it back into the glass like it had turned to vinegar.

STILL, I CANNOT SAVE YOU ～ 165

Mom and I looked at each other over Meghan's head. For the last few months, Meghan's love for Bernard had had the capacity to see-saw to anger, making it difficult to know which side we were meant to take. But then it had probably felt the same way for her. She wanted to be married, to die simply and lovingly.

"That's understandable, Meg, feeling that way," I said softly. "You're allowed to be angry sometimes."

"And he's wrecked this trip, too," she cried. "I don't even get to have this one nice thing."

And what was there to say to this? Because dying should have been the worst part.

"I'm exhausted," Meghan said finally. "I think I'm just going to go to bed."

"Do you want me to bring you a tea?" I offered. "There's a kazillion flavours stashed in the cupboards."

"No thanks. I think I want to be alone for a while." She padded off to the farthest bedroom and shut the door behind her.

Mom was stony faced, her wine glass empty.

"Well, this trip has been a wild success, hasn't it?" I took a gulp from my own glass and wrapped myself in a throw, even though the fire was giving off too much heat.

"No. Not what we had in mind."

We sat there saying nothing, but there was so much I wanted to say, so much anger that felt misplaced in my head. "Should we make the most of it and hit up this hot tub? It's only nine and we're clearly wild women out for a good time."

Mom peered behind me to view the steam that rose from underneath the outdoor cover and made a face of disgust. "I don't like the idea of stewing in strangers' dirt."

"It's just us, Ma. Heck, you could go in naked if you want."

"Oh, yeah right." She laughed though, and this felt like a win I could cling to when this horrible night was over. "Okay, I'll go get my suit on. If I'm not out in two hours, come find me. I'll be the one on the floor strangled by Lycra."

A few minutes later, helping Mom into the hot tub was an effort that made us both snort with a combination of laughter, exhaustion, and desperation. The MS made her body respond poorly to heat—we knew this—but still, she sat on the edge of the tub as I guided each leg in and the rest of her body followed with a splash. I slipped in beside her and turned on the timer so bubbles shot out from the jets. Mom positioned herself so she had a view of the room where Meghan slept.

"What if she needs us?"

"She'll come get us, Ma. Try and relax."

"I don't think any of us are finding this very relaxing." She tilted to one side to aim a jet of water at her back, wincing as it pulsed against her.

"That's an understatement." I adjusted the strap of my suit as it slipped off my shoulder. Perhaps I'd lost weight—self-care hadn't been a priority over the last year, much less a possibility, although all I seemed to do was eat. "What I don't get is all these lies she tells to protect him, which means she knows the way he treats her is wrong, and now she's whitewashing all these years of his garbage because he's ill." I knew Bernard was abusive because I had seen it, but I also knew Meghan was an excellent liar in her own right. It made me skeptical of whether or not she was telling me the whole truth about how bad it really was, because she was definitely quick to tell me the small moments in which it was good.

"Kelly, I don't think we'll ever understand how your sister feels about Bernard. Let's talk about something else."

What else was there even to talk about? All I could think about was the looming Labour Day deadline, the small window of time we had to ensure the safety of the kids. I patted at the bubbles that floated around my neck, suddenly aware of the bits of scum lining the edge of the hot tub. "We still have the kids to worry about, Mom. He was literally screaming that he was going to kill her and that she should hurry up and die because she was a burden. A burden." I let this sink in for a moment, but she didn't respond. "And that was while I was on the phone with her. What's he doing when we aren't around?"

Mom's focus on the suite doors softened and she leaned back into the headrest, letting her body float out in the water. "Parents have to support their kids, Kelly, even when they make choices we don't like." Her cheeks had gone too red from the heat, and she tried to hoist herself onto a higher seat before slapping the water in surrender. "She was so happy on her wedding day, wasn't she? I think it was one of the worst days of my life."

A light flickered on in the bedroom and both Mom and I stiffened. Maybe Meghan called my name, or I thought I heard it, but regardless, I sprang from the water into the chilly air, then paused halfway between the hot tub and the suite as I noticed Mom wrestling herself unsuccessfully from the water. I was overwhelmed with the urge to cry.

"Kelly!" Meghan's call was insistent and tight. I bobbed frantically back and forth between the two sets of patio doors, then turned back to Mom, but she shooed me away.

"Go help your sister. I'll manage."

When I rushed into the suite, Meghan was bent over the dining table in the dark, fumbling in the bag full of syringes. "I need another dose now." She gripped at her stomach, whimpering in agony. She held a needle to me. "Will you do it? I don't want to do it. Please don't make me do it."

Panic rose as I tore off the cap with my teeth, tugged her pyjamas down and plunged the needle into the sagging flesh of her bum. When I recapped it and dropped it into the portable sharps tub, Meghan wound her arms around my waist and squeezed so tight that air honked out of me like a dog toy.

"There. You okay?" I stroked her hair until her breathing steadied.

"Will you come lay with me until I fall asleep? I don't want to be alone. I'm freaking out."

"I'm soaking wet, Meg." A puddle had formed around my feet, and what if she slipped in the night? What if Mom did? Through the living room doors I could see Mom listless on the edge of the hot tub, as though girding herself to continue. "Let me change first."

"Now, please." Plaintive. She tugged me towards the king-sized bed, where only one side of the sheets were mussed and it was evident that her body took up so little space. There were so many pillows that when she tucked herself amongst them, she practically disappeared. "Will you spoon me?"

I curled my body around hers until we nested like quotation marks. "I don't remember you being so little," I said, tracing words on her back. *I love you. Sister. I love you. I love you.* It felt backwards, this comfort, when I thought of our childhood. I was the one then who would lay awake, anxious when tree branches scraped against my window or fretting about separation from Meghan at school the next day, and she would climb under my comforter and tell me stories until I fell asleep.

"That's because I never let you get close enough to figure it out." Her voice was dreamy and I felt her slip towards unconsciousness. I matched my breath to hers in the dark, listening to the rustle of the duvet, the buzz of incoming messages on her phone. It was such a small sliver of peace that I almost felt comforted enough to sleep, before remembering everything, startling myself awake.

Once she started to snore, I stuffed towels in my place to sop up the chlorinated damp. When I emerged into the adjoining bedroom, Mom was struggling over the boundary between the bedroom's patio door and the hardwood floors. I'd left the living room doors wide open and a humid bank of air was rushing through the suite.

"Shit, Mom, I left you out there. I'm sorry. She needed some morphine and then was anxious and wanted to be cuddled and I, well . . ."

"It's okay, Moo." Mom leaned into her cane and grasped the edge of the four-poster bed, huffing from the effort. "Maybe we should all get some sleep anyways. The gods are denying us relaxation. You sure you don't want this nice big bed?" She patted the covers and looked towards the living room where my own twin bed waited.

"I'm fine out there. The bed is comfy."

I kissed her cheek, drinking in her familiar smell of Chanel. She limped towards the bathroom, shutting the door so that a bar of light shone underneath.

I tossed and turned for an hour. Too hot. Then too cold. I contemplated calling Joe but worried he'd be sleeping. I wrote in my journal, used a headlamp to read a book until I realized I'd read the same five pages over and over without any plot sinking in.

"You awake out there, Moo?" Mom called in a hoarse whisper.

I stood in the doorway in the moonlight. "Yeah. Can't sleep."

"Me either." She lifted the blankets and I crawled in beside her. "We might as well not-sleep together."

The duvet rustled noisily as Meghan's snores echoed in the bedroom next to us. "I'm constantly panicked she'll need something. It's making me scared to close my eyes."

"We need to rest while we can, Moo. It's not going to let up any time soon." Sometimes I forgot how Mom and Dad had been here before, wide awake while Meghan fought off disease, panicked about the next need, the next dose, the next increase in suffering. And maybe it was a little different then, with Meghan so young and so much life spreading out ahead. What must it have been like, passing over their toddler for doctors to slice open, with such a limited chance of survival? What was it like now, knowing their daughter would die and they would live? All of this collided to make me feel impossibly, horribly heartsick.

"I'm scared, Mom."

She tucked me in close and we slept fitfully. We woke each time the other did, cried, and fell back asleep, only to repeat the cycle.

nineteen

The lawn surrounding Meghan and Bernard's bungalow was overgrown and littered with unused cars parked under trees and kids' toys abandoned mid-play. A copse of maples and oaks lined the perimeter, and the rest of the property consisted of worn grass that often flooded in heavy rain. Bernard's looming three-storey garage dwarfed the board-and-batten house, and the truck he had crashed weeks earlier sat behind the garage with its front end caved in like a pound of butter melted in the microwave.

"Home sweet home," Joe muttered as he parked. He sounded as tired as I was.

It was the end of May, only a week after the failed spa trip. With Bernard in hospital for nearly a month and Meghan in such steep decline, Joe and I had made countless trips between Trenton and Barrie to help. We rotated in and out like exhausted wrestling tag teams, alongside other family and friends, to ensure the kids had quality time with their mother and also to keep Meghan out of hospice care. Bernard had moved in with Phyllis when he'd been released a week earlier, and since Meghan couldn't physically care for the kids on her own, there was always someone designated to supervise.

For the most part, caregiving roles split down family lines—the children spent most of their time with Phyllis at her home, with an around-the-clock group of loved ones to watch them when Sam wasn't in daycare part-time. Complicating things was that Bernard was back to work full-time, and there were access limits in place. While Family Services said Bernard could have short periods of unsupervised time with the kids, Meghan couldn't be there at the same time. So they could not be together as a full family without a supervisory adult to monitor them. And then there was Mom, Dad, and me on Team Meghan, injecting medications and fluffing pillows. The arrangement was producing a natural bitterness between the two families.

I craned my neck from side to side to stretch the permanent knot that had taken up residence there. "I don't want to go in. That house is where happiness goes to die."

Joe took my cheeks and squished them together so that my lips formed a pout, then kissed me. "You want to take a break? Go to your parents' place for a nap? I can manage things here with your sister and the kids." Phyllis had just dropped Sam and Lily off with Meghan, and we had promised to be there to help. I was already stressed about the fact that we were twenty minutes late because Meghan had begged us to grab a Tim Hortons muffin on the way and I couldn't stand denying her something she craved.

A light switched on inside the dark house and shadows moved against the wall. From the car, I could pretend it was a happy family inside.

"Honestly, when I actually sit and think of how she's suffering, I can't even stand it, Joe. Like, I literally don't think I can take another breath." Watching her fill bags with vomit and wince in pain and miss the kids and panic as death neared was the source of our family's undoing. "And if one more person tells me it can always get worse, or to be positive, I will actually kick them in the fucking face."

"Maybe it's time for a break. Seriously, go to your parents' place and take a day or two to chill."

I shook my head. "She needs us. The kids need us." What I wanted was to not be needed. And yet, at the same time, being needed was a salve, because it allowed me to focus on small acts of care in place of the greater expanse of grief.

We picked our way through muddy puddles and stomped up the deck stairs. Sam saw me and I plastered on a smile as he ran into my arms and then zipped towards Joe, who swung him around in circles.

"Gunco Joe! Mum!" Sam cried, running back to Meghan. "Gunco Joe!"

"Yes, Mommy sees Uncle and Auntie, buddy." Then, in a less cheerful voice, directed at Joe and me, "Hey, guys." It wasn't the first time I'd seen her in the borrowed hospital bed that was in the centre of the living room, but she looked much thinner than the week prior, edging closer to an ending at frightening speed.

I went to give her and Lily each a kiss. The baby smiled a gummy grin from her spot nestled at Meghan's side while slapping two balls together like cymbals. She reached for me and I popped her on my hip and raspberried her belly.

"How's the sleeping palace? Hey, it even comes with a cute sidekick."

"My kingdom," Meghan said weakly, sweeping her arm over the arrangement. Toys littered the floor, Cheerios were stuck to everything, and grimy leftovers lingered in the sink, even though someone was at the house each day to help. "At least with me out here in the living room, the kids each have their own room." Sam now had bunkbeds in the primary bedroom, and Lily's crib was set up in the second bedroom, pushed against the wall to make a spot for a tiny dresser and a bin of toys. The seven-hundred square foot house had always made me claustrophobic, but the effect was now tenfold. I wondered where Bernard would sleep once Meghan was gone—a man who routinely lamented his need for alone time—now without a bedroom of his own.

"How about I take these two outside to burn off some beans?" Joe asked, taking Lily from me. He made silly faces at her while Sam jumped up and down in place and chanted. I watched my husband in that moment and ached over how lucky I was, to have chosen and found someone so inherently good. Since he returned from his deployment, I'd not been putting enough effort into my marriage, which was another barb of guilt lodged within me.

"Outside! Outside! Outside!"

"Make sure you put your rainboots on, bud," Meghan called to Sam. "And a coat. At least a fleece." Sam buried his head in the closet, hunting for some wellies.

Once they were outside, I settled into bed with my sister, wobbling awkwardly because the mattress was air-filled to accommodate the cancerous lumps that jutted from between her ribs. I took the remote from her lap and clicked off a cartoon character mid chatter. Meghan was always deaf to the constant blare of noise.

"Any update on Bernard?"

She punched at the bed controls, adjusting us to an erect position, and took up the large bundle of chenille for her latest crochet project. In the last month she'd spent hours with a hook, manipulating chubby acrylic into throw blankets—one for each family member. *Meghan Hugs*, she said, to wrap ourselves in when she was gone. We each picked our colour, but Mom couldn't settle on one, hemming and hawing in the Michaels aisle until she burst into tears; I had snatched four balls of blue-and-white blend and rushed up to the cashier before we both lost it.

"Well, we now know he's being charged with evading police and dangerous use of a vehicle." She didn't look up from the crocheting, looping yarn at an angry speed. "Maybe attempted assault for almost running over the cops. But based on what we read online, we think his behaviour that night was because of an allergic reaction to his medication, so that'll get him out of legal trouble, I hope." She nodded to herself, as though saying it would make it true. I gripped the comforter tight. Squeezed and released. Squeezed and released. I didn't ask if doctors had confirmed her research, or what she blamed all his previous years of abuse on, but it was the answer Meghan needed and so I left it there. "Although, things are going to get worse before they get better."

"What do you mean? There cannot be some vector of hell in which this situation gets worse."

Meghan cast the crocheting at her feet and rose from the bed slowly, all of her actions like moving through molasses. In the kitchen, she set a cup under the Keurig machine. "Bernard called Children's Aid on me and told them I was giving the kids my medicinal marijuana, so they came out here to investigate." She registered the horror on my face and changed tack. "It's hard to be mad at him though, because he's sick. He just wanted to get back at me for calling the cops on him."

"You mean, for calling the cops when he was threatening to kill you."

She went silent as the machine farted out the final few drops of acidic coffee. "Anyways, the social worker lady came, and they'll have to do regular assessments. Bernard still isn't allowed in the house with us unsupervised until things calm down." She blew her nose into a piece of paper towel. I couldn't tell if the towel had been used, since there was a crushed mess of them on the counter, along with a pile of dishes that could have been clean, or dirty, or somewhere in between. I wanted to pretend that this mess was merely a by-product of her illness, but her home had always looked this way. "So, I'm dying, and I don't even get to have my husband with me without supervision." She threw the paper towel into an open garbage bag that sat on the floor, because her garbage can was full to overflowing.

"If you were me—if you were dying—wouldn't you want to spend that time with your husband? As a family?" Meghan folded her arms across her chest and glared. Yet again, I'd failed her as a confidante and in my role as the supporter she always craved. But I looked to the patio doors and watched Sam and Lily playing with Joe and didn't know how to give what she wanted of me.

"I can't begin to imagine how hard this is, but more than anything, I'd want to know my kids were safe. This is why it's a big deal that you two keep sneaking in little family nights like the law doesn't matter. Because if you're endangering your children, the law doesn't care that you're dying or if he's mentally

ill. They care about Sam and Lily." I was so impossibly weary.
I rubbed at my cheeks, felt the heat rising there.

"It's so black-and-white for you, isn't it?" she snapped. "The
perfect daughter."

"Do you think I like this, Meg? Or that everything happening right now is because Mom, Dad, and I have a hate-on for
Bernard or something? Or that I don't have compassion for the
fact that he's mentally ill? Trust me, we want the kids to have
their father in their lives, especially when their mother isn't here
anymore. Yes, I think he'll level out once he's on the right meds,
but he has always treated you like shit. You said he's not been
looking for a counsellor like he was supposed to, or going to AA or
NA or support groups. Getting well takes work, Meg. Doesn't this
scare you?" She slurped sullenly on her drink, staring at the floor,
and paced by the overflowing garbage can, the stink wafting. My
voice was reaching a crescendo, but frustration rushed out of me
like a tide. "And if he's coming around here regardless, can't he be
bothered to help out a bit? Do some laundry? Clean? Or is that
fun stuff just for us? The people who actually show you they love
you?" I spat those last words and heaved, dizzy and disoriented.
The push-pull of anxiety and anger, caregiving and wanting to be
cared for, being an aunt, a sister, and a daughter—had me pressed
so tightly that I was practically screaming, knowing I was no better
than Bernard for it.

We both cried until we were gasping and depleted. After
wiping her face on the dishtowel, she joined me on the bed as
though someone had ordered us there to make up, sitting so that
our thighs touched even though we radiated animosity. As kids,
we'd stay angry and not speak to each other for days, throwing
snide glances across our childhood bedroom. Without fail, it was

me who apologized first, desperate for her good graces, but we'd always returned to one another—and the stakes then hadn't been nearly as high.

"Why can't you see we just want to help you?" I asked, softening my tone. "To protect you and the kids?"

"You can't save me from this, Kelly. Any of it. And it's never been your job anyways."

In that moment, all I could think of was the countless choices she'd made that sparked a hero complex within me—her addictions, her relationships, her denial. But it was facing her illness, the thing no one could control, that provided the reality check I needed: assuming Meghan needed saving robbed her of agency. Maybe I'd liked the role of protector because it made me feel good and strong and worthwhile, or because it let me forget my own failings. Sitting next to her, so close to death, I grieved all the spent energy that could have been channelled to love.

"What about the kids, though?"

"Bernard would never hurt the kids. Or me. Ever." She gazed out the window, watching as Joe bounced with Sam on the trampoline and Lily plodded across the grass in a plastic exersaucer. "I haven't been able to play outside with Sam for a while. This is nice for them."

For a long time, I had kept a note on my phone titled *Things Bernard Has Done*:

- *Kicks Sam's dinky cars across room. Says, "He might as well learn now. Life doesn't always work out the way you want it." Sam cries.*
- *Calls Meghan disgusting. Calls her a bitch.*
- *Swears and screams ALL THE TIME.*
- *Throws a glass across the room. Shatters on wall. Sam is home.*

- *Orders serrated hunting knives to house "for camping"—doesn't hunt or camp.*
- *Throws knife across the room & into the wall. Blames Meg for leaving knife out. Knife was in knife block.*

I thought of the list, burning a digital hole in my pocket, and could not make sense of how she believed he'd never hurt her or the children, simply because the only marks he left were in the Gyprock.

"I'm not going to die divorced, Kelly."

And there it was.

I opened my mouth and closed it again. I didn't understand and never would; but then, I'd never been in her position. She lay next to me with her lids closed to the sunlight, and I searched her face, wondering how far to push and what I hoped to achieve. Lily's delighted screams reached us from outside, and I watched her roll on a blanket with her brother, their bodies a ball of chubby limbs.

Meghan chewed at a fingernail, still watching her children in the yard. "Get this; Phyllis thinks that family and friends should rotate days taking Bernard for lunch so he has someone to talk to. She thinks that will make him better." She covered her mouth to stifle a smile.

"He tried to run over some cops, threatened to kill you, and she thinks he needs to be taken out to lunch? Who's the one out to fucking lunch?" We both smirked a bit at this. And right then, precisely then and a million other times as well, I was overwhelmed with how much I would miss her.

"I'm scared," she said, leaning into my shoulder. "I don't want to die, Kell. I don't want to leave them." It occurred to me that she might have been playing me, using her understandable fear to end the conversation she didn't want to have. She had done it many times before.

I tugged a blanket around her arms and placed her coffee on the table nearby before she fell asleep and spilled it. As her morphine doses increased, this had already happened three other times, and I'd had to dab Polysporin on her tender, blistered skin.

"I know you are, Meggie. I'm here. I'm always going to be here."

She dropped to sleep like a switch had been flipped, both of us aware that my presence, while welcomed, was never going to be enough.

twenty

A gaggle of kids ran around Meghan's yard screaming and dashing through sprinklers. A gigantic bounce house and waterslide dominated the yard, and the whirl of the inflating pump created a perpetual hum of bass while streamers and limp balloons dangled half-heartedly from the mailbox. It was July first, and Sam was turning four. Two more months until Labour Day.

"We're late," I said to Joe, putting the car in park. We had stopped at Costco to pick up the cake as Meghan had asked, but then I'd been stumped, standing sweat-sheened in Party City trying to choose between balloons in the shape of candles, animals, or numbers for Sam, panic swelling as the employee blasted gas with a squeal.

As soon as I emerged from the car, a wall of humidity hit, making the helium selection droop. "Kid birthday parties are literally my idea of hell." I manhandled the Mylar pig that had extricated itself from the ties, swatting it into compliance.

"Meg did say you didn't have to come." Joe heaved the sheet cake from the trunk.

I know it isn't your thing, she'd said as I stabbed another needle of morphine into her thigh. I didn't say that I was coming to support her, but we felt that sentiment linger. Plus, it was too hot for Mom to be outside safely, and she and Dad wanted a Thompson representative in the face of increased tension between us and the Montaignes.

As Bernard's court proceedings chugged along, Phyllis kept insisting that he was no threat to the kids and we were wrong for even thinking it. Whether she wanted to believe it or actually did, I couldn't say, but she was asking everyone who knew them to prepare letters of support for Bernard's upcoming trial, complete with question prompts she typed out for friends and family. I had found one of the printouts on Meghan's kitchen counter and had torn it into tiny pieces.

On the lawn, the partygoing adults were lined up in patio chairs like viewers at a UFC match, watching as their children hurled themselves down the air-filled slide and sent water spraying. Muddy puddles slopped at the kids' feet as they disentangled themselves before racing back up the stairs for another go. I searched for Bernard without success. Meghan, however, was easy to spot in her chair at the centre of the action. She was wearing a loose tunic I'd given her when she was pregnant, which disguised the lumps from the tumours, and she sported her new morphine pump belt looped over her shoulder like a purse, which meant no more painful needles. Sam stood at the top of the bounce house and waved at her, then shimmied on his bum, bounced down the slide, and ran to give Meghan a sopping hug, leaving a wet print on her front.

"How's my favourite birthday boy?" I called out as I approached.

"Auntie!" Sam jumped into my arms for a hug. He smelled deliciously of dirt and damp.

"For me! Birthday!" He reached for the knot of strings.

"Another pig for my Piggy." I grasped the foil animal and scrabbled the balloon around the ground like it was hunting for truffles. He gave it a gentle kiss on the snout before tearing back to his crew of friends.

"Kell, hey." Meghan beckoned me near, then reached to draw me close.

"Sorry I'm late. They couldn't find the cake in the back and then I had some kind of balloon existential crisis."

"Doesn't matter. I want to open gifts and cut cake, like, now. Right now. I have to go inside and lie down."

"Sure. Give me fifteen minutes and we'll sort everything out, okay? Where's Bernard?"

"Around somewhere." She gestured loosely to the area beyond the garage. "The kids can still play, I just ... everyone is looking, and I don't care about talking to anyone. Just want Sam to have fun." Her words came out staccato between pants of pain.

"Who are these people anyways?" I recognized only a few of the faces. Some parents from Sam's daycare as well as Meghan's hospital roommate, Beth, and her children. Meghan shrugged as if to say *who cares?*; then the pain erased emotion from her face.

"Hey, don't worry. Your official party wrangler is on duty." I gave a mock salute.

I snapped into the role of military logistics officer and issued orders to those standing nearby, sending one of the mothers for the plates, napkins, and utensils, and another to start corralling the children from the bounce house. Towels appeared, little ones were buffed dry, and Phyllis placed the boxed Costco cake on the picnic table. The icing instantly melted in the sun, sloping drunkenly sideways.

"Can you find where in the fuck Bernard is during his son's goddamned birthday party?" I said to Joe quietly, my face wrenched into a smile but my jaw clenched. "Meghan needs to wrap this thing up before she keels over."

"Yeah, I haven't seen him at all," Joe said, sending a spray of chip crumbs onto my shirt. "I'll find him."

As if summoned, Bernard emerged from behind his workshop holding barbecue tools, even though the grill was on the other side of the lawn and the lingering scent of hot dogs indicated the meal had finished a while ago. His face was sombre as he moved in front of the cake, took the knife, and lifted to slice it.

"We haven't sung 'Happy Birthday' yet," I said, my voice sharp. The candles still sat atop the buttercream, but they slanted towards the melting pool of icing.

He said nothing but blinked back at me lazily, reeking, as always, of marijuana. He looked like he had been crying, but I didn't know how to console him, or if I wanted to. We stood staring at one another until he leaned in to light the wax number four, which cast a wobbly shade onto the car-themed cake, and then carried it to where Meghan sat with Sam in her arms. "Happy Birthday" rang out and Sam blew the candles until they hissed curls of smoke from the wicks, then sank back into his mother.

"Hey, who wants cake!" I hollered, eliciting a dozen screams. I mindlessly carved out slices with Phyllis, tension tight between us, before we corralled the children in front of Sam and watched as he tore into packages like a dervish. By the time he finished examining all his gifts, paper and ribbon were strewn across the lawn, with chunks of glitter-wrap dissolving to mush in the splash pool where the kids had returned to play. All of this, in under twenty minutes.

"Kell, inside. Help me, eh?" Meghan reached for my elbow but stumbled and I caught her before she fell. Her friend Lucy rushed to take her other arm and Meghan said nothing as we half dragged her towards the house while everyone remained entranced by the bouncy castle, the screaming kids, food. We slipped through the patio doors and then eased Meghan into bed, and I brought the sheets to her chin while Lucy made tea. It felt like we were constantly, endlessly making tea, no matter the temperature or season, because it gave us something to do.

"Oh my God. I was dying out there." Meghan clutched at her stomach and leaned her head back into the pillow. One spindly leg hung off the side of the mattress and her neck was craned awkwardly to the side.

"Seriously, I don't know how you lasted that long," I said. "It's hotter than the hubs of hell out there and I'm like boob-sweat city. You want anything? I can go find Bernard if you want and he can come lie with you?"

Lucy brought the tea to the side table and then returned silently to cleaning the kitchen. The house was littered with party prep detritus—torn bits of streamer, plastic Marvel-themed cups in stacks, and open bags of hot dog buns.

"No, I'm good." Meghan's face creased as a tide of pain washed over her, but it was quickly replaced with a smile. "Sam had a good day, didn't he?"

"Are you kidding? He's in Shangri-La. Not to mention, I think he was gifted half of Toys "R" Us."

"I can't believe my baby is four." The morphine pump ground another shot of pain control through her bloodstream and her pupils widened as her body slackened. "I made it. I wanted to still be here when he turned four." And then she was asleep. I sat and stroked her arm, the clamminess of humidity sticking us together. I turned up the air conditioner, adjusted the blankets again.

In the kitchen, Lucy scrubbed at the countertops with a J Cloth, her breath huffing a tune. "She's been waiting for this," she said. Her knuckles were white on the spongy fabric, one of Lily's baby spoons clutched tight. "Holding on for today." Lucy was one of Meghan's few friends who had stuck around over the years, although she lived across the country, which I imagined made it easier to navigate the challenges of Meghan's torn loyalties. But having her here, someone else who loved my sister deeply, suddenly overwhelmed me with gratitude that I couldn't voice.

I wordlessly picked up the dishtowel and started drying items on the rack.

"I know it sounds awful, but I feel like now she's going to go downhill quickly, without something to look forward to. It freaks me out."

I didn't answer her, pretended to need the bathroom. I ran the water in the sink and stared at myself in the mirror. My blonde pixie cut was brittle, and lines streaked my eyelids and mouth. In four days I'd be thirty-four, but felt twice that. I dried my hands on a towel that smelled of mildew and ignored Bernard's razor by the faucet, his toothbrush lined up next to Meghan and Sam's. I could have asked about it—but then again, I couldn't handle more lies, and there didn't seem a point. The result was never going to change.

twenty-one

Meghan slept with her chin on her chest in a semi-seated position to manage her constant, raging nausea, and her laboured sighs echoed through the living room. There were no curtains, so moonlight filtered in and lit Mom's position on the lounge of the sectional couch and my feet dangling near her face, where the L-shape connected. Two days after Sam's birthday, the children had moved in permanently with Phyllis, and neither Mom nor I had wanted to sleep in their empty bedrooms, farther away from our charge.

"We can't keep doing this, Mom." I didn't bother whispering. Meghan would not wake. "This is the third night we haven't slept at all." The alarm on my phone did a digital countdown and I clicked it off before it chimed, then pressed the bolus button on the morphine pump and listened to the mechanical churn of the machine injecting the medicine into her bloodstream.

Lucy had been right. The day after Sam's birthday, Meghan's pain had become unmanageable, even with the constant stream of drugs through the port on her thigh and the fentanyl patch glued to her shoulder. Three times an hour—the programmable device set a limit to prevent an overdose—she could elect for a bolus, an extra shot of morphine for intense bouts of pain. While awake, she punched at the button whenever the timer allowed. But for the last three nights, Mom, Lucy, and I had rotated on Meghan's couch, setting an alarm to press the bolus for her so that she could get some rest. Otherwise, she woke every fifteen minutes writhing in a way that I felt in my marrow.

"She needs hospice, Mom."

Meghan had been in hospice just ten days earlier, before Sam's birthday, although it had been a false alarm. All signs indicated it was the end—she'd slipped into a coma and her breathing was shallow. When I'd rushed into her room, our entire family was crammed into the small space, but it was Bernard who was at Meghan's side, tears slipping down his face as he held tight to the bed rail, and then looked me in the eye for the first time in all the years I'd known him. *There's so much we didn't get a chance to do together*, he cried. I'd softened at his emotion, so rare and dazzling, like staring at an eclipse. When it turned out Meghan was not dying that day—it was an accidental overdose from the fentanyl patch—she returned home, and the memory of the desolation written on his face was erased by renewed bitterness.

"I wanted to keep her here, in her house, as long as we could." Mom's voice cracked.

"And we did, Ma. We did that. But it's time."

"Time for what?" Meghan said with perfect clarity, suddenly awake. She swung her legs from bed with shocking agility and stalked to the bathroom. Sometimes, she moved in a way that suggested miraculous healing, but the illusion was quickly erased when she dropped to her knees and retched, funnels of vomit splashing against the toilet water. We did not ask if she wanted company, someone to put a cold cloth to her neck, because she would only wave us away. Double-layered plastic bags hung everywhere in the house. We were all well-versed in dumping runny bags of her barf down the toilet, holding the plastic by pointer finger and thumb before shoving them in the trash.

Minutes passed and Meghan continued to throw up so violently that Mom could do nothing but shake her head over and over, dabbing her pyjama sleeve at her damp cheeks.

"It should be illegal, someone suffering like this," she whimpered.

Two days later, in the administrative office of Matthews House Hospice, I balled my soggy tissues and forced them into my already full pockets. The day had a surreal quality to it, as though I was dreaming, or watching a film of my own life.

An hour earlier, Mom, Dad, and I had picked Meghan up at home and carried her belongings to the car. Before we left, Meghan lingered in the doorway of each of the small rooms, caressed light switches, neatly folded the children's blankets on their beds, the ones she crocheted with such care. *Bye*, she whispered to her house, sobbing all the way to the car, where I eased her into the front seat of Dad's SUV. I followed in my Volkswagen and cried until my ribs hurt, a feeling of breaking open. What was it like to drive your daughter to the place where she would die? And what was it like to drive past shops where you'd bought diapers, farms where you'd let your son pick berries, and know you'd never see those things again?

"So, you're the power of attorney then?" the nurse asked while reading the form for what felt like the third time. I'd given the woman three documents, including standard POA paperwork issued by the Ontario government, the one-page will that named me as executor, and Meghan's burial plans with proof of payment. The funeral home director had arranged to meet Meghan and Bernard at their house, but Bernard called an hour prior to the appointment and said he wouldn't be coming. *I'm too tired. I'm going to have a nap.* When she challenged him, he'd screamed a string of profanity and hung up, leaving her holding the dead cell. I pretended not to hear while I washed the dishes, pretended I didn't want to drive over to Phyllis's to strangle him. It was Dad and I who opened the door to the director, accepted his glossy pamphlets, and sat at Meghan's side while she checked off the most basic items on the ordering form. She elected cremation in a plain pine box with no funeral, her ashes divided: one lot to Mom, Dad, and me, and the other to Bernard. Viewing? No. Embalming? No. Still, the $3,000 price tag concerned her, although she'd stashed money in a separate account and sent me to pay the invoice in advance.

"Yes. I'm POA." I snatched a tissue from the box of scratchy single-ply on the nurse's desk. Whenever I had a moment away from Mom, Dad, and Meghan, I melted, unable to contain everything I felt.

"But she's married. Your sister."

"Yes, well, he's an abusive asshole so she picked me instead." I left it there, this pregnant statement, in the space between us. I'd started to make this proclamation—that my sister was abused—without regard for decorum, liking the way the words slipped from my mouth after years of stifling them. But I hated being forced to say it, to voice what was already answered by legal forms.

"Is he out of the picture then? The husband? They separated?" The photocopier spat out copies of Meghan's documents. All the hard choices would be mine, Bernard absolved.

"No. Still together."

"And legally? You say he's abusive, but is he allowed to visit or are there any protection orders in place?" She held up a finger as if to silence me before I answered. "I'd remind you to think of what your sister wants here."

I wanted to slap her. It seemed that as a family, we'd spent a lifetime trying to figure out what Meghan wanted and how to give it to her, even when she'd been unsure herself. I tapped my pen on the table to some unheard beat, trying to tamp down the desire to answer in the negative. *No. Don't let him in.* The idea made me giddy.

"Yes, he's allowed to visit."

She nodded and passed me the admitting paperwork, writing Meghan's name on the whiteboard above the nursing station. Patient Name: Meghan Montaigne. Date Admitted: July 9, 2018. Diagnosis: Metastatic Leiomyosarcoma. Age: 37. The board was smeared with black and red, identities added and erased with the swipe of a felted brush.

"She's not thirty-seven for another two weeks," I said, fixated on the chart. "She wouldn't like that." The sobs rose again, and I had to lean forward, head between my knees. I wanted to tell the nurse our story so that she understood: how I was supposed to be born on Meghan's birthday, July 18, but she had chemo the week I was due, so Mom was induced and my sister had considered me the best of early birthday presents. I had turned thirty-four only days ago, and we'd always enjoyed this small window of time of being only two years apart instead of three. I wanted this stranger to know this tiny detail of our lives so she could glean just one, singular element of our sisterhood, see Meghan as the person beyond the patient. But Meghan was in her hospice room, settling into the place she had come to die, and how on earth could I be okay when next year I would turn thirty-five without a sister to turn thirty-eight?

The nurse sighed as though I'd caused her some great, pointless hardship. She wiped the seven from the board, replaced it with a six.

twenty-two

The hospice lobby was brand new, light-filled and colourful, with the gardens spread out past the window behind the registration desk. The volunteer, Shirley, stood and hugged me like we'd been friends for years and not just a week.

"Hi there, girl. How're you keeping?" Shirley spent more hours at the hospice than not, operating the visitor login sheet. "You on the late shift today?"

Never leave me alone. That was all Meghan had asked of us, and so I stopped shuttling back to Trenton and moved into Mom and Dad's so that my parents and I could rotate in twenty-four-hour shifts. Despite his boss's offer of compassionate leave, Bernard came only on Friday evenings and left early Saturday morning. A nurse was horrified to relay to me his complaint that Meghan was barely conscious most of the time. *What's the point in visiting?* he'd asked, as if he genuinely wanted to know.

"Nurse Kelly reporting for duty. Hey, did your son get that job he was after?"

"He did!" She adjusted my cardigan around my shoulders, and I felt the vibration of her palsy. "You're so kind to remember."

"Good for him. Also, I wanted to make sure you knew that Meghan has asked for no other visitors. From here on out it's just me, my parents, and her husband allowed."

"Yup, I've got that on my little notepad here. The nurses came by when she made the request this afternoon, so we'll ensure no one else is permitted. Taken a turn, has she?" Shirley still had my lapel gripped tight, with her knotted joints radiating heat.

"I think she's just tired, and people stay longer than she wants them to and don't really get the hint." When Meghan had posted on Facebook that she'd entered hospice, a host of visitors appeared, mostly people she hadn't seen in years. At first, she welcomed everyone and asked me to set up a roster so she didn't get overwhelmed. They arrived at the hospice with gifts—flowers that went crisp with lack of watering, photos she asked me to throw away afterwards, prayer beads—and stood at the end of her bed, afraid to touch her as they stumbled through strangled goodbyes. Meghan had started to wonder aloud where all these people had been when she'd been healthy. *What do they want from me?* she asked when they left. I was grateful the initial flurry had dissipated into a trickle—a handful of constant friends—because I was jealous, hungry for all of Meghan's time.

Shirley nudged me with her elbow. "It's like that, isn't it? People like to attach themselves to grief. Suddenly the person dying is their best friend, and they have all these 'memories' they have to share. Gimme a break." She tapped her forehead with a coral-painted fingertip. "That's experience talking."

"I should get to her now."

"Yes, you go. I'll bring you both a mint tea."

Meghan stirred when I opened the door to room ten and dropped my overnight bag by the windows. There had been a considered effort to make the room less clinical—gorgeous French doors swung onto a patio; a built-in twin bed, too short for me to stretch out in, was under the windowsill; there were quilts for bedding instead of hospital-like blankets and oversized recliners that seemed like an afterthought and didn't quite fit in the room. But it was impossible to ignore the sponge swabs for moistening dry mouths, sanitizing wipes, basins to hold vomit, and grab bars for accessibility. A chalkboard tacked to the wall behind Meghan's bed encouraged family to write loving missives in multicoloured chalk, but its presence, behind her head where she couldn't see it, was inexplicably offensive to me.

"Guess what I found?" I rattled the contents of a tote bag.

"You don't need to keep buying me stuff," Meghan said, struggling to sit up in bed. "But keep doing it."

"You said you wanted something different to drink." I counted the criteria on my fingers. "Not too sweet. Low acidity. Not dairy-based. No fizz. You complicated cow." I revealed a small jug of watermelon juice, gave it a shake so the pink liquid slopped back and forth in the plastic. "Ta-dah."

"I knew you were the one up to the task. Load me up." She gestured to a stack of waxed Dixie cups, the kind our grandparents used to keep in a dispenser in their bathroom and that Meghan and I would fight over who was next to tug one from the plastic tower. I filled a cup halfway and Meghan took a grateful sip and smacked her lips. "Oh, I needed that."

"You'll revisit it later when you barf it back up." I slurped straight from the container.

"Then it'll be tasty twice. Come sit with me." She patted the quilt on the bed and I snuggled in beside her. "You stink like chlorine."

"I did some laps at the pool this morning." At the gym, I had stretched my arms into a calm rhythm, but each time I cocked my neck to breathe, I felt like I was drowning. I'd only managed six lengths before I ran from the pool and had a panic attack in the changing stall. The attacks were getting more frequent; stress-induced, I imagined. But more than that, I didn't feel I deserved those quiet reprieves—not when everyone I loved was suffering so deeply.

"Remember when we used to play Little Mermaid?" Meghan asked. At the beach as kids, we took to re-enacting our favourite Disney movie, me always the villain, loping after my sister with my water wings in my best octopus-monster impression while Meghan flounced mermaid-like with delicately pointed toes. She had tiny, perfect feet that I'd always been jealous of. It felt silly, suddenly, to be jealous of feet.

"Of course. I'm just biding my time until you're gone so I finally get to be Ariel. No more sidekick for this girl."

"Oh, come on," Meghan said, laughing. The sound was a balm. "Younger sisters are supposed to come second. I wouldn't even be Ursula now. I'm like those mermaids she turned into creepy crawlies that sucked at people's arms." She flexed her hands into claws and pawed at my shirt, bulging her eyes like one of Ursula's sea polyps. I wanted to laugh and cry all at once.

"And yet, how are you still so beautiful?" My voice broke while I struggled to contain myself. There was nothing particularly beautiful about Meghan walking death's tightrope, but it still felt true. A few nights ago, the hospice superintendent had come by to install her bathroom mirror, working away while she slept. She'd be pleased, he thought, to have it replaced. Instead, she'd wandered into the bathroom and become so hysterical at the sight of her reflection that the doctor had had to sedate her. Each day was a stark difference in her appearance.

I watched as her pulse beat in her neck. She was still alive, still there. The air conditioning kicked in again, a constant, perpetual din. It made the space soggy with condensation—the blankets, the pyjamas in the drawer, the slippers I left neatly in the corner, my shower kit tucked away in the dresser.

"Hey, can you fix the picture for me?" She pointed to the TV stand, where the photo of Sam and Lily was knocked askew. It was sunny and warm the day Lucy had done the photoshoot for her. Meghan had had her makeup done, long fake eyelashes looking gaudy on her gaunt face. Bernard hadn't shown up that day, or hadn't been invited in the first place, I couldn't recall, but whatever the reason, he wasn't there, and, looking at the kids— Sam leaning in to kiss Lily's nose—resentment stirred inside me. The only other photo on display was one of Meghan and me at my wedding, me staring at the camera and Meghan looking up at me with something like awe—admiration, maybe. "Turn them towards me so I can see?"

I stood to tilt the frames in her direction. "Want me to find a picture of you and Bernard? I can grab one of your wedding shots from home."

She shook her head. "I have lots on my phone."

"Turning down a chance to fawn over your man? Has the world spun off its axis?" I crawled back in next to her as an overwhelming sweep of fear took over. When she stayed silent, a burp of watermelon juice lurched up my esophagus. I knew that if I didn't throw caution to the proverbial wind, I might never have another chance. "Why doesn't Bernard like us, Meg?" I knew we would never like Bernard, and he would never like us. Not even the kids, it seemed, created a space of neutrality.

"What? He likes you." Even she didn't sound convinced.

"You know he doesn't. He tolerates Mom, maybe. But not me. Not Dad."

"I know he was hurt by what you guys said when Children's Aid interviewed you. You know, that you thought he was a danger to the kids and stuff."

"I couldn't give a shit less if it hurt him, Meg, because it was true. Even you admitted that. It feels like everything is escalating, though, and we're worried that we won't be allowed to see the kids once you're gone."

"He would never. Ever." She sat up in bed, alert. "He knows what that would mean to me."

I swallowed hard, felt the unmoveable ball of emotion lodged in my throat. "Would you consider putting that down somewhere? Like, on paper? Legally?" I'd talked to a lawyer friend who'd said it might mean nothing in court, but still, it would show intent. I wanted to believe it would never get to a courtroom, but the closer we got to Meghan's death, the less sure I was. Bernard mostly ignored my texts, although he did take one of Mom's calls and had sobbed the entire time while Mom said soothing things to him and Dad and I stared in disbelief. I imagined, in the future, asking to take the kids camping or for a picnic and having the calls sent direct to voicemail.

"No way, Kell. No, I won't do that to him. What does that say about my husband?"

"This isn't about him, Meg. It's about making sure the kids

have a connection to their mother once she's gone." Part of her had to know. Somewhere deep that she didn't dare look, Meghan knew it would come to this, knew more than she would ever tell us. I wanted her to face that reality, even though I, too, was desperate to join her in her fantasy world of happiness. But we were running out of time, and as that hourglass drained of sand, it was clear that with it was Meghan's hope that once Bernard was properly medicated, he would change.

"Like I said, there's no need. He wouldn't do that to me or the kids. Ever. End of discussion."

I was painfully uncomfortable, edged in like a sardine. It had always been like this, really: me pressed against Meghan's choices. And then the words came and I could not stop them. "Meg, why didn't you ever leave?" My voice was soft. We'd had this argument so many times, but I'd never asked outright, always silenced by her anger. Thing was, it wasn't the dying that she was mad about: it was the shitty marriage, the arena of life in which she'd so wanted to succeed.

When I turned over to face her, Meghan was asleep, twitching in a medication-infused dream. I let her rest, my unanswered question dissipating into the air-conditioned void. I stared up at the dropped ceiling, counted the tiny perforations until she snapped awake, the medication having settled in her bloodstream. The moment was gone, which may have been her intention. Or maybe it was mine.

twenty-three

Meghan said, unequivocally, that we were not to acknowledge her birthday with her in hospice. Ten days there had not changed her mind: No cards. No presents. No celebration of any kind. Who wanted to celebrate a birthday when there would never be another? Still, Mom, Dad, and I gathered in her room to celebrate-not-celebrate her and made forced conversation.

Dad paced by the window, checking and rechecking the weather app on his phone, even though we spent almost every moment of every day inside. Mom sat on the daybed, her cane resting across her knee, watching her husband wander.

"Bill, why don't you sit?" Mom tugged on his shirt to gesture to the spot beside her, but he turned back to the window with his hands stuffed in his pockets.

"You guys going to sit and stare at me all day?" Meghan asked. "I'm not going anywhere. Still here, dying." Her ability to cling to humour impressed and surprised me. I'd changed her into a fresh nightie, a children's size that was shockingly loose, but the bright pop of pink was pretty against her pale skin.

"You might be the sassiest dying person alive," I said to her, flopping into the corduroy recliner by her bed.

"Will you two ever stop?" Mom couldn't suppress her smile.

"Yeah, I don't like this talk." Dad was staring at the spot where the smokers congregated near the green hydro box, and his orange fingertips tapped his chest pocket as if ensuring his pack was safe inside.

"Us? Nope. Death jokes to the bitter end." Meghan thrust a fist in the air. "Bitter end. Get it?"

I snorted and dramatically mouthed the words *Don't leave me alone with them.* Her grin of complicity washed over me like warm bathwater.

"Hello? Hello in there, birthday girl!" a familiar voice called from the hallway. Meghan's face widened in horror when Phyllis popped into the room with an exhausting level of energy, Sam and Lily following behind her. Mom, Dad, and I gawped at one another. Meghan had forbidden all visitors, Phyllis included, but it hadn't stopped the woman from pressing to bring the kids in because they missed their mother and she thought it was what Meghan wanted, too. Part of me understood—we were all fretting over the loss of connection Sam and Lily must have been feeling but were unsure of how to handle it because it was inevitable, devasting, too much to bear. What Phyllis didn't seem to appreciate was that seeing their mom wouldn't be the comfort she imagined for the children or my sister. If Meghan was frightened by her own reflection, what would her children see, especially when they were too young to understand the change? And what was it like for Meghan to see them and feel such impending grief of her own? So we left it to Meghan to dictate if she wanted Sam and Lily to visit, because she hated having parenting decisions made by others as though she wasn't still here, capable of making them herself. But she hadn't asked. Not once. *I'll scare them, Kell.*

There was no time to calculate how Phyllis had gained entry, because she launched into a round of birthday wishes. One of the nurses peeked into the room with a Dairy Queen log cake, the start of "Happy Birthday" echoing until Sam caught on. Mom, Dad, and I sang obligingly and smiled while feeling none of the emotions that usually went along with this ritual. We watched as Sam clambered up the hospital bed to help blow out the lone candle with a slobbery puff of air. Meghan pasted on a grin that belied countless emotions—fear, anger, love. She kissed Sam all over his face as the nurse sliced the dessert and we slurped at melting ice cream cake, unsure of what to say.

"They miss you so much," Phyllis said cheerfully. She had Lily balanced on her lap, but she lowered her to the ground where she wobbled but righted herself. "See how big they're getting? I bet you notice a huge change, right?"

Meghan didn't respond as she wiped a smear of ice cream from Sam's cheek. The tension in the room was thick.

"Lily, come see Mommy. Let's have a cuddle with your brother." Meghan held her spindly arms out, but it was as if the baby didn't hear. Lily wandered out the hall to test her new walking abilities, even as Meghan kept calling to her.

"Look at her go!" Phyllis laughed as she scooped another bite of cake. She was trying, I knew, but was so far off the mark that I had to fight the desire to kick her out.

"You know what kids are like, Meggie," Mom interjected.

"Once they learn how to move, nothing can keep them confined to one spot for long."

"That's right. You were the same way," Dad said. "Always on the go."

Meghan shook her head over and over, bottom lip wobbling. "She doesn't remember me."

Dad threw his cake in the garbage and left to chase Lily down the hall. I couldn't stand any of it, so I stared at the painting on the wall, some landscape thing, and dreamt of being in that grassy hedge, somewhere far away from room ten.

———————

Later, melted dairy coagulated on paper plates while the kids played in the grassy courtyard of the hospice. Stubby boxwoods formed a diamond pattern that criss-crossed with paving stones, capped by a cedar gazebo that smelled like summer docks heated by the sun. I chased Sam through the sunlight as he deked to the left and I ran towards his happy squeals. Then he halted in his tracks and whipped around to face me and I almost smacked right into him.

"Auntie, my truck has cancer like Mommy." He held a dinky car up as evidence, appearing stoic at this diagnosis. I had nothing to say to this, nothing at all, so I scooped him into my arms and held him upside down, marvelled at his face that was a perfect reflection of my sister's when she was four.

"Can someone take me inside?" Meghan called out. Despite the heat wave, Meghan was draped in blankets on the bench we'd managed to set her on. She was green with pain and nausea.

We'd had to balance her on a tuffet of pillows to accommodate her bed sores, but even so, she'd only lasted ten minutes.

"Mum, no!" Sam wriggled free from me and ran to Meghan, flinging himself into her arms. It made her wince, but she leaned into the hug, covering his cheeks with kisses.

"I'm sorry, Sammy, but Mommy's tummy hurts. She needs to go lie down."

Sam did not complain that Mommy always hurt, or that Mommy was always lying down. Instead, he watched as the nurses carried her indoors and laid her gently on her bed, tucked in the blankets, pressed the morphine bolus. Her eyes rolled drunkenly while Sam watched, his grip tight on the hospital sheets at her feet.

"You want to lie with Mommy for a while, bud?"

He nodded and reached for me to lift him, sinking into her as her arms reflexively snaked around his shoulders. They fell asleep holding one another and I watched them from the recliner, tears wet on my cheeks, while our parents managed Phyllis and Lily outside.

This was the reason she hadn't asked to see the children, because she knew it would be like this. Somehow it was clear to me that this would be the last time she would see them, but we never spoke of it. Of all the horrible things we'd had to endure in the past year, this was the harshest truth, the one we couldn't face.

twenty-four

"She's such an attention whore, am I right?" I said to Annie, our favourite nurse, while rubbing Meghan's cold feet with lavender oil. "My sister and her cancer, making it all about her." The jokes, I hoped, allowed Meghan to transport herself somewhere else as the nurse fiddled with the morphine pump settings. Despite hallucinations and a dosage that should have doped a farm animal, Meghan's pain management needs keep increasing. Earlier in the morning, she had woken me with detailed descriptions of her new magic beans. Did I want some? *And look, look, Kelly, at my new compact*, and she patted on invisible powder with a puff, then lined her pout with air lipstick.

"Everything in the world is all about me," Meghan croaked, pawing at her dry throat. She had grown too weak to hold a water glass, so I wiggled the straw until it met her lips, then used my sleeve to dab at the dribble down her chin. After four weeks in hospice, her body was failing by slow degrees. When I noticed she hadn't peed in more than twenty-four hours, the nurses inserted a catheter, and a gush of orange urine filled the waiting bag. Her pulse was slowing and her skin was taut against bone. When she slept, I took videos of her breathing, photos of her hands, documenting what I feared I'd miss when she was gone.

"Don't we know it, lady!" Annie tucked Meghan neatly into the blankets she'd brought fresh from the industrial warmer. The material filled the room with the scent of bleach. "Then again, as our longest-term resident, you get all the extra attention you want."

Even though it had only been a month, it felt like an impossibly long time. Other residents came and went, literally, within days. But in the context of dying, Meghan was young: her heart, at least, was healthy, and this kept her going even when Mom, Dad, and I dreamt—out of compassion, selfishness, exhaustion—that her pain would end. *I have never, ever seen anyone suffer like this*, Annie had said to me last week, tearing up as she folded me into a hug, her soft body like a favourite pillow. I was relieved, oddly, to know this was as bad as it could get, and yet part of me knew it could be, had been, so much worse outside of the hospice. In room ten she was loved, safe, could focus on the labour of dying. Death wasn't the saddest thing compared to all that came before.

"That's me," Meghan said, grimacing as she adjusted herself in bed. "Always knew I'd break some kind of record."

"And longest-lasting hospice resident is the record you wanted to set? You need loftier goals, Meg." I wiped excess oil onto the warm blanket, sinking my fingertips into the heat.

"Well, you and your parents have been here every day too," Annie said to me. "You two are like our sister warriors." She pressed to smooth Meghan's fentanyl patch on her upper arm and wiggled her fingers goodbye.

"She's right," Meghan said once we were alone. "You've practically moved in here. You should go home. Enjoy some time with Joe. Pot Roast, too."

I climbed into Meghan's bed as usual.

"Meg, wherever you are, that's where I am. Okay? I'm not going anywhere."

She patted my leg over and over until the gesture no longer felt intentional, more like a nervous tic. "I'm tired, Kell. I'm always so tired."

"We can clean you up before bed, if you want. Get you nice and warm."

"It's too much work."

"Stop being so lazy. Let's get you in the shower, eh? You stink." I held my nose for comedic effect.

"Do I?" She sniffed a pit in response, moving in perpetual slow-motion.

"Of course not." If she knew I was lying, she didn't say. My sister smelled of rot, likely because her coccyx was exposed from weight loss, gangrenous around the edges, with the rest of her covered in a scaly rash, weeping bedsores. When I handled these delicate edges of her, I tried to picture her former self—plump cheeks and dimpled thighs, just like mine. "But it'll make you feel better."

She acquiesced and raised her arms like a child reaching for her mother, and I lifted her up and into the wheelchair, then pushed her across the hall to the bathroom. I lay a towel across her for modesty and then tugged the nightgown over her head, leaving it in a heap for laundry.

"You've seen a lot more of me than anyone wants to see of their sister." Meghan signalled to her nudity. "I'm starting to lose count of how many times you've literally had to wash me."

I set the water on warm and dangled fingertips in the stream to test the heat, then locked the shower seat into place, stepping over the tiled lip that kept the water from seeping out the door.

"I am but your lowly servant. Ready?" I squatted in front of her and held my arms out for her to grab.

"I'm not sure I'll be able to step over that," she said, looking towards the shower curb. Tension tipped her voice upwards.

"We'll manage, Meg, don't worry. I've got you." I imagined she didn't even weigh seventy pounds, not even as much as Pot Roast. I wrapped my arms under her armpits, lifted up until she was standing facing me. Together, we waddled, me moving backwards towards the spray. Slowly, like she was gliding across water, Meghan lifted one leg, then another, across the boundary before she started to shake with weakness.

"Kelly, oh my God, no." Meghan let out a long, continuous wail as her legs gave way beneath her, strength seeping towards the drain. "I'm falling, Kell. I'm gonna fall. Don't let me fall!" I widened my stance, which set me directly in front of the water's stream, and as I tightened my arms around her, her face pressed into my chest so that I worried I would smother her. Water poured over us, into our mouths, and still, she wailed this animalistic sound.

"Meg. Meghan! Calm down. I'm not going to drop you. You're safe. You're okay." Her skin slipped against mine, but I somehow managed to ease her into the shower seat and tilt the nozzle towards her lap instead of her face. Placed there, she breathed heavily to recover. My heart raced with abject terror.

"I'm sorry," she said, voice small as she held tight to the edges of the seat. "I freaked out."

"Hey, we made it, right?" I gave a weak smile and stepped out of the water to grab body wash and a cloth.

"Oh my God. Your clothes are soaked."

"I have other clothes here. Not a big deal."

"No, Kell." She kissed my knuckles like I was a princess. "It's a big deal. The biggest."

I kissed the crown of her head and then gently glided a soapy washcloth across her fragile skin. Meghan leaned into the spray, murmuring with pleasure from the heat, opening her mouth to let water trickle in, then allowing it to dribble down her front. I took tender care around her new sharp edges. The terrycloth, I feared, was scraping her skin, so eventually I abandoned the cloth to allow my hands to do the work, savouring the strange intimacy of her naked body so boldly bared. After soaping and conditioning her hair, we laboured through the process in reverse, getting her dry and back into the wheelchair in a new pair of pyjamas before I tucked her back into bed and changed my own clothes.

"That was exhausting," she said, tugging the blankets to her chin. "But worth it. I'm snug as a bug. Will you read to me to help me fall asleep? From your book?"

"I thought you just wanted to listen to me type all day." In the brief moments when she slept soundly, I worked on my book, determined, out of some sense of duty to Meghan, not to ask my publisher for an extension. We didn't talk about how she'd be long dead by the time my dream would actualize. A year away.

"I just like the sound of you working, doing what you love. You know, your next book should be about you and me. Christ knows I've given you enough material. You'd have to tell it all, though. All the ugliness." She grunted a laugh but clutched her sore stomach. The sun dipped behind the horizon and the room sank into semi-darkness.

"Knock, knock." Annie popped her head in. "Hey, dolls. Meg, you up for something to help you get to la-la-land tonight?" She rattled a pill in a tiny plastic cup and wobbled a thumbs-up.

"Oh, I'm fine. I don't need anything," Meghan said.

"You sure, hun? Might help with the anxiety."

No matter who was spending the night, Meghan woke us countless times, panic taking over. My subconscious had started to wait for these tides of fear so that I was prepared to get up from the daybed and snap on the TV to distract, crack a joke, get a cup of tea. But my tactics were waning in their efficacy.

"I just don't think I should," she said uneasily. "I don't want sedatives to become my way of coping. It's not healthy, right?"

"Healthy? You mean because you did drugs seven years ago?" I rubbed fingertips up and down her arm. She nodded, looking ashamed. I couldn't help snorting. "Geez, Meg, I admire the dedication, but I think when you're dying you get to throw addiction caution to the wind."

"Really?" She fiddled nervously with the edge of the sheet and looked to Annie. "You sure?"

"What's the worst that can happen? An overdose?"

"Think of me as your dealer, gorgeous. A legal dealer." She gave Meghan's foot a loving squeeze and put the plastic cup on her lap. "It's all about peace and comfort now. Let us give you that. Let the Gucci meds give you that."

Once Annie left, Meghan pointed for some water, then strained to ease a slip of liquid up the straw to make the pill disappear.

"I hope that works. God, Kell, I'm freaking out." What was there to say to this? She swallowed over and over until I brought the barf bucket to her chest, but she shook her head and pushed it away. Each day, she heaved litre upon litre of barf into the plastic tubs we held for her. Sometimes I willed myself in place despite my phobia; other times I ran down the hall in a panic, calling for a nurse. When I returned to the hospice after a night at Mom and Dad's, I approached the room anxious, tired, desperate for the end, and then hated myself for that horrible, dark desire. "I wish there was something they could give me to just knock me out. I mean, what am I waiting for?" Her eyelids bobbed and so did her chin, the medication taking effect. "But then, I guess that would be asking them to kill me, wouldn't it?"

How many times had I wondered what she was waiting for? Because there was no perfect ending to hold out for. The kids would lose their mother and Bernard was not going to suddenly atone so that she could slip peacefully towards some cheesy light. It felt like she was waiting for a fairy tale.

"So, not just something to help you sleep," I said carefully. "Is that what you mean?" I wanted her to mean it, wanted the pain-free release of an assisted death, for her, and for us.

"I don't know what I mean, Kell."

"If you're ready for that, then I'll talk to the doctor for you tomorrow, okay?"

"Yeah. Maybe."

When I asked her about the conversation the following morning, she claimed to not remember. But my sister had never been good at lying to me.

twenty-five

"So," Dr. Mohabi said, leaning into Meghan's bedside, bobbing a loafered foot up and down. Her neat blonde hair and tidy grooming was a stark contrast to the rest of us, who looked post-apocalyptic from lack of sleep and showering. Mom, Dad, Meghan, some nurses, and I had collected in room ten for the meeting the doctor had called, and we were packed in tight and uncomfortable. "I think it's time we talked palliative sedation to help ease your suffering here, Meghan."

The doctor explained that Meghan would receive the drug Versed through a continuous pump, much like her morphine, which would slip her into a twilight zone of consciousness, somewhat aware of her surroundings but unable to communicate. She would not be able to eat or drink and would die in days. *To help ease your suffering.* In the past week, in addition to the litres of vomit, Meghan steadily spat up bile like tobacco juice into a spittoon. She was in constant, moan-filled pain. She couldn't stand. Couldn't shower. Had a catheter and a diaper, her dignity disintegrating like her skin.

Dr. Mohabi barely had time to finish her sentence. "Yup. I'm ready," Meghan croaked, lids squeezed shut. I looked to her, shocked, having expected some fight, for her to ask questions. To say she needed more time. To ask to see the kids. To wait for Bernard. I'd been waiting for this—some guaranteed end-state— but now it was happening so fast.

Mom and Dad were clutching one another awkwardly at their elbows, tears sneaking down their cheeks, while I leaned into the wall and pressed myself against the cold in the hope that I would find something tangible and assured. Meghan retched another glob of black bile into a kidney basin, and Mom leaned in to smooth her hair from her face.

"It's just barf," Meghan said, her mouth curved into a weak smile. "I'm not dead yet, guys." She tried to waggle her fingers like a ghost, but the effect was too limp to be funny. Still, we laughed anyways.

This is the right choice. This is the right choice. I repeated this over and over in my head, because the doctor had said it would stop her pain. But all I could think of was how Meghan wouldn't be able to communicate. If she couldn't talk, how would we know if she was hurting? And then it dawned on me that this was the very last day I would hear her voice or feel her touch me or listen as she cracked some horrible, death-themed joke that only we would understand. I pulled my sweater close and leaned in to rub Meghan's feet, sitting gingerly on the edge of the mattress. She gave a thumbs-up.

"Okay, let's get this party started," she said, her gaze not leaving mine. "Ready when you are." The doctor and nurses shuffled into action, disappearing to leave our family alone. The moment they left the room, Meghan pointed at me weakly. "I didn't like that. All those people at once. I was like a circus sideshow or something. Everyone staring."

I watched her, uncertain if she was legitimately angry or just wanted to focus on something beyond what was about to happen.

"They just wanted you to feel supported."

Sisters, I'd read once, can communicate telekinetically if they concentrate hard enough and can form a bond akin to that between twins. I tried to tell her without words how brave she was, how effervescently funny, how much I couldn't stand to let her go.

"Hey, can you take this?" She pushed her phone to me. It had remained at her side the entire time we'd been in hospice, texts serving as her only connection to Bernard. She had written the passcode down weeks ago and sealed it in an envelope but I had left that at Mom and Dad's, hoping, somehow, I'd never need to use it. "You know, for my passwords and stuff when you're exec-utor." When I took it, our fingertips touched: mine warm and clammy; hers bony, cold, and dry. Always opposites. "There's stuff on here, Kell. Stuff to keep."

"Sure, Meg." I dropped it into my purse as if it had burnt me. "Stuff?"

She didn't answer my question and, instead, wiped at her mouth with the corner of the quilt. "Can you tell Bernard what's going on?"

I sat at the end of the bed and rubbed the callous on the ball of her foot, pressing gently as I parsed her words. She did not ask me to have him to come. She did not ask to say goodbye to her husband, to have us call so she could hear his voice. She didn't dial his number right then and ask for a private moment.

"Of course I will, Meg. I'll call right now."

"Not now. Just wait, for a few minutes." Only then did she look afraid, and Mom and Dad each reached out to hold a section of her arm. "A few more minutes."

"We're all here, Meggie," Dad said. "We're not going anywhere." He looked so tired, aged two decades in the last two months. His head tilted towards Meghan's, and Mom stood to his left, their pain caught in the light like dust motes. But I couldn't think of it, couldn't focus on them because it was too much. All of it, too much.

The nurse approached with the Versed pump and touched me on the shoulder. "Excuse me, sweetheart." I stood to make room, hovering as the nurse slipped another IV into Meghan's deflated thigh. I leaned against the wall to catch my breath, tried to time mine to Meghan's, but hers was so shallow that I soon felt faint from the effort. The pump whirled and Meghan's body relaxed into the mattress as we told her over and over what we needed her to hear.

"I love you."

"We love you, Meggie."

"Love you so much."

She looked to have fallen asleep. The room heaved a sigh of relief but the tension remained hungry and consuming. Meghan had taught each of us the frustration and regret that came with ending conversations angry or not at all. We couldn't bear it happening one last time.

———

"Kelly, can I see you a minute?"

Mallory, the RN on duty the next morning, must have heard me coming down the hall, the buckle on my sandals making a sharp slap with each step. Mom had stayed the night and Dad and I had returned with a duffle of belongings from home, not intending to leave until we left as a family.

"Sure," I said, wheeling into the nursing station. Dad continued ahead to join Mom and Meghan. "What's up?"

Several staff members sat together in the station while some lingered in the office doorways. Five friendly faces greeted me, faces I knew and loved. I knew that Sarah the RPN had a son who needed expensive dental work, that Beverly was about to run a marathon, that Max and his wife had dreamed of being parents, but when they couldn't conceive, they chose to care for the residents in the hospice. In six weeks, these people, my sister's caregivers, had become more like family than people paid to offer support.

"The sedation level isn't quite where we need it, and Meghan is still awake and chatting away." Mallory stopped, leaving me to fill in the space.

"She needs a higher dose then? Of the Versed?" The answer seemed logical to me.

"Yes, well, that's the thing. I went in to up it and Meghan waved me off. Said she was fine. But she's still in a lot of pain. She's still dealing with all that bile, which is exactly why she's on the sedation—so that she doesn't have to suffer. I turned to your mom to see what she thought was best, but she just defers to your sister. At this point, we think Meghan doesn't want to up the dose out of fear, which we understand, but we also know she's in agony and not necessarily in the right state of mind, considering she agreed to this so assuredly yesterday and, to be honest, is medicated to a point she's not fully capable of making such a big decision."

"So, what you're saying is I have to decide. As power of attorney." I clung to the strap of my purse. So close. I had been so close to not having to make any hard choices.

"We support both you and Meghan, of course, in whatever you decide. But she chose the sedation, and now she might need you to be strong enough to choose to increase it."

I swallowed, but the ball in my throat would not move. "Can I just pop in and see her first? Go from there?"

"Of course." Mallory gave me a sympathetic smile.

I didn't move though, rooted there biting my lip, wanting to say something else, wanting to ask more questions I already knew the answer to. In making this choice, was I stifling her spirit? Robbing her of peace? Putting her down like a dog? Taking away chances for more goodbyes and last-minute visits with the kids? What if there were more things to say and we hadn't yet said them?

"We get it, honey," said Annie. "There's no right answer here. Go have a chat with your sister. You know where we are."

I spun on my heel and rushed into Meghan's room. "Hi, Meg." Her lids opened lazily, her irises rolling to the ceiling. Mom sat uncomfortably on a hard plastic chair, her forearms resting on the bed where she traced faint lines up and down Meghan's arms with her nails. Through the patio doors I could see Dad hauling on the business end of a cigarette so that it burned an inch with his inhale.

"Hey," she said. It was a croak of pain and thirst and exhaustion. Mom squeezed her eyes shut until they crinkled and then opened them again. "Mom." Meghan's tone was an urgent warning. "Now. Quick." Mom held the kidney basin next to Meg's lips as another burp of inky bile squirted from her mouth.

"Looks like good times in here."

"Well, you know, woot woot." Meghan tried to lift her arms into a raise-the-roof pump but her muscles drooped and the effort sagged. Three months ago, we'd been teaching Lily to "raise the roof," hooting as she revealed a gummy mouth while palming upwards. I winced at the memory.

"What are you doing awake, anyways?" I asked as I slung my bag onto the floor by the daybed. "Aren't you supposed to be in a nice little coma by now?"

More bile, spitting. Mom wiped a glisten of sweat from Meghan's forehead and rinsed the basin in the sink, returning it right before another burp that led to a steaming stream of vomit. I turned to face the wall, but not seeing did not stop me from hearing, smelling, feeling. I was ashamed, knowing how many times I'd abandoned my sister while she heaved and heaved, fleeing the room like a frightened child until one of the nurses came to tell me it was over. I'd left her alone while she assured me that she was fine, that she knew that my emetophobia was real, as real as her cancer, she said once. But I didn't know what I feared anymore, what I should force myself to witness and what I truly could not bear.

"It's okay, Meg. Let it out," Mom said soothingly, but loud enough to be heard over the sound of gagging. I willed my feet to stay in place.

As Meghan requested, I had called Phyllis the night before and told her about the sedation. Explained that this meant no intake of food or liquids. That she should tell Bernard the end was coming. Phyllis had promised to relay the message, and so maybe I'd expected to enter room ten and find Bernard by her bed with that same panicked look he'd had the first time she went into hospice. But I could not picture making space for him now, to pretend his abuse and anger was anything but exactly that.

Meghan leaned back, defeated. "God," she said. "That was a tough one."

I went to kiss her sweaty forehead, mopping at her brow with my sleeve. She smelled acidic and tart. "I'm going to make some tea, and I'll bring you a mint for your tummy, okay? Be right back. Anyone want anything from the kitchen? Mom?"

Mom shook her head, and I blazed a wide smile, all cheerful and supportive. Ten steps down the hall, I diverted to the nurses' station, where I found Mallory documenting charts from her swivel chair.

"She's suffering, isn't she, Mal?"

"Yes." Mallory was curt but empathetic.

I fiddled with my tissue before the tears came in earnest and I was gasping for air. In private with the nurses, I could bare my weakness because no one needed me to be calm or funny or capable. "Increase the dose, please." I sank to the floor, clutching myself.

"It's the right thing to do," Mallory said. "You're caring for her by reaffirming the choice she already made. She knew you'd back her up."

We returned to Meghan's bedside and Mallory slipped in and increased the dose on the Versed pump.

"Don't mind me, sweetie," she said to Meghan. "Just have to get a reading off this thing." Mallory gave me an okay sign with her fingers, along with a sad tilt of her head.

And so our vigil began.

twenty-six

It was a Friday, day four of sedation, and Mom, Dad, and I had all moved into room ten to stay as a family. We catnapped in shifts and looked borderline psychotic—hair sticking up in greasy patches, unshowered, clothes full of the musty stink of over-wear and exhaustion. Each day, I dressed and wondered if this was the last outfit I would wear while I had a sister, then slopped down the hall to the kitchen to take my morning medications. The expiry date on the carton of milk in the hospice's fridge was in three weeks. My sister would be dead by then, but I would still be here. I shook the milk and then could not shake the panic—soon, any minute, my sister would die, and then what? My functioning was predicated on what was happening in room ten, right at that moment. Anything outside of that—the kids, work, Joe—was beyond comprehension. There was a constant, palpable fear of leaving the room in case that moment was it, or the next one, or the one after that.

Since her full sedation, Meghan had done nothing but consistently moan in what I was convinced was pain but what the nurses insisted was likely hallucinatory or "death sounds," which I had to google. In hopes of preparing myself, I spent a lot of time researching the process the body goes through in death, my iPhone glare illuminating my face while everyone slept.

What to expect when someone dies.

What to look for when someone dies.

What happens when someone dies?

Apparently, we might witness little exhalations of breath that were not actually breath, but rather the releasing and purging of gases, the body giving itself up to the next stage. Her chest might move in this process, I read, but that was normal. *Often, this is upsetting to loved ones.* Her body would let go, literally, figuratively. She would need certain parts of her washed, and so I laid out the pyjamas and robe we wanted her sent off in, complete with underwear, which she hadn't been able to wear for months because the elastic waistbands pinched at the cancerous lumps. I'd turn off my phone and sit in the dark, wondering what it felt like for Mom, as a nurse who'd sat countless death vigils, to already have the knowledge of what would happen to her daughter. And then Dad. As a soldier, he'd seen so many dead bodies, but none of them part of his own body. How would they survive this?

Now, in the light of day, I rubbed Blistex across Meghan's lips, selecting from one of the five tubes of balms that littered her bed tray, the one I knew was her favourite scent. "Here we go, Meg. Don't want you getting chapped. I know you'd hate that."

A grunt emanated in return. The lip balm jerked erratically when her lips moved with the tube, as though her flesh were made of wax. "Fuck," I whispered under my breath as I wiped the excess away with my thumb. Mom and Dad didn't know how much Meghan and I swore together, and I wanted to keep this a special secret between us. "Sorry, Meggie. Got it all over the place." She moaned again and I stroked her cheeks in an attempt to soothe us both. Another moan, this one like nails on a chalkboard. "Now," I said, narrating my steps of care as I replaced the cap on the lip balm. "I know you like to be clean." I nearly expected her to answer. Even the day before, despite the shockingly high dose of Versed, her bony arm had reached around Dad's neck as she told him she loved him. Dad waited until her arm fell limp before hurrying out, his tears echoing in the hallway. I hoped they were the last words she'd utter. I wanted him to have that.

I tugged a Burt's Bees face wipe from its resealable package, snapped it in the air to unfurl it. I'd been spending, on average, more than fifty dollars a week on these damn wipes because she liked the smell, relished the fake cucumber fragrance that had come to turn my stomach. "Here we go, Meggie." I swiped at her face. Her mouth hung slack, lids closed halfway, skin pale and yellow, far beyond the reach of the brightening wipe. "Nearly done." I spread her skin taut to get into the folds of her face, both wrinkled and yet somehow ageless, a natural by-product not of age but of a sinking into oneself, fat eviscerated. In the hollow of her neck, I dabbed away blackish-brown slurry that had pooled from her open mouth. I held my breath because a smell emanated from Meghan—through her mouth, skin, pores. It was the smell of death, and each day, I found I was unable to wash it from my own skin. "Let's get this all cleaned up," I said as I pulled another wipe from the packet, soaking this one too, until it was brownish black with back-tracked feces, vomit, and bile.

Next, I took a bony hand and cleaned it as she'd done for her children, digging underneath her fingernails, suddenly unsure if she would rather be left alone, if I was bugging her or if my touch was a comfort. Mom watched us, lip wobbling, and I had to turn away. Focus. My sister needed me to focus.

"There. Clean as a whistle." I tossed my pile of used wipes into the garbage and returned to the fold-out cot we'd wrestled into the room alongside the hospital bed, the recliner chair Dad slept in, and the daybed where Mom spent the wakeful nights. The space was orderly and neat, even though our belongings clung to every corner, every surface, four people in a room for one. The cot was firm, wildly uncomfortable. But then it didn't matter. I never slept for long.

———

Somehow, I napped, snapping awake to the click of the patio door lock turning and Dad stepping through into the room. It struck me then, as I stirred, that it was the last time we would be together as a family of four.

"Joe just called. Said he texted you but you didn't answer," Dad said. He'd been chain-smoking, and a waft of nicotine odour followed him. "He's going to be here in a few minutes with dinner." Joe had been cooking us meals and delivering them daily, sticking Post-it love notes onto the Glasslock containers. *Please eat. Love you all! The dog misses you!*

I groaned. "I'm not really hungry."

"None of us are," Dad said with a sigh, although he'd been obsessively snacking on the baked goods made by volunteers. He chewed mindlessly and, once finished, could never say whether the cookie was good or what flavour it was. "But we have to eat."

"How's she doing?" I forced the hope from my voice, no longer sure what I was hoping for. Meghan's head was craned at a horrible angle that made me nauseated, her neck wrenched towards the pillow.

"No change." Mom's voice was a croak.

Just parked! A text from Joe pinged to my cell. *Come meet me?*

"Joe's here." I held up my phone and stuffed my feet into sneakers. "Maybe Meg is one of those people who needs everyone to leave the room before she finally goes?" I let the questioning tone linger, knit my fingers into a braid. I felt woozy, wobbling in place before righting myself on the dresser.

"I saw that a lot at work," Mom said from her plastic chair next to the hospital bed. She'd barely left it in days.

"I'll ask Sandra to sit with her while we eat," I offered. Meghan liked Sandra, the personal support worker who called herself white trash but cared for my sister with such gentle kindness that I was often overwhelmed at the sight. *I'm just going to change this medication bag, Meg,* Sandra would say, narrating as she worked, just as I did. *I'm just flushing this line, okay?* She didn't wait for the permission that never came, but I liked the way she made Meghan a part of the process.

Once Sandra arrived and assured us she wouldn't leave, I clapped my hands against my thighs, rallying my parents like a sports coach. "Let's all go eat, okay?" We fussed to make ourselves presentable, tucking in shirts and smoothing gobs of hair, but on the brink of leaving the room, none of us moved to open the door. "What if . . . ?" I couldn't finish, my words choked.

Dad patted my arm knowingly. "We love you, Meg."

"Love you, Meggie."

"We'll be right back. We love you."

Down in the open kitchen and dining area, Joe had laid out pork tenderloin with cheesy potatoes, baked cauliflower, and gravy. He hugged me tight when I approached, then passed out plates and unloaded his cooler full of tomorrow's breakfast, lunch, and dinner. "Just in case," he said.

We ate in silence. Joe did not ask how we were, because what kind of answer could we possibly give? I wanted to thank him for all of it—for the effort, for the chocolate bars he pushed into my purse, for being him—but the thoughts swirled through my plate of gravy and I couldn't muster the energy.

"Joe, thanks for that," Dad said after a few mouthfuls, "but I think I'll head back to Meg." Dad pushed back from the table and swiped a mini muffin from the coffee tray as he went. I watched him all the way down the hall, and as he pulled on the door-handle to room ten and disappeared inside.

"You guys must be so tired," Joe said.

"It's been so, you know." Mom bit her lip and shook her head over and over, dark lashes sweeping her cheeks.

"Try to eat, Ma."

"Look who's talking, bossy pants." She gestured at my nearly full plate.

I looked up just as Dad burst through Meghan's door and flapped his arms wildly at the opposite end of the corridor, like he was doing snow angels.

"What?" I hollered, stifling laughter. He looked ridiculous. *Always overreacting*, Meghan and I would say, nudging one another conspiratorially. But then Sandra peeked from the doorway and waved too, a hand swooping inward. *Come. Now.*

"It's time," she yelled, miming at her watch.

It was time.

The hospice blurs in scene. And I am ready, or I am not ready, and I feel sick but purposeful, anxious but calm. All of it. I feel everything as I abandon the table and run towards my sister, not even thinking about how Mom can barely walk on her own. Joe, instinctively, waits behind with our discarded meal.

"Hurry!" Dad jogs down the hall to help Mom and I run ahead of them both because she cannot die alone, she can't. I explode into room ten to find Meghan taking short, raspy breaths, her chest barely rising with that incessant, agonizing moan. It's hot in here, sticky even, and oh my God there is brownish mucous oozing from the corner of her mouth where her ear is pressed against a pillow. She would not want to go like this. She would not.

"I need a Kleenex!" I cry out, but the voice doesn't sound like mine. It is a demand, not a request, and I am snapping my fingers as though a tissue will materialize. She would not want this, and Mom and Dad can't see this and oh my fucking God it is happening.

"I'm so sorry. I didn't notice," the nurse says. She passes the tissue and I snatch it without looking, wipe at my sister's mouth, because I can give this to her, a modicum of the dignity she's been clutching for, the last time I will touch her living body. My hand lingers on her face, cupping her sunken cheeks in my palm. "I love you, Meg." In the softest of whispers.

Mom and Dad burst into the room looking harried, and I take my place at Meghan's feet, Dad on Meghan's right, Mom on her left. The nurses slip away, but Mom, ever the medical professional, keeps her fingertips on Meghan's wrist for a pulse while we watch her chest. Has she stopped breathing? I can't tell. I want to get close and press my cheek to her lips, feel the puff of air there, or lack of it. I want to know for myself, and more than that, I want to be the first to know because I have always known Meghan's truths and this is the most honest thing we will ever experience together simply because it is the last thing we will experience together.

"It's okay, Meggie," I say. "We're all here. We love you. We love you so much." I want the last words she hears to be the thing she has always longed for: Love. *We love you. You have always been so very loved, even when you made it hard. Your children love you. Your friends love you. You have left a legacy. You matter.*

"Yes. We're all here. Mom, and Dad. Your sister." Dad cannot keep his voice even. Meghan breathes in raggedly and we go silent.

"Is she gone?"

"Not yet," Mom squeaks, fingers still at Meghan's wrist. "It's okay, Meg. It's okay. You can go."

We are quiet. Unsure of what else to say beyond the panic.

And then it is done, known. Something missing. For a moment, pure silence as we listen. An absence I can feel on the tip of my tongue. A roar rises but I swallow it down, stare at my knuckles gone white in their grip on Meghan's feet like I could hold on to her and keep her here.

"She's gone," Mom says with a nod, naturally looking to the clock to call it like she would have done at the nursing home:

1605 hrs, 17 August 2018. Weeks before Labour Day. And just like that, we've become a family of three, and as we look at one another, it's clear that none of us knows how to process this new fact. My tears drip onto the warmed blanket atop Meghan's feet and disappear into the quilted pattern. I watch the damp spot bloom like a mushroom cloud.

Dad throws himself on top of Meghan, arms snaking gently under her body to tug her close. For the first time in weeks, she will not moan in pain, and I am so relieved by this. He cries out her name in a way that scrapes at my heart, guttural and simultaneously pinched, and I cover my ears and grit my teeth as his sobs fill the room. Mom rocks slightly back and forth, staring at Meghan as though she might come back any minute now, half here, half somewhere else.

"God," Dad says after a moment, rising to his feet. He swipes at his face. "I have to get myself together."

"Bill, it's fine."

"Dad. Just let yourself be sad."

"Don't tell me what to do," he growls. Mom cries harder at this, her lips sputtering and body trembling.

I don't want Meghan to hear us fight, which is stupid, right? It's stupid. "I'll go tell the nurses," I say, standing unsteadily. But more than that, I want to give Mom and Dad time with their daughter, alone.

Don't think of what they lost. Don't think of it.

I step out of the room and into the incandescent lighting of the hallway, blinking into the reality outside of room ten. Nothing has changed. The hospice continues to hum with activity, the world actively spins, and this revelatory moment of death has revealed nothing new, nothing meaningful. Just the pang of loss felt in every of the ten rooms several times a week. We are no different, but we are so different.

I peek around the corner into the nursing station where the caregivers are sitting somberly, waiting for me. I pause in the door-frame, fiddling with the tie of my pants, because if I don't say it aloud, don't give voice to this horrible thing, then for another few moments I can live in a world in which my sister shares that world.

"It's, um, she's done. I think. Gone." The nurse with the curly blonde bob nods. I want to fold myself into her, listen to her stories about softball and stare at the scar on her lip and ask her how it happened. I want anything but this. As if sensing that, she stands and hugs me, and I feel her hands rub up and down my spine until I sag into her, sobbing. I pry myself from her, sud-denly worried for my parents, for my sister's body, for Joe, and our family scattered to these hallways. "Do you think we could call the funeral home now?"

"We can wait, honey," she says. "Give you all some peaceful time with her."

I can think of nothing I want less. I want to shed this place like a snakeskin. "We've had our time. I think I just want her . . ." What? Gone? Done with? "At peace, or whatever."

"Okay. We'll just go in and prepare her for you to say good-bye then." I nod, praying they will not go into details about what it means to prepare her. "We'll give the funeral home a ring and maybe you want to take your parents down to the living room there?"

I bob my head unenthusiastically, glad for the task. Once back in Meghan's room, my heart wants to avoid looking at her body, but she is there, looking unrested and unpeaceful and anger bubbles up inside me because peacefulness ought to be a consolation prize for all this. A promise that the person is in a better place, whatever that means, free of suffering and pain. But her eyes are still half open, her mouth in the form of a circle, skin yellower, blood already pooling to bruises in her extremities. She looks frozen in a tableau of pain, and my powerlessness to change this is excruciating.

Mom is in the bathroom blowing her nose while Dad wrestles with the cot I've been sleeping on. The unwieldy metal legs of it clank against the hospital bed, jostling Meghan's body in a way that makes me nauseous.

"Goddammit," he mutters, slamming the frame into place like he's trying to refold a map the way you found it in the package.

"Dad, that can wait. The nurses need to get Meghan ready. Clean her up."

Mom emerges from the bathroom and looks at me pleadingly, her face puffy and red. Dad is trying to ram the cot into the carry bag it came in, but like in a cartoon, each time he tries, a new section pops into the air, stubborn and refusing—just like how Meghan and Dad spent a lifetime trying to fit each other into imperfect spaces. They never did fit. I want to tell him this is okay, that all of us have been there, willing Meghan to something she isn't, and look at all of us—exhausted for the effort.

"Dad," I say, a palm gentle on his shoulder as he whacks the cot against the floor. "Dad!" This time, sterner. He stops, drops the cot, his eyes wild when they meet mine. And then his shoulders sink as his lip trembles.

"Moo, I'm sorry I yelled at you. I'm so sorry." He falls into my shoulder and we stand there a moment, silently sharing tears.

"It's okay, Dad. I get it." I try to calm my own voice through sobs. We were so ready, weren't we? But still, the shock of it.

"You should take Mom home, get some rest. I'll wait for the funeral home guys."

"No way," Dad says. "We're not leaving you."

My role in the family has never felt so certain and in contrast, my parents have never seemed so frail. And I realize now, with a horrible certainty, that I will exhaust myself filling the space my sister has left, even while knowing it is impossible. But this is how we show love. And caregiving is, in some fucked-up way, a gift.

"I have paperwork to sign and stuff, as executor. Plus, Joe will be with me, so I won't be alone."

"We don't want you to have to do this," Mom says, dabbing at her nose.

"None of us want any of us to have to do this," I respond. She shrugs, blows her nose again.

"If you're sure then." Dad gathers their bags, their pillows, reaches his arms out to Meghan as though he can't bear to leave her behind.

"I won't leave her alone, Dad. I promise."

"Did you want more time?" The nurse is here, with a bucket of warm water in her arm and Sandra at her side, carrying a stack of towels and some cleaner. We collectively shake our heads no. "We'll get her ready for you."

We shuffle into the hallway and find Joe there, waiting to help my parents carry their things to the car, and then we walk silently to the Lincoln, where we squeeze each other tightly.

"I'll see you guys at home, okay? I should go call Phyllis and Bernard to let them know."

"You don't have to do that, Moo," Mom says tearfully. She says the words, but I can hear her gratefulness to not have to be a part of it.

"It's fine. It's my job, right? Executor and all that. Joe and I will be home in a bit."

I return to the hallway, hovering outside room ten where I can hear Sandra and the nurse bustling. I try not to imagine what is involved in their work as I stare at Phyllis's contact info on my phone, finger hovering over the call button. I rub at my raw nostrils. It's almost dinnertime, and I picture Sam and Lily running around Phyllis's kitchen, still unaware. The image stabs me in the gut.

Phyllis answers on the third ring, sounding out of breath. "Kelly, hi."

I rub at my throat, hoping to dispel the lump that sits there. It doesn't work, and I start bellowing sobs into the phone. "Hi. I, um, you asked me to call you when Meghan died. Instead of calling Bernard, right?" I'm uncertain, suddenly, of the instructions, if I have them quite right, because nothing makes sense anymore, this new limit on contact with Bernard, especially. It should be a time for reaching out, for belonging, for family, even when those connections are fraught.

"Yes, that's right." Phyllis is matter-of-fact. Pots and pans clang in the background and Lily squeals a high pitch. "I think it's best if we communicate through me for now, while emotions are running so high." I wait for Phyllis to fill in the obvious reason for my call, but she lingers on the line, saying nothing.

"Well, Meghan died today. Just now."

"Oh, my." The distance between us yawns wide and I can't tell if I hate it or love it—space I've wanted from a family for whom I feel such animosity. Part of me expected all this anger to dissipate when delivering this news, so I'm unprepared for more of the same strain. "Well, that certainly wasn't the news I was expecting today."

I sputter a snarky laugh. "She's been palliatively sedated since Monday, Phyllis. Five days. It was exactly what we were all expecting." Phyllis and Bernard didn't have to see how bad it got. They didn't ride the waves of thinking Meghan's suffering was easing, only to have it take another unbearable turn. They got to escape it all, and I hate him for it especially because it is Friday, which means Bernard has the day off. He could have been there, at his wife's side. My face is hot with sudden rage.

"Right." Again, the silence.

Meghan would know what to say, so well-versed in keeping the peace. I focus on how happy the kids sound in the background to make sense of Phyllis's desire to believe in Bernard's goodness. "So, you'll tell Bernard then?"

"Yes, I'll tell him."

"I hope he'll be okay, Phyllis." They are words I say but maybe-kind-of-don't-want-to-perhaps-don't mean, and yet, if I'm being insincere, if I don't hope for the safety and health of the person my sister loved, the father of my niece and nephew, then what does that say of me?

"I'll let him know. We'll get through this." That voice again, the certainty that is bossy but also assured in a way that gives me odd comfort.

I wait, lingering for something else I can't place. Meghan is dead. It is over, and yet part of me knows the pain is only getting started. "Will you kiss the kids for me? Tell them their auntie loves them?" My chest heaves and then I am uncontained, ugly tears spilling. "I love them so much. Please tell them."

The kids, the tie between us, softens her. "I will. Give my best to your parents." She hangs up then, leaving me there alone in the hallway.

"How'd it go?" Joe says as he approaches. He's been lingering down in the kitchen, cleaning up our abandoned meal.

I don't have time to answer before the staff call us back into Meghan's room. We find Meghan lying with her hands folded neatly as though in prayer, but her mouth and eyes still agape in that horrific stare. I try to close her springy eyelids only to have them pop back open with an elasticity that makes me shudder. The room smells strongly of floral cleaner, windows wide open to the warm August evening. Joe shuffles in behind me and I lean onto the railing at the foot of the bed to catch my breath and swallow down the hysteria that threatens.

"I'm here," Joe whispers into my neck. I sense him looking at my sister and suddenly want to shield her because she wouldn't want to be seen like this. She would want some mascara on those impossibly long lashes, some blush to bring her skin to life. A bra for her now tiny breasts, or a pretty sweater in a nice blue. "She looks so . . ."

"Dead." I cough to stifle the tears, desperate to get home before the breakdown begins in earnest.

"Thin," Joe says instead, his voice a soft wobble. "I guess it's been a few weeks since I've seen her."

I look between my husband and my sister, aware I've lost all sense of what a body should be, how much fat should pad the bones. Joe stares at her now, his own eyes welling in grief or horror, I can't be sure, and I want to comfort him but also to do something, because doing has been my saviour and now there is nothing but thoughts and pain and my sister's corpse. There is my husband at my back, and heat radiating from my scapula.

"I have to. I need . . ." The rest of the words don't come and so I move, gently pushing Joe away. I pack what I can donate, chucking what I cannot, arms and legs moving independent of my mind as I toss the cheap junk that it is—the polyester pyjamas, the dirty slippers, the lotions and creams, the endless tubes of half-used lip balm. The smell of the lavender oil—how many times did I rub that scent into her skin?—makes me gag before I shove that in the garbage bag too, shaking as I wrench the plastic shut. It takes mere minutes to finish, and that recognition stabs the air; her whole life tidied up in three minutes and a bin bag.

The nurse pops her head in. "The gentlemen from the funeral home are here. They're just bringing the vehicle around now but they have some paperwork for you."

I go to follow and then my throat catches. "You'll stay, Joe? Stay with her? Don't leave her." The tears heave then, swelling up in my chest. He folds me in his arms and nods, ushering me into the hallway, where I take the clipboard from the nurse and mindlessly sign papers, mutter words that barely register. I've been preparing, preparing so much. My paperwork is in order, signatures in all the right places. This is what I do: make necessary arrangements—logistics, planning, execution. *Meghan, I did all of it, kept it all together for you. Look. Look how your life of disarray is so tidy and neat now.*

"We'd like to do the walking-out ceremony with you," says the nurse. She is standing too close. The smell of her shampoo overwhelms, combining with the cookies she was eating earlier, butter tinging her breath. "We have a ceremony here where the staff walk out with you and Meghan to the vehicle to see her off. It's one of the ways we say goodbye. Closure."

Closure. What a thing. I picture this parade of thirty people down the hall, and my nose scrunches in distaste, at the weird pomp and circumstance, the ritual she wouldn't want.

"No. No, I don't want that," I manage. My voice tightens until I am almost yelling at these wonderful people who have literally wiped our tears and kissed my forehead while I slept. "She would hate that. She hates stuff like that!"

She is already nodding placatingly. "I understand, Kelly. Everyone will understand. We don't have to do it."

I sink to the floor, fold my head to my knees as the men from the funeral home, wearing black suits, approach. Dread swells because this means the end and goodbye. I want me and my sister and the way things were. I want us against the world. I want to be Ursula to her Ariel. I want her to read my book. I want her to admit her lies about her husband and her finances and her choices. I want her to choose her children above all else. I want my parents to have two children. More than that, I want Sam and Lily to have two parents. I want so many things I'll never have.

"Mrs. Thompson?" the older man asks gently. His voice has a soft timbre that I imagine has put countless families at ease. "So sorry for your loss. Your sister talked about you with such pride." They introduce themselves, owners of the parlour up the road, a father-and-son duo I didn't meet during the planning.

I stand and wipe my palms down my pants. "That's nice of you, thanks." They wait, expectant. "She's, um, in there." I gesture to her room. Meghan's room that will now become someone else's room, and this is another injustice I cannot stand.

The men disappear and Joe comes to my side to wait until they wheel the gurney—my sister—out into the hallway. She is in a black body bag, a quilt laid over the plastic to humanize the experience somehow. It doesn't work.

"Ready?" the younger man asks. Everything about the way he moves is respectful, and I want to tell him this, how good he clearly is at his job, how I trust him just by the way his hair sweeps his brow and his hands fold in respectful compliance when he speaks. But words have left me, and I can only follow their lead towards the front doors, Joe following closely behind. My sister is in there, under the protective bag, wrapped up in the dark and alone and I will never hate anything more than this fact, this horrific, painful knowledge of her loneliness. I walk alongside Meghan, the two of us, always the two of us, reaching out to touch her as we move, fingering the plasticky coating of the bag for something familiar, but everything feels padded and lumpy, not like human flesh and bone and sister. We keep walking, and I turn away from the other families, the volunteers, the people I know keenly because we're all here losing someone, sharing the grief, but they don't understand this grief, this pain that is unique to us, and I don't want to share it. I turn towards her protectively, shielding her from view.

It feels like an hour, but in a minute we arrive outside the front doors and to the waiting van. An ordinary van, industrial even, white and cubed. I expected a hearse, more dignified, but this is just a nondescript van of the type owned by contractors.

Cicadas chirp noisily as the sun beats the pavement and pollen wafts by on the end of a summer's breeze. A beautiful day to die, but I don't want to let her go. Panic blooms, my throat tight, tears dampening the front of my banana-printed T-shirt. In this outfit I went from a sister to a sister without a sister and I hate this stupid T-shirt even though it was on sale and it fits perfectly and Meghan loved it. I am a thirty-four-year-old woman wearing bananas and my sister is dead and none of this makes sense.

"Wait!" I yell, although there is no reason to yell, the air around us calm. The men stop rolling and I frantically grab at the body bag, plucking but not really wanting to find the opening. "Can I kiss her goodbye?" I just want to touch her one last time. Countless, endless last times. I want to see her tiny toes, the delicate, pointed fingers, the rosebud lips speckled with freckles.

"Of course," the older man says. "Do you want us to unwrap her?"

"Yes, please." I don't get what he is really asking. *Just open the fucking bag.*

There are layers. The bag. Blankets. Fleece. Inside all this, a white shroud, and I have never seen a shroud or known they were this real, modern-day thing not meant for mummies or religious traditions, but it is there, semi-sheer, with her body underneath, the pink striped robe knotted over her stomach. I lean in, unprepared for the smell to already be so pungent, for Meghan's skin the colour of mud.

"I love you, Meggie." I kiss her forehead, place my hand on her heart. "I love you so much." I drip tears onto her skin but leave them there. She will take this with her somewhere new, this love in liquid form.

I step back and the men rewrap her. They've seen this all before. They pack Meghan into a van. I am left behind, a sister without a sister. A protector without something to protect.

twenty-seven

Hours later, Joe, Mom, Dad, and I sat in the living room nursing teas, Pot Roast nuzzled into my side. The sun was beginning to set and the living room glowed Creamsicle orange. It was a beautiful evening, the humidity having given way to the gentle call of autumn.

"You called Phyllis, right? To tell Bernard?" Mom asked blankly. She and Dad were nestled together on the couch, thigh to thigh. I'd spent the forty-minute drive from the hospice to Mom and Dad's relaying the news of Meghan's death to anyone I thought might need it—grandparents, aunts, uncles, close friends—wanting to get that part of things over before I could allow myself the withdrawal I craved.

"Yes, of course."

"What did she say?"

"That it was 'not news she was expecting,'" I said bitterly. "Like her death was some surprise. She's going to tell Bernard, since apparently we're not allowed to call him anymore. I literally don't get this."

"Right. Maybe that's for the best."

"It's ridiculous, Ma. What in the hell does he get to be mad about? We're the ones who should be mad." It felt good. It felt so good to say this all aloud when we'd had to be so, so quiet.

"Maybe we should have made more of an effort," Mom said, fretting with the edges of the blanket Meghan had crocheted for her, a twisted blue-and-white yarn. She had finished it the week before her sedation, and I had helped darn in the loose ends because Meghan's vision was so blurred by drugs that she couldn't see the loops. She asked me to keep the leftover yarn from each of our blankets in case they ever needed repair. *No one else in the family knows how to crochet. No one else will be able to fix them when I'm dead.* And now the blanket was there, existing, and Meghan was not. I couldn't stand it. How were any of us standing it? "Maybe we should have explained what the sedation would mean."

My shoulders dropped, energy draining like someone had pulled the plug in the bath. "And by we, you mean me. That I should have made more effort." Meghan would have defended me. She would have told them—our parents who always considered her to be the wounded bird in need of care and me the gladiator of logistics—that I was doing enough, that I couldn't handle one more burden, even while knowing Mom and Dad were carrying the life-altering truth of burying their daughter. And yet the hardest nugget of knowledge had laid itself bare: even though it felt like everything should be different following a loved one's death, nothing actually was. The world remained unchanged even if your own world combusted. "Bernard and

Phyllis can google as much as the next person. Unlike him, I was a little busy actually supporting Meghan." Joe gave me a look, encouraging me to temper my nastiness, but it was an overflow I could no longer contain.

Mom lifted her hands up in question, then dropped them into her lap. "It all feels so horribly fractured. Us against them. Meghan would hate this."

"Sadly, Meghan's the one who put us and left us here, squarely in the middle. Or rather, with the kids in the middle."

The doorbell rang and startled us all.

"Who the hell could that be?"

"Don't answer it," Dad said, his voice a grunt. His eyes were bloodshot and watery, his lips chapped.

"Well, whoever it is can see me," I said, leaning back in my chair to find two people peering through the glass front door that made me feel exposed. "Hopefully they'll take one look at my swollen face and get the hint." I walked to the entryway where Meghan's possessions lay jumbled, stuffed in black garbage bags. My heart surged at the possibility that she was returning to us, even while simultaneously recognizing the impossibility. How many times had she arrived at that very door—fresh from a breakup or a bender—with her belongings slung over her shoulder?

I swung the door open to a couple in their twenties, dressed in business casual. The woman wore a knee-length skirt and a light, summery cardigan the colour of dishwater, while the man's starched white shirt collar was tight around his sweating neck. His skin was still pimpled and his scant beard was a work in progress, evidenced by the rash on his neck. They held pamphlets outstretched, simple gold wedding rings glinting in the sun.

"Can I help you?"

"Good evening. We were hoping you had some time to discuss the teachings of Jehovah," said the man, his voice calm and measured. He looked kind but tired in the fading summer light. The woman next to him, his wife, I presumed, nodded with encouragement, whether at me or her spouse, I couldn't be sure. The man thrust a folded paper at me.

"This really isn't a good time," I said as quietly but forcefully as I could. "We've had a death in the family." I did not, under any circumstances, want Dad to hear me whispering through the door.

My parents had always been staunch supporters of freedom of worship and were polite to anyone who attempted to preach at their door. But their inability to entertain the Jehovah's Witnesses was legendary in our house, all because of their knock on our door when Meghan was almost three, just finishing her chemo and radiation. She was bald, with a feeding tube snaking out from her nose as she toddled towards the friendly strangers on the front step. Seeing she was sick, the Witness informed Mom that Meghan was sick because Jehovah was punishing her for her sins. Dad's raging response had ensured no one from that church ever returned to our house.

And here they were. On the day Meghan died, with their brochure. I stifled a laugh despite myself. She would have liked this serendipitous event.

"We understand," the man said. "But the word of Jehovah can be a comfort in hard times." He wiggled the paper a little, making the illustrated pious man wobble in the breeze. I'd sometimes wondered if Meghan was being punished for something, but then serial killers lived, people made mistakes, and Meghan was more than the bad things she'd done. Would this man and his pamphlet believe in that?

"I don't mean to be rude, but like I said, she died today. Like, actually today. Hours ago. So, we'd like to be alone with family."

"Then that literature will be more applicable to you than ever," the man countered, his head bobbling.

"Who is it?" Dad called from the living room. I could hear his footsteps nearing, and with them, a sense of doom and hilarity took over. I was laughing and crying at the same time, which was how it often started with Meghan and me: setting off one another's laughing fits—a game of emotional telephone.

"No, I'm sorry." I shut the door on the faces of the earnest visitors. They stood there a moment before stepping delicately towards the next home, crossing the small grass boulevard between us and our neighbours with little hops. When I came back to the kitchen, Dad was pouring glasses of wine. He watched as I dropped the pamphlet into the recycle bin.

"So?" Mom dabbed at her face with a tissue. "Who was it?"

"It's almost funny. You won't believe it." I was laughing still—or crying, maybe—and dammit, I felt like an asshole. My sister was dead. Dead. And already, I was laughing. "It was Jehovah's Witnesses."

"You're kidding me," Dad said, voice monotone. His moustache bristled with a twinge of a smile.

We let our laughter spill out unabashed until we were swiping tears from our faces. Meghan would have liked it.

twenty-eight

It had been two weeks since she died. I pressed back into the velour car seat while Joe navigated Newfoundland's rolling roads. I reminded myself of my promise to Meghan. *Yes, I'll go. Yes, I'll take pictures.* But standing at the edge of Canada, gasping back grief among the Jellybean Row houses, I wondered why I'd bothered when all I thought of was her and suffering and dying. *You'll need a vacation,* Meghan had said, *after all of this.* She had gestured to the hospice room and her withering body. Joe and I had booked our visit to Newfoundland nine months earlier, before Meghan's surgery, before chemo, before death. *You'll need time to look after yourself.*

"Well, that was something, wasn't it?" Joe said as he drove, his cheeks red and wind-whipped.

Now that I had a signal, I pressed send on my text message to Mom, including a photo of Joe and me on the edge of Cape Spear. A few months earlier, a woman had made the news by plunging to her death after she ignored the countless signs to stay clear of the cliffs. *Don't linger near the edge*, Mom had yelled into the phone that morning, pitch bordering on operatic. I'd pulled the cell from my ear and winced. Since we'd landed days earlier, my raging head cold had turned into an ear infection and everything ached.

See! my message said, underneath the bubble of Joe and me with our faces pressed into grins. *Not fish bait at the bottom of the ocean! I stayed on the path.*

She instantly replied with a heart emoji, as if she'd been waiting by her cell. Mom had only recently started employing emojis. A month ago, Meghan and I were laughing about this new tendency, along with her propensity for calling town streets "the main drag" and her use of slang like "vacay." *Is Mom secretly a valley girl, or what?* Meghan had whispered, and we'd laughed so hard. The memory bloomed like a taste on my tongue.

I stared out at the views, forcing back the tide of sadness, holding my sobs in my throat so that I didn't hamper another part of our vacation. *Vacay.*

"I don't mean to mess with our plans, but I definitely need to see a doctor." I rubbed at my jaw and neck where the pain had spread. For days, I had been mistaking the ear pain for a physical manifestation of grief, allowing it to grow angrier and more insistent, ignorant to the idea that I might be ill and my body depleted of any possible resource to repair itself.

"We'll be going through Gander in a few hours," Joe said lightly. "We can stop there, no problem. They'll give you some antibiotics and get the ball rolling." He patted my bare thigh where my shorts had edged up. I hadn't worn shorts in years—too embarrassed about chubby thighs—but I'd promised Meghan that, too. Chubby thighs were something to embrace because they meant nourishment and health and that I was alive. "You'll be better in no time."

———————

Joe dropped me off at the hospital while he went to get groceries for the next stage of our trip. I didn't have to wait long in the emergency room, although the nurse practitioner chided me for letting the infection get so far gone as she wrote me a script for penicillin.

In the hospital lobby, I waited for Joe to pick me up. Our next destination was Gros Morne National Park, where I wanted to lose myself in the scrubby landscape and present as openly depressed as I was without having to make anyone comfortable with it.

"Quite the day out there, isn't it?" The elderly man sitting next to me leaned into my line of sight, using his chin to point at the rain falling in torrents. We could barely see across the road except for a span of pines that bent sideways in the wind. "The kind of weather that soaks you in seconds!"

"I'm not minding it too much." It suited my mood, although I didn't voice this. I felt wrung out, like a sopping sweater.

"Ah, you're from away then. Whereabouts?" He wore a thick wool sweater despite the heat, but had it pushed up to his elbows. Veins lined his skin like a purplish road map, with liver spots pocking the terrain.

"Ontario. Toronto area right now, but I'm an army brat. Moved around lots."

"Ah, I once lived out that way, but no longer. Me, now, I live on Fogo. You know Fogo? Been a fisherman all my life. It's in my bones. Fred's the name." He gave a semi-toothless grin. Fred, in his pageboy hat and thick corduroys worn at the tail end of summer, looked like a caricature of a Newfoundlander. All that was missing was a cod dangling from one hand and a sou'wester in the other.

"I'm Kelly. Nice to meet you."

"Kelly, it's a pleasure. I'm waiting on my niece. She's taking me back after my checkup with the surgeon. Got me a new knee, you see?" Fred lifted his trouser leg to reveal a shiny line of staples that swirled around his joint. "Good as new!"

I gulped, thought of the criss-cross of staples down Meghan's abdomen. "Your knee feels better then, after surgery?" Normal Kelly would have loved this exchange with a stranger. *I think you were stolen from out east as a baby,* Meghan had said once. *You can make conversation with anyone.* But this was Grieving Kelly. I wanted to mean nothing to anyone and I had no desire to chat.

"By far, by far, girly. I'm a new man." He slapped his good knee, as though testing his own mettle. "You waiting on someone? Need a ride somewhere?"

"Oh, that's nice of you, thank you. But my husband is coming. He's just running some errands before he picks me up. We have a long drive ahead."

"Where you off to?"

"Gros Morne. My husband wants to do some hiking and I plan on getting some writing done. I'm a writer." I had edits due. On my book. A book that Meghan would never see. My publisher had said to hold off, that the deadline could be pushed as long as I needed, but I owed this to Meghan. I owed it to her to work through whatever hurt I was feeling to make something beautiful instead. I was choked with the possibility of it.

Fred nodded pensively. "It's good to be married. He a good man, your husband?"

I couldn't suppress the tug of a smile. "He's the best. The best of men."

"Ah, my Gabby. Now she was a good wife. She was a good cook, too. Mind you, nothing fancy. She didn't do fancy, but always had the seasoning just right. Never too much salt. You can wreck a meal with too much salt, isn't that right? Gabby, I lost her eight years ago. To the cancer. Terrible disease." At this, Fred's eyes welled up and he pulled a handkerchief from his pocket to dab at his face. But he turned to me then and let me witness the tears still brimming, and then he took my hands in his and held them, giving gentle pats like he was comforting me, not himself. His honesty was a salve, peeling back layers of my own bare grief.

"My sister." I gulped. "She just died of cancer. Two weeks ago."

"Mere weeks!" At this, he let himself cry in full force, tears lodging themselves amongst his weathered wrinkles. "Oh my, dear Kelly. She must have been some young by the looks of you."

"Thirty-seven. Just turned." I let my own tears fall and felt them drip between our entwined knuckles.

"Cancer, it be a nasty beast."

I couldn't say how long we sat there, but we snapped to when a horn honked two quick taps. Outside beyond the glass, a young woman leaned over the steering wheel of a sedan and waved through the windshield, a swirl of red hair falling in loose curls. Fred waved back and wiped his face with his handkerchief. "That's my niece there. She's a good girl." He sniffled and returned my hands to my lap like he was putting a kitten there and not a part of my own body. "You take care now, Kelly. You come to Fogo anytime and I'll see you right. Just on the northwest edge is where you'll find me. Just ask after me and folks will direct you the rest of the way."

I stood and hugged my new companion in the lobby of the Gander emergency room, the last place I'd expected to find comfort. I watched him drive away in the little red car just as Joe pulled up. I flung myself into the rental, turned up the heat, and instantly fell asleep.

That night, I had a nightmare that seemed to start the minute I closed my eyes.

The plan was that a week after our return from Newfoundland, we would scatter Meghan's remains from a cliff in Grundy Lake Provincial Park north of Parry Sound, the destination of our last family camping trip. Meghan had seemed happy on that vacation, nineteen years old but still reading her favourite young adult books and feeding chipmunks while stretched on her belly, patiently waiting for hours at a time. She was already into drugs by then, testing her own boundaries. It was the start of the end of our sisterhood, which I now knew was just a temporary stay.

Back home, we had put Meghan's ashes in an urn Joe made in his pottery classes, after having promised to make it the colour of the Thompson sister eyes. The glaze was a swirl of sage green with flecks of blue, and there was a Celtic-style pattern pressed into the clay lid, a nod to our Scottish roots. A temporary home for my sister until we set her free. Until then, she had been in a cardboard box held in a garish velvet bag, with a plastic bag inside that. Resting on top of the grey pile of ash was a silver disc with Meghan's name, the date of cremation, and the cremation number. *In case you want to travel with her at some point,* said the funeral home employee, *when it goes through the X-ray machine it identifies the remains. Otherwise, they can look like, well, explosives.* The idea had seemed ludicrous. I lifted the bag, which weighed just a few pounds, and felt a heaviness sink into me before uncertainty took over. Should I use a funnel? My hands? A spoon? Eventually, I opened the urn, nestled the mouth of the bag into the opening, and started shaking, gently, until a pile of Meghan built up like a powdery mountain. But she didn't fit, and I had to push her ashes inside with my hand spread flat like a paddle. And then I was laughing, knowing Meghan would have loved the weirdness.

I didn't tell Joe, because it seemed so strange, but I had brought Meghan's remains to Newfoundland, grateful that before applying the seal of silicone to the lid, I had placed the proof-of-cremation disc atop her ashes.

So, Grundy Lake was the plan. But in my dream, we scattered her into the wind, only for her to splash back into our faces. I woke sweating and called our parents, praying for the reception to hold, grateful Joe had put earplugs in before bed.

"I'm not ready," I gasped into my cell. "I'm not ready to let her go."

"Neither are we, Moo," Mom replied. "Neither are we."

I held her urn to my chest as I clicked the television on. "Well, Meg, for once I get to control the remote. I'm not watching any teenage vampire movies." I didn't expect a response, but I couldn't stand an end to the conversation.

———

At Gros Morne, the skies opened to reveal a stunning landscape that did nothing to stem my despondency. For days, I skipped rocks and sat motionless on cliffs writing letters to Meghan that I'd never send while Joe hiked the mountaintops, returning to tell me about his encounters with caribou and deer. I always kept the letters with me, folded into tidy squares and tucked inside my windbreaker pocket where I could finger the pages. A tangible proof of our connection that I carried like a talisman.

While Joe hadn't pressed me to join him on any of his adventures, I'd agreed to a boat tour in the national park, thinking it would be mindless, if nothing else. We walked the wide gravel path to Western Brook Pond, but I kept tripping, the tip of my sandal catching because of my dragging feet. I couldn't bother to lift my feet up, to commit to each step, so my toes glowed red from rubbing against rocks.

"Glad I wore sunscreen," Joe said, tugging his baseball cap lower. He'd spread the lotion so thickly across his face that he'd gone chalky white amid his beard stubble. "Feels good, the sun."

The walk to the pond from the parking lot was three kilometres and nicely groomed with marshland surrounding us on both sides. While the path was flat, cliffs jutted upwards in the distance to meet the sun like an open mouth, with the lake sandwiched between the two expanses of rock and invisible from the trail. People returning from their tours filtered in the opposite direction, and we bid constant polite hellos as we passed.

"This feels like a long walk to potter about a pond." I chided myself for voicing my thoughts. Joe had done all the planning for this trip, all the arrangements, all the research into noteworthy sites. He'd brought me to an island roost of chubby puffins, to plays at Trinity's Rising Tide Theatre, to seafood meals that stuffed me full of crab and lobster until I felt ill. And yet I could not find it within me to give myself to the living, as though energy was a reserve I needed all to myself.

"Oh, come on, it'll be worth it. It's supposed to be gorgeous. The water is low in nutrients and algae, so apparently it's super clear, almost untouched by humans except these boat tours. They do a lot of environmental certification to keep it that way." Joe went into an extensive explanation of fjords and water feeds and oxygen content, his environmental physics degree springing to life. I feigned interest, gave the right *mmm-hmms*, and *uh-huhs*, focusing on the winding curve of the path that would lead us to some end state. I just wanted to get back to doing nothing. Ideally with a glass of wine. I pushed my sunglasses up my nose and kept moving.

Half an hour later, we arrived at the reception area to purchase tickets. Tourists poured off two big boats down at the dock to queue up for the washrooms, flitter through the collection of cheap souvenirs, buy iced tea spurted out of a noisy machine. Conversation burst from every corner and anxiety niggled up my spine. I rubbed at my jaw, the infection aching from the wind.

"You take your penicillin today? Do you need something to eat to settle your stomach?" When I waved Joe off, annoyed at the fuss, he shook his head at me. "I'll see if we can fit on the next scheduled trip." He shrugged his messenger bag from his shoulder and adjusted it onto mine. "Wanna grab us a drink while we wait?"

"That's all I need. Something to make me pee while I'm stuck in a boat for two hours."

Joe raised his brows in a look that told me to suit myself, then wandered off to buy our tickets. Feeling confined, I pushed my way outdoors to the deck, which expanded around the little shelter like a fan. It was only then that I realized calling Western Brook a pond was a considerable misnomer. The water sparkled in the light, with sheets of rock gliding upwards and slashes of trees rising to the sky. Everything in the surrounding area was splashed vibrant green, untouched except by the throaty rumble of nearby boat engines. I turned my face to the sun's warmth, listened to the delightful timbre of foreign languages being spoken nearby.

"It's something, eh?" Joe appeared behind me and wound an arm around my waist. He pulled me close, kissed the top of my forehead, and I nestled into his neck and breathed in deep.

"I'm being so horrible. I'm sorry."

"I told you, no need to apologize. I get it."

"Still. I'm wrecking everything with my shitty attitude."

"Pretty sure anyone in your boat would have a shitty attitude. Boat, get it?" He squeezed the back of my neck and I felt the warmth spread. "We're on the next tour. Should we head down to the dock? Get some good seats?"

I let him guide me towards the waiting vessel. We took seats at the back, exposed to the elements, whereas others tucked into the protected interior of the boat, braced against the unpredictable blasts of maritime wind, Gore-Tex zipped to their chins. Two women in their late twenties plonked down beside us, lugging heavy rucksacks that they placed at their feet.

"Gawd, it'll be nice to sit on our arses for a wee while," said one to the other in a northern British accent. She tucked errant stands of hair into her bandana and passed a tube of sunscreen to her friend. "Slather this on. You'll be a tomato in no time."

"Bossy cow." They snickered at this, but the woman did as she was told, smearing the cream up her arms and down white legs spotted with a week's worth of shaving stubble.

More people crowded onto the craft, and I had to press closer to this stranger, bumping into her lotioned legs.

"Whoops, sorry. We're getting a bit squeezy here."

"No need, no need," she replied, waving me off. She waggled the bottle in the air and flipped the cap back into place. "I know what you're thinking. This delicate English rose is so pale that she's wearing far too much sun cream already, but I'll go redder than a lobster and then the next day, poof"—she popped her fingertips like a magician casting a spell—"back to lily white."

"That's just like me," Joe said, shaking his own bottle of Coppertone, which he reapplied onto his exposed shins.

"I'm Tara," said the lady with the bandana. "This is Bridget."

"Joe and Kelly. Nice to meet you." We shook hands just as the captain boarded and a tour guide took up the microphone.

"Welcome onboard this tour of the Western Brook Pond. We'll be on the water for approximately two hours, but you won't be bored, folks. You'll see and hear about local legends, watch waterfalls cascade into some of the cleanest water in Canada, and marvel at the beauty of Mother Nature!" The man's voice bubbled with life and interest, unlike the robotic scripts I'd heard from so many other guides. I settled into the fibreglass seat as the boat lurched forward, engine puttering until we reached a greater expanse of water and picked up speed.

The magnitude of the lake lulled Joe and me into cuddly silence, nestled against one another and half-listening to the staticky voice of the guide indicating landmarks. A man's face in the stone. The history of the fjord. Legends of a waterfall that plummeted at such a speed that the water looked like a gentle mist as it tumbled downwards. Joe snapped endless photos with his phone while I stared in a trance. If my mind wandered too far, it filled with visions of Meghan, decrepit and suffering. Every time I closed my eyes, the vision followed me—hospice room ten with its smells and sounds and misery.

"Western Brook Pond is an ultraoligotrophic environment, folks, which means there are very few nutrients available to support and sustain life. There aren't many organisms that can thrive here, except incredibly hardy plants and fish."

We turned a corner and the water opened to vastness, pushing me to focus on the image before me instead of the ones in my head. When the guide stopped talking, calmness swept over me as I was surrounded by the sounds of the engine, birds cawing overhead, the slosh of water against the boat. I turned to sit on my heels, trail my fingers through the icy water. The shock of the cold moved up my arm, cramped my neck into satisfying tightness.

As a family, camping was the only vacation we could afford, but we went each year, even once it was clear that Meghan would rather have been with friends back home. Still, she could be lured by a stack of books and the promise of marshmallows. The one time Dad let us take out the rental boat to paddle within his view, she'd found the oar so unwieldly that she whacked my cap off my head, and when she tried to retrieve it, a snapping turtle rose up from underneath and swallowed it whole. After that, she'd refused to let her hands dangle over the edge of the canoe and harboured a fear of lake water. It was a strange comfort, knowing that some environments simply weren't hospitable. Not conducive to life. And somehow I felt her there, in this inhospitable place.

When the captain wheeled the boat back south, panic bubbled up to replace the calm I'd just felt. I squeezed at Joe's knee and he held me tighter, his entire body curled protectively around mine like a conch. I didn't want to leave, fantasized about

256 ~ KELLY S. THOMPSON

diving off into the water that would not sustain me, would pull me somewhere deep and dark.

And there, again. *Brown mucous from her rosebud mouth. Air conditioning dampening the quilts. The sound of retching. Goodbyes scraped across the chalkboard.*

"Gosh, it's a dream here," Tara said to us. "Shame we're turning back." Her hair had escaped her bandana and whipped around her face. She kept pushing it back to little effect as she focused her thirty-five-millimetre lens on the rock faces.

"Do you want me to take a picture of you both?" I offered. "I'm not bad with film, actually."

"That would be grand, thanks." She passed the camera to me while Bridget thrust her iPhone out, too.

"And one with this, please, so I have it when I go home and this one never gets around to developing it." I snapped photos of them pressed into each other, then passed their devices back.

"You're a star, thanks. You lot Canadian then?" Bridget blew a mint-scented bubble of gum and snapped it back into her mouth. Tiny webs stayed stuck to her lips. "I imagine this is all the norm for you then. This kind of gorgeousness." She swirled her pointer finger to gesture around us.

"Canadian, yup," Joe said with a laugh. "Newfoundland is the last province we haven't travelled through, so we're trying to take it all in."

"On a vacation?" Bridget popped another snap of gum.

"Yeah," I muttered. "Just a vacation."

"You two seem awful smitten. Newlyweds?"

"Hardly. Been married six years now."

"I hope I like my husband that much whenever I get married," Tara said, tucking the camera into a protective bag. "Or maybe I'll stay an old maid with this gal." She pushed Bridget's shoulder jokingly.

"What about you two?" I swallowed, goading myself into more conversation that would distract from the retreating fjord, the beauty we were leaving behind, my sister lost in the murk.

"Yorkshire girls, us two," Tara replied. "We live far apart now, so we get together every year for a trip like this. Made a promise that no matter where we went or what jobs we had or what guy was in our lives, we'd make the time. Sister bonding and all that."

"Oh." My voice tightened, and I leaned to dangle an arm back into water, felt the shock of it shimmy from the ripples. "You're sisters then?" I reached into my pocket and worried the edges of the letters—five thick pages crisp with dried fountain pen ink. Still there. She was still there.

"She's the oldest, clearly," Bridget said. "Just look at those wrinkles! Almost thirty, the old bat. We've been touring about most of the summer. This is the last stop before home. And what a last stop it is, am I right?" Bridget ruffled Tara's hair, messing it even further until it knotted in her fingertips. Tara pushed her away but they fell back into one another, laughing. The intimacy made my mouth water, like an acidic food hitting my tastebuds.

"My sister just died." I blurted, then immediately regretted it. I felt Joe's arms snake tighter, reassuring and present as I blushed, hoping the redness would be disguised by the whipping wind. The two women blinked back at me, mouths open. Yes, they looked alike. I'd only just noticed. "I'm sorry. That was a weird thing to announce."

"Oh, love, what a thing for you," Tara said. She pressed closer into her sister at the news. "I'd be lost without this one here. Don't tell her though. She'll get a big head." She winked at me and the effort scrunched her nose up into a wrinkled ball. "I've always thought that sisters have a way of communicating no matter what keeps them apart. If this gal is suffering in some way, I know it. That doesn't just go away, you know. Even in death."

"She's a physicist," Tara said. "I trust her brain with the science bits."

I edged the corner of one of the letters underneath my nail until I was certain I'd drawn blood, holding back sobs. I was so tired of crying. Tired period. The exhaustion made it easy to embrace the idea that the conversation, the secrets, the love stayed. The proof was wedged underneath my nail.

"Maybe," Joe said, leaning around from behind me to interject, "this could be a sign you two should never stop going on these trips together."

I could only nod, my lips pressed together, the sisters' foreheads raised into compassionate domes.

"Well, folks." The guide's voice popped over the speaker system. "We'll be finishing up the tour now, but not without a great Newfoundland tradition!" He brandished a pair of connected wooden spoons and knocked them in a beat against his thigh, whacking the other side with an open palm. The effect was musically folk-like and mesmerizing, and soon the whole tour audience was clapping along. The merriment was infectious.

When the guide approached Joe and passed him the spoons for a try, Joe took the instrument and used his wrist and my thigh, and together we made something close to music.

twenty-nine

Within a week of arriving home from Newfoundland, I started my executor tasks. The first was to have Meghan's mail forwarded to my home, so I stood in line at Canada Post, moving ahead a customer at a time. I kept a long piece of foolscap in my purse to track everything else I had to do: get access to her bank accounts, pay the throng of bills she and Bernard had ignored, advertise her death in the paper to bring creditors out of the woodwork. I approached the list like I had her death—a step at a time, the only way that seemed possible. As the line snaked slowly forward, I jammed headphones into my ears to stave off conversations with anyone nearby.

I should have been listening to soothing music to ease the process, but instead I obsessively played the recordings I'd found on Meghan's phone and then transferred to my own to ensure they wouldn't be lost. I had plugged her phone in to fulfill my promise to shut down her social media and answer emails

lingering in her inbox—another one of the items on my long list
of to-dos. When the screen chugged to life, it told me the device's
memory was nearly maxed out, which was no surprise, really,
since Meghan was always bad at organizing. I sorted through
everything from audiobooks to reels of photos of the kids and
then earlier, pouty selfies, usually taken in the front seat of her
car. What surprised me were all the audio files, saved one after
another with dates, not titles, some of them recent and others
going back years. I tapped the button to play and had spent all
my time since both regretting it and listening to them on a repetitive loop—in the bathtub on speakerphone, in the living room
on the surround sound, or through my tinny headphones while
running errands. The hunger for confirmation of my suspicions
left me feeling dirty and deceitful.

The MP3 files varied in content and context except for one
constant—Bernard's slow baritone.

You're such a stupid, fucking idiot.

When he speaks of Sam, who coos nearby: *He'll be lucky if he
remembers you existed.*

Or in a mocking, sing-song voice: *"I'm not getting enough help."
What the fuck?*

Are you that dense? Do I have to get you a fucking dictionary?

And then Meghan, quietly defiant: *I can't have the kids watching
their dad treat their mother like this when she's dying.*

Worst of all was Sam interjecting, *Mommy? Play-Doh?*

Once I found the recordings, I was a bloodhound with a scent.
I dug through her emails, typed notes, text messages. I only found
one piece of vital proof, but it was all I needed. A month after
they'd married, three years earlier, she'd written an email to
Bernard and titled it: *I can't believe you used your fist,* insisting that she

wouldn't stay with a man who hit her with a closed fist. But she did stay. She always stayed.

Did she know I would find her breadcrumb trail? Hope for it, even? I remembered her passing me the phone from her hospice bed, her insistent stare, her words now layered with meaning. *There's stuff on here, Kell. Stuff to keep.*

Another customer stepped up to the counter and I cranked up the volume to the worst of the files, where Sam asked for his Play-Doh. I imagined him holding up the plastic tubs of clay and trying to make sense of everything while Meghan secretly pressed the bright red Record button, hoping to capture it all.

The postal employee waved me up to the counter and I approached to fan out my documents, popping my headphones out so they dangled around my neck. She recognized me, I knew, from our previous witty banter over my online shopping package pickups. *Do you get one in every colour, honey?* she'd ask as she stacked my boxes on the counter.

I girded myself and cleared my throat. "I just need to buy your forwarding service. For my sister."

"She moving in?" the clerk asked as she picked up my forms. "Getting a roomie?" The grin melted from her face when she found a copy of Meghan's will, her death certificate, my identification, all as required. My block printing on the form looked messy and childlike, and yet being executor was comforting, in a way, with its checklists and facts, paperwork and financials. "Oh, hon, I'm so sorry," she said, scanning the will. "How old was she?"

"Thirty-seven." I looked towards the window and the brilliant cascade of light that shone in, glinting off the Royal Canadian Mint coins in their glass case. I was getting used to this question; at thirty-four, people didn't expect me to be serving in this role.

"Gosh, too young to die." As though Meghan's young age was the greatest injustice. "Well," the clerk said with a thwack of a stamp on paper. "She knew you'd look after her and her estate. I'm sure that gave her comfort." She patted the forms into an envelope and stapled on a receipt. Eighty dollars to get my dead sister's mail. I snorted at the strangeness of it before collecting my papers and rushing out to the parking lot, where I slumped breathless into the front seat of my car, desperate for an antidote to the panic. I plugged my phone into the car Bluetooth, allowing Meghan's voice to blast through the Bose speakers.

Hey Kelly, I love you, lots.

Kelly, I love you so much. More than anything in the whole world.

Her tone wavered at the end of this recording, the tightness in her vocal cords straining against tears. Still, she hadn't minded me asking, when I thrust my iPhone at her, *Tell me something you want me to know forever*—and she shakily held it near her lips as she spoke, holding my gaze. Next, she took the tiny devices destined for the palms of two Build-A-Bear stuffed animals, one each for Lily and Sam, and made those recordings, too. *Mommy loves you so much, Lily. Mommy is always with you, Sammy.* A legacy in a single megabyte.

———————

I brought our plates to the table, my wrists wobbling under the weight of two obscenely large steaks. "I had a meat craving."

"Shit, did you have it with five other people at the same time?" Joe lifted the plate with his palm flattened and bicep curled. "Whew, there's my workout for the day."

"You're hilarious." I sat to plot my attack on the sirloin, moving my knife from one grain to the other, then back again. "They are a little big, aren't they? I should know better than to grief shop. I just buy a bunch of stuff to get out of there."

After the post office, I'd stood in the aisle of the grocery store and sobbed amongst peas and frozen waffles, filling my cart with four family-size jugs of watermelon juice. It was all I craved, and yet I could never bring myself to drink it, the memory of the hospice too stark. Meghan and I had spent half of our lives hating each other, so I hadn't expected her death to be so damn hard. The depth of the loss was breath-stealing like an ice bath.

"Still can't figure out what to do with the recordings?" Joe sliced into a piece of roasted broccoli and pointed at my phone with his fork.

The prosecutor in Bernard's criminal case had gotten in touch when I expressed interest in providing an impact statement. Did the courts know about all the things swept under the carpet? And if not, if I kept quiet, would the kids grow up to learn that love was anger and screaming and breaking things and court cases and closed fists? Worst was that I couldn't discern what Meghan actually wanted of me: To tell the truth and hope it resulted in change she couldn't enact herself, or to be silent like she'd been, because sometimes silence was the only way to peace?

I stared at the hunk of meat on my plate, still unsure. "I wrote out a statement along with the copies of the recordings. But I don't know. I can't tell if I want to punish him or if I actually want him to get help."

Joe rested his knife and fork against his plate and leaned towards me. "It's because you love the kids that you're feeling bad about wanting to punish him. But it's also because of the kids that you're considering it. Whatever choice you make will be the right one."

I'm alive because of what you told the judge. It wasn't an MP3 file, but it might as well have been—I remembered it word for word from the night of her bachelorette party. I writhed in anger, furious at having been put in this position. Why hadn't Meghan sent in the recordings herself? Why did she leave me to clean up her mess?

Kelly, I love you so much. More than anything in the whole world.

I unlocked my phone, finger hovering. Finally, I pressed Send.

———————

Months later at the trial, Bernard managed to plea down his case to a summary conviction of dangerous driving, with his lawyer leaning on Bernard's grief over his wife's death. His sentence was a temporary driving limit that only allowed him to go to and from work, some probation, and a minor fine. "You told the truth, Mooster," Dad said. "That was all you could do." As with so many moments over the last few years, I knew this had to be enough to get by on. One more day. And then another. And another.

thirty

I checked the rear-view mirror obsessively, looking for signs that I'd not buckled my niece's and nephew's car seats properly. I'd googled the procedure before I left the house, watched a few YouTube videos, but I was still uncertain, even after Phyllis helped me double-check when I picked Sam and Lily up from their new home with her. All of it—the diaper bag, the mini monkey-printed mittens, the plasticky buckles of their winter coats—felt uncertain.

"Who wants to sing a song?" I asked, my voice high and tight. I swallowed hard as a spate of emotion overwhelmed me in the face of these walking, talking Meghan look-alikes. It'd been six months since their mother died and, equally, six months since Mom, Dad, and I had been allowed to see them.

Since Meghan's death, we'd asked countless times to visit the children and were always denied—until Phyllis finally admitted that she and Bernard feared we'd alienate the kids from their father. *Your dad seems to hate Bernard so much,* Phyllis said on the phone when she finally answered one of my calls. There was confusion in her voice, as if she really couldn't comprehend the source of our bitterness. *Phyllis, first of all, we would never, ever do that. Second, try to imagine Bernard dying while being screamed at, abused, and threatened. Think of what that must feel like for us.* She responded so coolly and with such matter-of-factness that she might as well have been ordering dinner. *Well, he was sick.* Without a hint of irony. Her dismissiveness piqued something inside me—an awareness that we were standing on opposite sides of the horrible place Meghan had inhabited, the no man's land where the kids remained. Phyllis had a son she loved as much as we loved Meghan and all the ugliness that came with her, and Phyllis was protecting her son while mired in an impossible, horrific situation. We were all just trying to save someone. It was a state of loving despite instead of loving because.

"Hello back there?" In the mirror, Lily smiled shyly. The kids had been keen to show me their new rooms in their nana's house, Lily's covered in splashes of pink and purple and Sammy's a veritable Hot Wheels parking lot, both seeming happy and loved. The fireplace mantle showcased photos of their adventures with Phyllis—ice skating, kayaking, and swimming. I reached out to touch the snapshots and tried to not envisage Meghan's face in place of Phyllis's, by the children's sides. No matter my anger towards her, Phyllis was a lovingly involved guardian to my niece and nephew, which made it easy for me to admire her. "No one wants to sing for Auntie?"

"Auntie," Sam said, his voice serious as he stared out the window at the passing fields of snow-covered corn. "My mommy is in heaven." He was certain in this, bordering on emotionless. A typical four-year-old's comprehension of death that sparked from nowhere.

I focused on the lane in front of me and tried not to be thrown by the randomness of his statement, but then I was a reminder of that former life with his mother. The yellow line warbled like a mirage. "I know, Piggy. We miss Mommy, don't we?"

He bobbed his head. "She's an angel now. You smell like her, Auntie Kelly."

A few tears slipped down my cheeks, and I swiped at my face, annoyed. *Keep yourself together.* I didn't know if Meghan believed in angels and heaven and all that, or if it was something we told the kids to help them cope. She'd never gone to church, didn't pray, not even in supplication for an end. "You know, your mommy was Auntie's sister. Just like Lily is your sister."

"You have a sister?" Sam leaned forward against the confines of his booster seat. His eyes were the same colour as Meghan's. As mine.

"That's right. My sister was your mommy." He tried to compute this, looking to Lily and then back to me.

"I'm sorry your sister died, Auntie." And then he reached across the expanse of the car and took his sister's mittened hand. "Hey!" Sam cried out. "It's Daddy's house!" He pointed out the window and pressed his lips to the glass, fogging up the pane. As we passed, I couldn't bear to look at the house where Meghan had suffered, trying so hard to make it a home. When I thought of Bernard living there again—imagined him using her favourite mug or climbing into their shared bed with the sheets she'd picked out—an aneurysm of pain shot through me. I knew the kids spent some weekends with Bernard and his girlfriend, but it was Phyllis who took Sammy to school and Lily to daycare, Phyllis who tucked them into bed.

"Are we at Grandpa's now, Auntie?"

"Almost, buddy. We're almost there."

———

When we got to Mom and Dad's house, Sam and Lily launched into my parents' arms. They did not make strange with them. They did not cry or complain. They did not get upset about being in a house they had only ever visited with their mother and had not seen since. All of our worst-case scenarios dissipated with their laughter. We did puzzles, played hide-and-go-seek, coloured cards for Bernard's birthday, coming up in a week. Mom and Dad's faces filled with the same emotion I felt, a mixture of joy and devastation.

Sam slapped puzzle pieces in place at the kitchen table. He paused occasionally, bringing Lily a toy she might want, a crayon colour she should see, and held these things out to her like little offerings.

"Thank you, So-So," she responded. As they interacted, I thought of how they would look after one another, maybe until puberty hit. I wanted to warn them that it would be rocky then, for a while, but they'd find themselves again, discover a route that led home to each other. The idea washed over me with warmth.

Lily and I played on the living room carpet at Mom's feet, balancing wooden blocks on top of one another. When the tower reached her desired height, she toppled it, and we laughed together as I poked her belly. She stood and took in the scene around her—the plastic train set, the soft-covered books, the trucks and plush animals—and pushed hair from her face, toddling over to the entertainment cabinet where a photo of Meghan was framed. In the picture, Meghan's hair is shoulder-length and bouncy in soft waves, and her cheeks are plump, with freckles sprayed across her nose and cheeks. It is the way I liked to remember her.

"Mama." Lily took the photo from the cabinet and pressed it to her chest. "Mama." She held the frame in the air now, triumphant.

"That's right, sweetie," I said, the only one capable of uttering a word, although my chest was paralyzed. Both Mom and Dad fought tears. "That's Mommy."

She waddled to my side, having spent most of the day glued to me, a little human Velcro piece. "Mama?" Lily held the photo to me, as if asking a question. *You? Mommy?* No, no that couldn't be it, because Meghan and I looked nothing alike, right? Or maybe she was saying, *Where is she? Where is this person?* Yet I sounded like my sister, or, like Sam had, she smelled something in our shared DNA.

I pulled my niece into my arms and snuggled her shaggy curls. I didn't correct her. Didn't offer her an answer to the question she did not ask. I tried to remain content to let the words remain unsaid, unknown, to offer comfort that there was a Mommy, and that, in some ways, pieces remained.

thirty-one

"Okay, so I've got the lasagna ready for tonight." I dried the final dish and slung the dishtowel over my shoulder. "I'll pop it in the oven when I get home from my walk. Takes about an hour." I sealed the tray with a thick layer of foil and pushed sweaty hair from my forehead. Mom and Dad's house was a perpetual pressure cooker. "I made a couple extras to freeze for when I'm gone. Wrote heating instructions on each one." I buried each casserole in the freezer.

"There's no ricotta in it, is there?" Dad glared suspiciously from his new recliner, a heating pad draped across his aching knees. Mom was slumped in her matching chair in the opposite corner of the room. The new layout of their living space—a chair in each corner—created the impression of four opponents bracing for a boxing match. Over the past few weeks, we'd sold the couch, the coffee table, the bar-height dining set. Anything that might get in the way of Mom's wheelchair.

"You always try to hide stuff in my food. Things I don't

like," Dad continued, wagging a finger in my direction but not bothering to turn away from the television newscaster. It was the first of four nightly news programs they watched in masochistic succession, ambivalent to my pleas for something uplifting. It was a perpetual loop of war, hunger, anger. Hadn't we had enough of that? "You think you can hide stuff, but I taste it. I know it's there."

"You don't taste anything, Dad." I wrung the dishtowel until my fingers ached. Every muscle in my body was twisted in knots. "You just see something you think you don't like, and then refuse to touch it." I thwacked the towel on the counter with a snap that startled Pot Roast, who'd been waiting at my feet for dropped chunks of mozzarella.

Dad's teeth ground together so that the words came out like his jaw was wired shut. "Don't speak to me like I'm a child."

Then stop acting like one. I kept silent. In Meghan's absence, Dad was unable to abide the slightest difference in opinion from his now only child, and I found myself less willing to capitulate in an effort to soothe him. *I put the garbage out on the left side of the street, not the right. You're not folding that towel properly—in thirds, not in half. The mail needs to be checked every day. Yes, every day.* Maybe he needed the friction as a reminder, and I was the only one left to give it.

"I didn't use ricotta, Dad." I pressed on the bridge of my nose and then stooped to scratch Pot Roast behind the ear. "Want to get out of here, buddy?" He wagged his tail at the attention.

"I'm not sure I feel like eating," Mom said listlessly. She stared outside and watched two squirrels battle over a peanut in the backyard. Next to her was the wheelchair that she now required, a change in her MS status so sudden it was like a light switch had turned her body off.

My chest tightened with a push-pull of frustration and compassion. "Ma, you said you were hungry when I asked an hour ago. I made this big meal." I gestured about the kitchen, garlic scent still fragrant, sauce splattered on the perfect white backsplash. I took a sponge and scrubbed at the tile because no matter the effort I'd made, for my parents this stain would mar the work, would become the focus for their nitpicking. I swiped at the tomato chunks until my reflection appeared in the glaze. She was older, this woman staring back, than the me I remembered. Meghan hadn't even been gone a year and there was no end in sight to the heavy weight we all carried in our own way.

"Yeah, sorry, maybe." Mom shook her head like an answer might rattle loose. "Maybe I'll be hungry later."

"The doctor said you have to eat, Mom. Especially during a flare."

"Eating dinner won't make my legs miraculously work." She flicked angry fingertips at the wheelchair. Until the occupational therapist finished his assessment, we were stuck with an old transport chair model, one we'd used only to shuttle my now deceased grandma to medical appointments in her last year of life. It was large and unwieldy, making Mom appear childlike in the seat, arms barely able to reach over the sides to spin the wheels.

I sat on the floor and took her limp, purple feet to rub them warm and was instantly overwhelmed with the imagined scent of lavender oil. Grief swept over me despite my effort to bite it back. "Still. You have to take care of yourself." Seeing me on the floor, Pot Roast sidled up and rested his anvil head on Mom's lap. "You have us still."

"I know. I know, Mooster." Mom stroked the dog absentmindedly. "I don't mean to be a grump. You're doing so much."

"Look on the bright side." I gently pinched the skin on the back of her arm. Meghan and I used to jokingly threaten her with mimed pincher claws, and we'd end up in a heap of laughter after chasing her through the house. *Remember?* "It could be Meghan looking after you. You'd be waiting until sometime tomorrow for a meal and it would probably taste like sand."

She burped out a strangled snort. "Lord, can you imagine? I'd be living off Kraft Dinner and sleeping in sheets unwashed for a month." Mom tugged a tissue from her sleeve and wiped her running nose. "She used to tell me not to worry, that she and Bernard would move me into their house when I got sicker, and I'd feel such dread." She dabbed the tissue at the corner of her lash line. "I don't know if it was the idea of her being my caregiver or living anywhere close to Bernard that scared me. That sounds awful, right?"

Mom glanced between me and Meghan's photo on the TV stand. She'd have been mad to hear us carrying on, or she'd have grown up enough to see the truth in it. Or she'd stomp across the floor and say no one in this family gave Bernard a chance. Or she'd laugh. Or she'd squeeze the muscles around my neck and tell me we'd face our aging parents and their declining health together. It was the lack of certainty that really stung.

"Another reason to be nice to me," I said as I stood. "I'm all you've got left to keep you out of the nursing home. I expect that to be reflected in my inheritance."

"Oh," she swatted at my arm and laughed. "You're awful."

"Hey, without Meg around I need someone to appreciate my death jokes."

Mom suppressed a grin as she attempted to wrestle herself into a comfy position. Her muscles had atrophied, and I vacillated between offering assistance and making space for her independence, settling on doing nothing. Because really, there was nothing to do but lean into the reality of each day arriving after the next. Illness would creep in. We would continue aging. Dinner would need to be made and the sheets would need washing.

"Pot Roast needs a walk." The dog followed my every step, tail wagging as I clipped the leash onto his collar. "I'll be back in a while."

"But what about the lasagna?" Mom called as I strode towards the front foyer.

"Oh my God! I thought you weren't hungry?" I froze in place, grip on the leash tightening like a noose. *Our parents are so annoying. Yeah, and aren't they the best?* No one else would understand.

"Should we preheat the oven or anything?"

I willed myself towards the front hall. One step. Then another. "Just leave it, guys. I'll take care of it when I'm back." I shrugged into a sweater and laced my sneakers as fast as I could.

"What if we're hungry before then?" This time, Dad's voice, as he finally broke his attention from the screen.

I slipped out the front door as though I'd not heard, stuffing headphones into my ears but not bothering to turn on any music. Mom and Dad's neighbourhood was typical city suburban. It was so close to Kempenfelt Bay that sometimes I caught the scent of the water I grew up swimming in, Meghan and I predictably emerging with swimmer's itch. We'd trace the outlines of our hives in pen, leaving inky routes on our bellies once the swelling subsided.

Pot Roast ambled at a slow pace, stopping to sniff every post, every blade of grass longer than four inches high. He didn't particularly like going for walks, preferring instead to nap by a fire or bake himself on the deck. But during my stay in Barrie he'd been my companion during my daily escape from caregiving, looping around cookie-cutter streets as the temperature rose and fell in the unpredictable pattern of Ontario weather.

We approached the end of the road and the house that often stirred Dad to rage, a heap of a building that was crumbling with neglect and wrecking local property values. The fence barely stood vertical, shingles peeled from the roof, and junk sat in haphazard piles on a lawn blanketed in weeds. Pot Roast jerked the leash towards a cluster of dandelions and ruffled his nose in the patch of yellow. I chided him, reminded him in pointless human language of his allergies. He'd develop a rash, require Benadryl, and need aloe spread onto his hot spots. More care. He tugged again, sending a tuft of puffy seeds aloft and turned to me proudly, snout tinted mustard, then sneezed a glob of saliva onto the pavement.

Dandelions were said to be the flower of the military child because of their resiliency, travelling on the wind to new places, always able to take root. *Sure*, Meghan said, *some people get named after the rose, or a daisy. Us army brats get labelled with a weed.* Still, she never missed a chance to make a wish on one.

I picked up a puff and blew it into the wind. I didn't watch the seeds land, certain only that they would find their place.

acknowledgements

Thanks to:

The entire McClelland & Stewart/Penguin Random House Canada team. For support and compassion in this emotionally tricky book, and during an equally emotional time releasing my first book while my family was in tatters. Special thanks to the dear Jenny Bradshaw, Jared Bland, Erin Kelly, Linda Pruessen, Linda Friedner, Kate Sinclair, Erin Cooper, Ruta Liormonas, Trudy Fegan, Jaclyn Gruenberger, Kimberlee Kemp, Tonia Addison, Sarah Howland, the glorious sales team, and every single intern who brings sparkle to the office.

Stephanie Sinclair. For being my agent, yes, but also a champion of my books and an owner of the kindest heart.

Suzanne Brandreth. For picking up the agenting helm with kindness, grace, and pizzazz.

Dr. Lania Knight, Dr. Bea Hitchman, and Dr. Martin Randall at the University of Gloucestershire. For helping me examine the complex, beautiful landscape of grief.

Tod Augusta-Scott. For insight and education into domestic abuse and how we view intimate partner violence.

Art Henry. For guidance and counselling to cope with writing this book as well as all that came before and since. Never once have you mansplained.

Marissa Stapley—my grief book buddy. WE. Also, other literary sisters in crime, including Eden Boudreau, Caitlin Crawshaw, Shannon Webb-Campbell, Megan Cole, Zoe Grams, and other cheerleaders near and far who let me whine and share as needed.

My creative nonfiction students. For reminding me why we tell true stories.

The Banff Centre. For a creative place to create the first draft of this book.

Jessica Dozois. For being there. Always.

Friends and family. For supporting us in this grief journey in myriad ways, be it food, kindness, hugs, bent ears. Special thanks to June Roser, Kathy McNeil, Trish Lipsitt, Debra Gafford, Dave Leahy, and BJ Melnyk.

The nurses and staff of Matthew's House Hospice. Gems of the world, every single one of you.

My Nikki K. For wine. For Post-Its directing me to the wine. For reminding me some sisters are made.

Mom and Dad. For giving me the most complicated, beautiful, maddening, magical sister.

My Joe. For loving me back. For too many reasons to count.

Meghan. For telling me to write it, and not to leave out the ugly parts. For you. Always, for you.